RESISTING ORDERS

ADVANCING STUDIES IN RELIGION
Series editor: Sarah Wilkins-Laflamme

Advancing Studies in Religion catalyzes and provokes original research in the study of religion with a critical edge. The series advances the study of religion in method and theory, textual interpretation, theological studies, and the understanding of lived religious experience. Rooted in the long and diverse traditions of the study of religion in Canada, the series demonstrates awareness of the complex genealogy of religion as a category and as a discipline. ASR welcomes submissions from authors researching religion in varied contexts and with diverse methodologies.

The series is sponsored by the Canadian Corporation for Studies in Religion whose constituent societies include the Canadian Society of Biblical Studies, Canadian Society for the Study of Religion, Canadian Society of Patristic Studies, Canadian Theological Society, Société canadienne de théologie, and Société québécoise pour l'étude de la religion.

8 Identities Under Construction
Religion, Gender, and Sexuality among Youth in Canada
Pamela Dickey Young and Heather Shipley

9 Prayer as Transgression?
The Social Relations of Prayer in Healthcare Settings
Sheryl Reimer-Kirkham, Sonya Sharma, Rachel Brown, and Melania Calestani

10 Relation and Resistance
Racialized Women, Religion, and Diaspora
Edited by *Sailaja V. Krishnamurti and Becky R. Lee*

11 Sacred as Secular
Secularization under Theocracy in Iran
Abdolmohammad Kazemipur

12 Under Siege Islamophobia and the 9/11 Generation
Jasmin Zine

13 Sacred Cyberspaces
Catholicism, New Media, and the Religious Experience
Oren Golan and Michele Martini

14 Caught in the Current
British and Canadian Evangelicals in an Age of Self-Spirituality
Sam Reimer

15 Prophets of Love
The Unlikely Kinship of Leonard Cohen and the Apostle Paul
Matthew R. Anderson

16 The Holy Spirit and the Eagle Feather
The Struggle for Indigenous Pentecostalism in Canada
Aaron A.M. Ross

17 Resisting Orders
Catholic Sisters Contest Their Church
Christine Gervais, Amanda Watson, and Shanisse Kleuskens

Resisting Orders

Catholic Sisters Contest Their Church

CHRISTINE GERVAIS
AMANDA WATSON
and SHANISSE KLEUSKENS

McGill-Queen's University Press
Montreal & Kingston • London • Chicago

ISBN 978-0-2280-2370-8 (paper)
ISBN 978-0-2280-2502-3 (ePDF)
ISBN 978-0-2280-2503-0 (ePUB)

Legal deposit second quarter 2025
Bibliothèque et Archives nationales du Québec

Printed in Canada on acid-free paper that is 100% ancient-forest-free, containing 100% sustainable, recycled fibre, and processed chlorine-free.

This book has been published with the help of a grant from the Federation for the Humanities and Social Sciences, through the Awards to Scholarly Publications Program, using funds provided by the Social Sciences and Humanities Research Council of Canada. Funding was also received from the Faculty of Social Sciences at the University of Ottawa.

Funded by the Government of Canada | Financé par le gouvernement du Canada | Canada | Canada Council for the Arts | Conseil des arts du Canada

We acknowledge the support of the Canada Council for the Arts.

Nous remercions le Conseil des arts du Canada de son soutien.

McGill-Queen's University Press in Montreal is on land which long served as a site of meeting and exchange amongst Indigenous Peoples, including the Haudenosaunee and Anishinabeg nations. In Kingston it is situated on the territory of the Haudenosaunee and Anishinaabek. We acknowledge and thank the diverse Indigenous Peoples whose footsteps have marked these territories on which peoples of the world now gather.

Library and Archives Canada Cataloguing in Publication

Title: Resisting orders: Catholic sisters contest their church / Christine Gervais, Amanda Watson, Shanisse Kleuskens.

Names: Gervais, Christine L. M., author | Watson, Amanda D., 1986- author | Kleuskens, Shanisse, author.

Series: Advancing studies in religion; 17.

Description: Series statement: Advancing studies in religion; 17 | Includes bibliographical references and index.

Identifiers: Canadiana (print) 20240529820 | Canadiana (ebook) 20240529952 | ISBN 9780228023708 (paper) | ISBN 9780228025023 (ePDF) | ISBN 9780228025030 (ePUB)

Subjects: LCSH: Catholic women—Ontario. | LCSH: Women in the Catholic Church—Ontario. | LCSH: Feminism—Religious aspects—Catholic Church. | LCSH: Social justice—Religious aspects—Catholic Church.

Classification: LCC BX1422.06 G47 2025 | DDC 282/.713082—dc23

This book was designed and typeset by Marquis Interscript in 10.5/13 Sabon. Copyediting by Grace Seybold.

McGill-Queen's University Press
Suite 1720, 1010 Sherbrooke St West, Montreal, QC, H3A 2R7

Authorized safety representative in the EU: Mare Nostrum Group BV, Mauritskade 21D, 1091 GC Amsterdam, the Netherlands, gpsr@mare-nostrum.co.uk

To all whose resistance in the present glimmers
with hope for a more expansive future.

Contents

PREFACE

Pursuing Co-Authorship

Writing this book was a highly collaborative process resulting in our unique co-authoring arrangement. Over several years, we grappled with the significance of what the sisters had shared in their interviews, meeting in person and eventually over phone and video calls, and through threads of comments tracked within numerous living documents. The first author, Christine Gervais, is the study's primary researcher, who invited former research assistants to co-author the manuscript, echoing women religious' own evolving approaches towards decentralized leadership, democratic governance, and diverse engagement represented here. Thus, this co-authorship is intended to model inclusivity in terms of both its content and its mode. No single paragraph within this work was written by only one author. This multi-generational co-authorship also offers a unique lens through which to deliberate and analyze gender injustice within a religious institution, bearing in mind both continuity and evolving dynamics that may resonate with, and impact, girls and women of all ages.

The timing of this writing has been shaped by work- and pandemic-related disruptions to family life. We are three women authors with various employment commitments, one of which is outside of academia, as well as caregiving and community service obligations; this compression of time and the emotional toll of caregiving through intersecting crises (pandemic, wars, conflicts, occupations, and the confirmation of Indigenous children's graves at former residential school sites) are relevant to our analyses of the gendered labour of care and service described by the sisters. Furthermore, they provide continuity when thinking about the historical settings the interviewees describe, and about how some things have changed while many others pertaining to women's work, obligations, and status have remained entrenched.

Such commitments, crises, and especially some church-related controversies throughout the decade and a half since the original interviews from 2008 to 2011 also resulted in extended writing delays as we sometimes felt compelled to pause and discern our ambivalence vis-à-vis our analyses, as well as any association with Catholic Church–related matters. Yet we persisted in our writing to further expose the contradictions and various forms of church-based discrimination, including sisters' own retrospective realizations of, and concerted efforts to mitigate, those issues.

We also raise the disturbing occupations of various locations across Canada by the so-called "Freedom Convoy" in 2022 to provide additional political context for the later stages of writing.[1] Notions of freedom described herein recuperate liberation and autonomy from neoliberal individualist logics that reject accountability, service, and care. Relatedly, the notions of resistance that were both renewed and muddled in the context of countless crises and worrisome world events over the last decade have also informed our (re)considerations of how sisters contemplate controversies and confront contradictions.

Given that we are not experts in theology, history, liturgy, canon law, or religious studies, there are inevitably many conceptual and contextual aspects from these fields of study and areas of religious practice that, while relevant, are not mentioned, engaged with, or developed in this book. We recognize that such omissions may disappoint and even frustrate certain readers and reviewers, but our purpose is to share the sisters' experiential accounts in such a way that their thought-provoking and change-oriented perspectives can be accessible, relatable, and thus hopefully impactful for a wider audience.

Throughout the book, we engage with academic scholarship, particularly that which is advanced by serious sister-scholars, while also drawing on media and grassroots organizational sources, some of which are led by women religious.[2] Although some academic critics may presume that we view such mixed sources with the same credence, of course we recognize the differences between them. Yet, as critical, advocacy-oriented, and collaboratively minded scholars, we draw upon a range of sources because they provide relevant contexts and timely updates, and most importantly, if our fundamental and common purpose is to raise change-generating awareness about inequalities within and beyond the church, then it is essential to engage with a multiplicity of sources – both academic and societal, as well as religious and secular – in order to keep the required conversations flowing fully and freely.

Acknowledgments

This book is the outcome of shared labour, intentional reflection, and mutual care. We extend our deepest gratitude to the women who gave generously of their time and trust during the original interviews and in meaningful follow-up conversations over the years. Their courage has been exemplary and their inspiration will be enduring.

At McGill-Queen's University Press, we especially thank senior editor Kyla Madden for her insightful feedback and sustained support throughout the extended preparation of this book. We also thank the editing, copy-editing, production, and marketing staff at the press who supported this publication endeavour so thoughtfully and professionally behind the scenes.

We are grateful to the anonymous peer reviewers for their constructive comments and encouragement, which were welcome reminders of the importance of sharing the stories of women who have been silenced for too long.

At the University of Ottawa, we acknowledge the Centre for Academic Leadership's invaluable support via its writing days and retreats, as well as the Faculty of Social Sciences, the Undergraduate Research Opportunity Program, the Professional Expenses Reimbursement Program, and the former Laboratory on Justice Studies and Research in the Department of Criminology for their financial support.

At Simon Fraser University, we acknowledge support from the University Publication Fund and the Academic Women writing group.

Christine recognizes that this project benefited tremendously from a very dedicated team of research assistants. She is particularly grateful to her former assistants turned co-authors, Amanda Watson and Shanisse Kleuskens, whose analytical and administrative contributions have been infinitely impressive, insightful, and inspiring and whose steadfastness has been sustaining beyond measure.

At the same time, Amanda and Shanisse wish to thank Christine for taking a leap of faith and inviting us to work on this project as students at various early stages of our scholarly training. We have each grown alongside this project thanks to Christine's inclusive leadership and feminist research ethics – beyond the ethics required by university research boards.

Collectively, we are indebted to editor Sarah Gilliss for her contributions beyond copy-editing. Her supportive editorial guidance through the complexities associated with discrimination, power, and rights-respecting matters in this context helped us to clarify arguments and undoubtedly brought this manuscript to press. We are thus pleased to consider her an honorary co-author.

Together, we also thank our relatives, both immediate and extended, for their ongoing and unwavering support on a variety of fronts (relational, analytical, emotional, domestic, editorial), which has been vital to the completion of this book.

Amanda would especially like to acknowledge her father and grandmother for listening to arguments and brainstorming titles over morning coffee. She also thanks her departmental colleagues for invaluable hallway chats about the tensions inherent to writing within and about powerful colonial institutions.

Shanisse would especially like to thank her partner Dave, for continuously setting an example of how to remain curious about the world around you, and to her parents for instilling in their daughters the confidence needed to navigate patriarchal institutions on their own terms. Shanisse would also like to tell her darling Sam that she loves her "beaucoup beaucoup beaucoup," and that she hopes that her world will see more justice by the time she can read this!

Christine would especially like to thank her partner Grant, whose sense of practicality and humour are always uplifting and whose modelling of gender parity to their sons remains exemplary. She also extends profound gratitude to her late father not only for his helpful clarifications, which appear in more than a few footnotes herein, but also and especially for his critical stance vis-à-vis the institutional Church; for his timely sharing of thought-provoking books from his personal library, along with the meaningful conversations about them; for his special recollections of sisters' contributions in his own life; and for his everlasting reminders of the importance of love for all.

RESISTING ORDERS

Introduction

Christine Gervais and Amanda Watson

Father, that's not God … you're not teaching them right. God is love.

This emphatic declaration was expressed by a "very tiny" six-year-old girl[1] as she "stood up and put [her] hand up" in the front pew to protest the "hell, fire and brimstone" sermon by a "big burly … missionary priest"[2] in her family's home parish in the early 1940s. She recalled that while her "mother nearly had a stroke … and [her] father didn't say a word … [she] wouldn't sit down." What came next was a young girl's daring defiance against a powerful patriarchal pastor in the Roman Catholic Church:[3]

> Do you know what he [the priest] did? This is how he knew how to deal with a child. He said, "You sit down or leave the church." I said, "Fine, I'll leave" and I stomped all the way down the aisle. And you can imagine a little country church … Everybody kinda looked at … this kid who's totally undisciplined and I stand on the steps, and I just went like this [crossing her arms] and I was all mixed up. What's happening here, you know, as a little child? … My father came out and he put his arm around me … and … he said, "You're right; you're right; you tell him."

This riveting story of resistance animates the spirit of this book. The girl, whose critique was met with an ultimatum from the priest at the pulpit, dared to march down the long centre aisle and out the doors while adults looked on in surprise because of her conviction that love should be at the centre of religious discourse. Of course, this little girl went on to become an outspoken nun!

This child's demonstrated capacity to contest at such a young age forecast her life-long resistance against patriarchal Church orders and institutional practices throughout the entirety of her sisterhood.[4] Her life story finds company with those of many women religious[5] as they persistently call attention to the myriad of inequalities and injustices still plaguing the Catholic Church. And her feelings that day – "all mixed up" – are echoed in the ambivalence that women religious express in these and other pages as they have sought to manage their "feminist" and "social justice" identities vis-à-vis their "Catholic" selves (Gervais 2012; Holtmann 2008; Huygens 2023). Receiving conflicting messages from the priestly "father" and her dad that day – the former alienating, the latter affirming – nuances the ways in which sisters experienced and navigated patriarchal authority throughout their lives.[6] Of particular interest to us now, as we think in ecological and more-than-human ways about solidarity and justice on a warming and warring planet, the certainty of this woman's faith remained rooted in the nature-based lessons that her family father had imparted: "My father taught me about God by looking at the stars and the earth ... by walking through the fields ... and he'd show me the blades of grass and how God was all loving, you know, and so I was free." Finding spiritual liberation in a sense of awe at the world around us renders the vengeful God particularly confusing.

That sense of freedom, the clarity of conviction, along with her spirited personality, clearly emboldened the future sister's moves, not only to challenge the priest, but also to exit the church instead of being silenced. Both acts – the contestation and the exit – and the gendered nature of the event are of particular interest to this book's overall emphasis on women's religious resistance and their distinct feminist and social justice orientations to navigating the harms resulting from patriarchal and hierarchical Church policies and practices.

Bringing to light the unheard stories of sisters and former sisters based in Ontario, Canada, we underscore the ways in which these women reckoned with contradictions they faced both within and beyond the confines of Roman Catholic Church doctrine. We also attend to their diversity as a group as we unfold the extent to which some sisters embraced the language and associations of feminist activism while advocating for social justice and gender equality. In so doing, we recount some complicated stories of women religious in Canada who have variously navigated two competing devotions: to the Catholic Church, and to serving their community with equity and compassion.[7] In each chapter, we bring together attempts to reconcile their obligations, and corresponding glimmers of feminist solidarity, against a backdrop of overt sexism and patriarchal rule. We thus reject stereotypes of women religious as compliant, subservient, and rigid in their thinking (Brock 2010; Jackowski 2004, 1; Kristof 2010; Mangion 2008; Wexler 2016).[8] Instead, we attend to their varied ambivalence and resistance – making space for the evolving, unexpected, and diverse perspectives of Catholic women religious to break through.

The sisters occupy a complicated social position with respect to resistance and power. While the case of the six-year-old's defiance of a missionary priest seems clear, the various forms and varying degrees of resistance and compliance in which sisters have engaged are often more ambiguous or fraught.[9] Indeed, Catholic nuns have, in various contexts, actively advanced colonial and racist mandates led by various Christian churches (Burns 1999; Kinew 2017; Michaelson 2021; Williams 2022), abused children in their care (Araujo-Hawkins 2021a, 2021b; Böhm et al. 2014; McDonald 2009; Truth and Reconciliation Commission of Canada 2015a, 2015b, 2015c; Watts 2024), *and* perpetuated sexist subjugation (CBC Radio 2014, 2017; O'Malley 2016; Gott 2021, 2022).[10] It is with these historical correctives in mind that we untangle Catholic sisters' power and resistance in the ongoing colonial and hierarchical context of the Roman Catholic Church.

Each chapter of this book represents a site of resistance in the lives of the sisters interviewed. Whether it be quietly strategizing or publicly agitating, the sisters who have lent their voices herein reflect on oftentimes painful issues, from resisting state repression in nations under authoritarian regimes, to denouncing clerical abuse, to challenging the ban on and criminalization of women's ordination, to supporting women's reproductive justice, to rallying against homophobia. It is through their stories of resistance that we explore in greater depth what Johnson (2002a, 61) intimated two decades ago: how "living within patriarchal [religious] systems … [has] forge[d] among women [religious] recognizable experiences of suffering along with typical patterns of … victoriously resisting, strategies that enable women to survive." Thinking with the words of these sisters has been vital for our own understanding of institutional power and resistance in our lives as feminist authors who aspire to advance social justice in our respective communities amid daunting and at times overwhelming systems of oppression. These women, while pushing and agitating, did not mistake reverence for deference.

Defining and tracing tactics of resistance involves taking a position on the extent to which subordinated people and groups act to "apprehend the conditions of one's subordination, to endure or withstand those conditions in everyday life" (Chandra 2015, 565). In addressing sisters' resistance to monastic discipline in previous work (Gervais and Watson 2014), we have regarded resistance rather broadly "as the practice of going against an order by action, argument or critical reflection," yet we specified how it encompassed a wide range of overt and covert forms, as well as individual and collective efforts, including tactical strategies (involving physical, verbal, and psychological dimensions), open defiance, negotiation, creativity, innovation, humour, fun, and solidarity. We intend to push our own thinking here, informed by decolonial questions about how to "read" resistance with attention to specific historical contexts and scale (see Lilja 2022). For example, as women and women religious who added their voices to the #MeToo and #NunsToo movements contribute to a broad network of resistance (Meyer 2021; Poggioli 2019; Wagner 2018), so too do the range of activities by Indigenous Peoples maintaining their presence, language, and livelihood on unceded lands amount to daily forms of spatial and spiritual resistance. We wonder about intentional forms of resistance in the sisters' examples, such as when they strategized to circumvent the authority of priests on various issues, as well as moments when the sisters may have found greater access to power and autonomy (Brock 2010) – for example, by avoiding the patriarchal confines of heterosexual marriage, strategically or not (Hidalgo 2007).

To consider the context of religious affiliation in particular, we draw on Holtmann's (2008) frame of resistance among Catholic women as broadly involving the acquisition of analytical tools and language initially, followed by critiques of religious rules and teachings, public protests, refusals to remain silent about or participate in patriarchal practices, and outspoken challenges of injustices paired with persistent pursuits of justice. Holtmann also brings forth an understanding of Catholic women's resistance to Church dogma, not as an indication of their unfaithfulness, but rather as an exemplification "of their fidelity to the gospel" and thus of their faithfulness (Holtmann 2008, 216). As such, by engaging Holtmann's flipside and faith-informed conception, we illustrate how, in the case of feminist and social justice–oriented sisters, not only do their religious beliefs ground their resistance efforts, but resistance itself constitutes "an important part of their religious practice" (Holtmann 2008, 202–3).

Given the relevant parallels, wherever applicable, we complement Holtmann's consideration with Ó'Murchú's (1997, 113–15) affirmation of feminist-informed resistance consisting of four strategies, including conscientization (i.e., education and information-sharing to change attitudes), active protests (i.e., embodied action to counter injustices), loyal disobedience (i.e., wisdom-informed decision[s] to undermine dominant "man-made system[s]" and strive for "greater justice"), and alternative communities (i.e., diverse models for creative interaction and mutual engagement beyond patriarchy's monolithic approach). As evidenced across this broad range of tactics, Ó'Murchú's (1997) conception of resistance is especially pertinent as it is grounded not only in a feminist critique of patriarchy and religious practice, but also in an expansive sense of spiritual life, and an inclusive model of justice and solidarity.[11]

To extend understandings of the context specific to the Catholic women religious herein, we consider Murphy's (2022) application of Avishai's (2008) and Burke's (2012) feminist concept of resistance agency as it pertains to how a congregation of sisters manoeuvred twenty-first-century patriarchal constraints through a Vatican investigation and diocesan interference. While Murphy (2022) demonstrated how most of the investigation-affected sisters primarily exercised empowerment agency by intentionally focusing their attention elsewhere on the needs of marginalized populations, he also illustrated how some sisters engaged in resistance agency as they challenged the patriarchal Church structures by variously rejecting the status quo. In so doing, he generated a more nuanced understanding of sisters' agency that entails interrelated layers of both empowerment and resistance, as well as what may be perceived as subversion and submission experienced simultaneously or at least in complex and sometimes non-binary ways (Ammerman 2003; Avishai 2008; Burke 2012 in Murphy 2022; Brock 2010; Mahmood 2006, 2009, 2012; Osiek 1986; Wexler 2016).[12]

To situate the sisters' experiences on a broader canvas of women's rights and feminist agency, we also draw inspiration from Faulkner and MacDonald's (2009) conception of women's resistance that challenges perceptions of women as solely victims of patriarchal structures, and offers instead a framework to consider "the moments *beyond* victimization" in which women "move on, build and grow" through a range of individual and collective forms of resistance against overbearing political, legal, and cultural systems (10). By employing Faulkner and MacDonald's more emancipatory conception, we attend to the multiple ways in which sisters have resisted dominant religious and societal practices by scrutinizing patriarchal discourses and hierarchical policies and have also engaged in "life-giving strategies to enable change in their own [and others'] lives" (11). To understand these strategies in context, we engage where relevant with what Munn and Bruckert (2010) represent as a "resistance pyramid," which reflects the extent to which resistance efforts contain particular objectives, purposes, strategies, tactics, skills, and (in)actions.[13] In so doing, and mainly in chapters 1 and 2, we consider not only what Church-based and, in some cases, state-based discourses, policies, and practices the sisters have intentionally challenged for both their individual and collective benefit (Munn and Bruckert 2010, 145), but also *how* they have done so in ways that were either spirited, subtle, or stealthy (Bonavoglia 2006; Chittister 2004; Wexler 2016).

It is not our intention to shape the contours of these concepts of resistance here. Instead, our thinking on resistance is intended to contribute to broader scholarly analysis and public commentary about sisters' resistance against patriarchal Church powers across time and space (Brock 2010; Caspary 2003; Chittister 2004; Mangion 2020; McPhillips and McEwan 2022; Thompson 2022a, 2022b). We also aim to write accessibly on the sisters' many forms of resistance, in order to invite readers to reflect on their own positions and capacities for resistance within patriarchal and colonial institutions.

The sisters' stories presented herein also include expressions of ambivalence and ambiguity in the face of systemic oppression (Huygens 2023; Wexler 2016), which is instructive. When pertaining to patriarchal oppression in particular, their expressions of ambivalence resonate with, and at times run parallel to, what psychologists Glick and Fiske (2018) have termed *ambivalent sexism*. For Glick and Fiske, sexism in a patriarchal society is more often marked by deep ambivalence than outright hostility or hatred, as cultural representations of women are "revered as well as reviled" (116). This frame helps us understand the deeply sexist context of the sisters' complicated position as women within the Roman Catholic Church, from their outright subordination and criminalization by the Church to the ways in which their presumably essential feminine virtues are admired in Catholic doctrine (Case 2016; Elliott 2004, 2016; Schüssler Fiorenza 2016). In the women's stories presented here, we carefully witness the ambiguity voiced by some of the sisters in order to present the complex negotiations of power required in their positions throughout their lives (McPhillips and McEwan 2022).

The power and privilege of the sisters in this study are conditional as they navigate patriarchal oppression, economic precarity, and labour exploitation while also enjoying relative safety as white settlers in a settler-colonial nation-state and in a dominant religious institution. In this and other contexts related to Church-based exploitation and exclusion, we invoke Aleta Payne's (2021) critique of the biblical "wise men" to consider the times when the sisters may have witnessed or been complicit in colonial and patriarchal violence and "packed up their privilege and slipped out the back." We stay with "feeling mixed up" when hearing their ambivalence or ambiguity so that we might continue to deepen our historical understanding of institutional power in the Church and in this setting of colonial Canada in the latter half of the twentieth century and into the present. With this feeling as our starting point, we aim to stay alive to the complicated position of sisters and resist the urge to resolve their activities one way or another, seeking to deepen our understanding of why and how people within dominant and sometimes violent institutions make meaning of their practices of resistance and complicity.

We align this set of stories in response to questions about resistance activities by women in the familiar position of outsider-insiders with respect to their faith institution and broader culture. What shape does resistance take among the Catholic women religious interviewed here and what does this realization help us understand about resistance, feminist and otherwise, more broadly? What can be gleaned from expressions of ambivalence? And how can these questions lend insight to our view of social movements and institutions in a time when the future of democratic governance and social progress is uncertain? These queries guide our study of the sisters' stories of resistance.

A NOTE ON WOMEN-CENTRED METHODS AND ETHICS

Who are the women in this book?

This book tells the stories of twenty-six women religious and six former women religious who were affiliated with eight women's religious congregations located in the eastern, central, northern, and southwestern regions of the province of Ontario. The women's accounts were derived from qualitative interviews, questionnaires, and participant observation carried out by Christine Gervais, the primary author, between December 2008 and September 2013.[14]

As shown in tables 1.1 and 1.2, at the time of their interviews, their ages ranged from forty-nine to ninety-one, and their years as women religious extended from twenty-four to seventy-three. The specific year they entered religious life ranged from as early as 1937 to as recently as 1985, while their age upon entry was as young as seventeen and as mature as thirty-four. In terms of their ethnocultural heritage, nineteen were of Irish descent, five were of French descent, two were English-Irish, one was Irish-German, one was Irish-Scottish, two were Irish-French, one was French-German, and one was Indigenous-French-German. Regarding their primary language, two women self-identified as Francophone.

The women religious herein were well-educated, some having completed multiple post-secondary qualifications. For two of the sisters, the highest level of education they attained was a high school diploma; eleven of the sisters completed a bachelor's degree; fourteen sisters obtained a master's degree, and five of them earned a doctorate. In addition, the majority – twenty-six of the thirty-two women – also completed teacher education programs. In their professional lives, the sisters worked primarily in the education sector as teachers, principals, and librarians, while others worked in health care, social work, and hospitality sectors as a nurse, psychologist, social worker, and chef, respectively.

They all contributed to varying extents in their religious communities and in their parishes on committees, on leadership teams, in vocations, and as pastoral associates, choir members, and spiritual directors. At the time of their interviews, twenty-four participants had served as councillors on leadership teams and five served as general superiors of their communities; several sisters did so multiple times, illustrating how women's religious orders are sustained by the numerous roles in which sisters serve in their communities over the course of their lives.[15] For most, their diverse commitments were still being carried out during their "retirement" years, as some were serving in these roles in their seventies, eighties, and even nineties. For many participants, spiritual direction represents a second career and one through which they conduct specialized counselling and healing based on other traditions within psychology, theology, social work, and beyond.[16]

Table 1.1
Current women religious

Pseudonym	*Age at interview*	*Profile*	*Decade of entry*	*Years as a sister*
Adele	68	Teacher, spiritual director, pastoral associate	1950s	51
Agnes	72	Teacher, leadership team	1950s	51
Benita	80	Teacher, alternative education	1940s	62
Carmen	84	Teacher, principal, pastoral associate, counsellor	1940s	65
Clara	72	Teacher, principal, leadership team	1950s	53
Corinne	74	Teacher, librarian, provincial councillor, local superior, support staff	1950s	54
Edna	73	Teacher, religious education, pastoral services	1950s	55
Ella	74	Teacher, spiritual direction, leadership team, general superior	1950s	56
Edith	76	Teacher, professor	1950s	57
Jeanette	63	Chef, leadership team	1960s	44
Joelle	67	Teacher, editor, parish service, program coordination, formation, leadership, general superior	1960s	49
Josephine	76	Teacher, principal, spiritual direction	1950s	57
Kelly	80	Teacher, spiritual direction, therapist, leadership council member	1940s	62
Loretta	73	Teacher, principal, leadership team, general superior, formation director	1950s	53
Mabel	71	Psychologist, public health, leadership team, councillor, general superior	1950s	55
Marian	80	Teacher, treasurer, health care administration	1950s	50
Maureen	80	Teacher, leader of associates program	1960s	46
Mona	70	Leadership team member	1960s	48
Nellie	81	Teacher, parish service	1940s	63
Noreen	68	Teacher, social worker, novice director, leadership team	1960s	48
Penelope	62	Teacher, formation, leadership	1960s	44
Rita	76	Teacher, pastoral care, local leader, convent superior	1950s	52
Sarah	49	Pastoral work, leadership team	1980s	24

Table 1.1
Current women religious (*continued*)

Pseudonym	*Age at interview*	*Profile*	*Decade of entry*	*Years as a sister*
Shannon	91	Teacher, catechetics, adult education, superior of convent in mission	1930s	73
Sophie	82	Teacher, principal, pastoral care in health care, pastoral assistant	1950s	50
Theresa	80	Teacher, principal, leadership team	1950s	54

Notes to tables 1.1 and 1.2: Details as of the date of the interviews or questionnaires. For anonymity purposes, we are not including the specific year or age of entry.

All interviews or questionnaires were completed between 2008 and 2011 (two in 2008, twenty-five in 2009, one in 2010, and four in 2011).

When they entered religious life, the women ranged in age from seventeen to thirty-four: twenty were in their late teens, ten were in their twenties, and two were in their thirties.

Table 1.2
Former women religious

Pseudonym	*Age at interview*	*Profile*	*Decade of entry*	*Years as a sister*
Carol	62	Teacher, principal, youth ministry	1960s	14
Charlotte	75	Teacher	1940s	26
Darlene	68	Teacher, spiritual direction	1960s	42
Judith	76	Teacher	1950s	20
Mildred	73	Teacher, psychotherapist	1950s	33
Naomi	64	Teacher, parish ministry, counselling, formation, holistic practitioner	1960s	28

Why protect their identities?

To preserve the women's anonymity, pseudonyms are employed and the names of the congregations and their specific geographic locations both in Ontario and on various continents where they held foreign missions are omitted. While this concealment of identity may be unusual in writing in which personal accounts are contextualized historically, the women only agreed to participate in the study on the condition of anonymity due to concerns pertaining to their gendered experiences, and to fear of reprisals within the patriarchal Roman Catholic Church (Chittister 2014; Johnson 2002a; Ó'Murchú 1997; Schneiders 2013; Stone 1976). Despite the loss of historical, geographical, and socio-economic specificity resulting from the ethical agreement between the principal researcher and the participants, the women's verbatim accounts, paired with dates, ages, locations, and duties documented herein, provide credible and illuminating sources of oral history and counternarratives that are otherwise fated to be unspoken and subsequently lost to the past.

Our methodological sensibility is consistent with historical literature that argues for the validity of oral history while protecting informants' identities, particularly in research settings fraught with political tensions and past traumas (Jessee 2011; Nì Laoire 2007). While naming participants and providing identifying details lends credibility to historical research participants' accounts, such an approach was not employed in this study due to the aforementioned risks (Nì Laoire 2007). Anonymity offered a safe space for the women interviewed to share "unspoken or hidden narratives" that they otherwise might not have divulged if identified out of fear of reprisal or compromise to their safety (Nì Laoire 2007, 377; Jessee 2011), providing in return a nuanced understanding of the history of the Catholic women's religious orders featured herein. As such, and contrary to Rolph's contention that anonymity results in "condemning participants to remain hidden,"[17] the use of anonymity provided safe conditions to *unhide* the historical accounts of women religious that are undeniably absent from androcentric Catholic Church records (Bruno-Jofré 2007; Johnson 2002a), and that conventional historical methodologies risk losing. Thus, at the cost of missing a measure of historical specificity, these women's previously hidden narratives are brought to light.

Why employ women-centred methods?

Since sisters' experiences have been both denied and disparaged in the androcentric traditions of the Roman Catholic Church (Briggs 2006; Chittister 2004; Daly 1973; Johnson 2002a; Romey 2022; Schneiders 2004; Ó'Murchú 1997), our consideration of how women religious voice their own feminist resistance within some of the world's most striking patriarchal policies and practices constitutes an important contribution to scholarship that seeks to illuminate their spiritual and institutional realities (Murphy 2014; Smyth 2007). By enabling women religious to tell their own stories, as well as genuinely consulting and respecting their standpoint, this study provided women religious with a more secure opportunity to relate the concerns and critiques that are significant to them (Johnson 2002b; Schneiders 2004). In doing so, we seek to contribute to broader scholarly considerations of sisters' experiences that are conducted collaboratively, rather than competitively, and thus with a view to prioritizing sisters' voices as widely, profoundly, and respectfully as possible (Thompson 2018).

Why publish their stories now?

We are publishing these women's stories more than a decade after they were shared in interviews for a few reasons. Since the first author conducted interviews and participant observation from 2008 to 2013, the role of the Catholic Church in advancing settler colonialism through its administration of residential schools has become more widely known and condemned among settlers, particularly in light of the confirmation of Indigenous children's unmarked graves at residential schools across Canada beginning in 2021. This writing accounts for this new social context, interrogating the subjugated position of women within a violent colonial institution as its many atrocities continue to become more tangible.

Women religious remain uniquely positioned given their affiliation with the Roman Catholic Church, yet they remain systematically excluded from official leadership roles and oppressed by patriarchal violence (Chittister 2022b; Wexler 2016). Thus, their simultaneously privileged yet marginalized position has both shaped and limited the lens through which they have observed and experienced (in)equity. Relatedly, both the Church's patriarchal conditions and their own feminist quests have inevitably influenced who they are, what they prioritize, and how they prefer to engage socially and spiritually. The interviews from over a decade ago remain valuable source material because they provide a rare yet clear window into both the historical contexts and the then-current considerations significant to the women at that point in time, and that have not yet been fully analyzed or published. Regrettably, thirteen of the thirty-two women interviewed have died since the data collection phase; thus, in addition to the sociological reasons underpinning this book, we were motivated to publish these accounts out of respect for the women who spent time telling their stories, including those who may still be able to see their thought-provoking words in print.

Finally, we contend that the issues of inequality and exclusion raised in the primary author's first book, *Beyond the Altar* (2018), and in other co-authored publications based on the same interviews, remain not only present and problematic (Evangelista 2022), but in some cases particularly pronounced in this third decade of the twenty-first century (Chittister 2022b; Romey 2022), and thus warrant ongoing scrutiny. In addition, in many regards, the interview conversations between 2008 and 2011 appear to have prefigured various societal and Church-related developments, or more importantly a lack thereof, since then. There is no doubt that with a shift in papal leadership in 2013,[18] there have been gestures towards inclusivity and initial accountability on the part of Roman Catholic Church officials, including Pope Francis's non-judgmental and apparently grateful approach towards members of the 2SLGBTQI+[19] community and the women religious who advocate on their behalf within the Church (Fraga 2021; Yeagle 2022); his openness towards women deacons (Giangravé 2023; Glatz 2022; Zagano 2021a); his 2021 signing of a decree officially allowing girls and women to be readers, altar servers, and communion ministers (*Vatican News* 2021); his inclusion of women's greater participation in the most recent synod (Giangravé 2023; Romey 2022); and his initial, yet historic, apology to the survivors of Canadian residential schools in Rome in the spring of 2022 (O'Kane 2022), followed by the long-awaited official and somewhat more comprehensive apology on Canadian soil in the summer of 2022 (Pauls 2022).

Yet, there is still considerable cause for concern and critique given recent indicators of the ongoing entrenchment of patriarchal supremacy within the Church (Schneiders 2021, 2014; Stone 1976; Wexler 2016). First, considerations of women as deacons are still uncertain given that deliberations of the Vatican's 2016 and 2020 study commissions have stalled (Barlow 2022; Zagano 2021b), and, as some critics have contended, were inevitably "set up to fail" (Giangravé 2023).[20] Such critiques are not without merit, given how Pope Francis seemed to have closed the door on the possibility of ordained women deacons (or priests) during a media interview in the spring of 2024 (Hertzler-McCain 2024; Hunt 2024; White 2024a) and he has postponed discussions on the matter until 2025 (Giangravé 2024; Wooden 2024). Second, the official permission for women to serve in specific positions during Mass does not reflect a significant shift because they have already been serving in such roles for decades (Davidson 2021; Women's Ordination Conference 2021b). Third, while women's input is included in the preparatory phases of the 2023 Synod, and the first woman – a sister – is being granted the right to vote, among other nonordained members' involvement (White 2023a), it cannot be overlooked that such progress is the result of sustained advocacy (Hertzler-McCain 2023),[21] and it remains to be seen to what extent women will actually be part of the main decision-making processes "behind the closed doors where the final draft of Church documents are written, or the pronouns are determined" (Chittister 2004, 170–1, 2023; Romey 2022).

Fourth, and of the utmost concern, we cannot overlook Pope Francis's reinforcement of Pope Benedict XVI's 2010's criminalization of women's ordination through an official canonical codification in 2021 (Holy See Press Office 2021; Women's Ordination Conference 2021a; Zagano 2021b)[22] – which constitutes yet another example of how the patriarchal exclusiveness in the Roman Catholic Church has been written and re-written in religious law for over two millennia (Roll 2015a; Stone 1976).

Arguably worse still, and adding insult to injury – literally, as was seen in the case involving an allegation of repeated sexual violence by a bishop against a nun in India (Kavi 2022) – not only do women and women religious remain barred from certain spaces by men clerics, but when they are allegedly assaulted by them, they are not only unsupported by the male hierarchy, but they are also disparaged by them, including as recently as 2022 (Fernandes 2022; Kavi 2022; McPhillips and McEwan 2022; Thomas 2022).[23] Furthermore, despite Pope Francis's openness to blessing same-sex unions in 2023 (The Associated Press 2023), there is also much to be done in terms of full inclusion of the 2SLGBTQI+ community, including papal use of language (Thomson Reuters 2024).[24]

Moreover, given the Church's extensive and longstanding history of cover-ups and counterlitigation to avoid responsibility and reparation (Stefanovich 2022),[25] and given the perceived partiality of the original papal apologies in both the spring and summer of 2022 in which neither full institutional accountability nor sexual abuse related to residential schools were specifically acknowledged (Bergen 2022; Forester 2022; Pauls 2022),[26] and regardless of the overall progress implied in Pope Francis's penitential pilgrimage across Canada in July 2022 (CBC News Edmonton 2022; CBC News Manitoba 2022; Tucker 2022),[27] it remains to be seen what concrete steps the Church will actually take towards full accountability for its role in orchestrating and facilitating the abuse of Indigenous children in residential schools, as well as for its broader role in authorizing a range of destructive colonial tactics through the Doctrine of Discovery – the latter of which many Indigenous people expected to see officially repealed (Bergen 2022).[28] While the Vatican's long-awaited repudiation of the doctrine in early 2023 was viewed as "a symbolic step forward," it remains to be seen whether actions leading to change on the part of church and government leaders will follow (Winfield 2023).

Ultimately, such struggles towards full equality in all its forms remain an "uphill battle" – to say the least – not only in the Roman Catholic Church and other religious institutions, but also in countless other societal spheres worldwide, including political, economic, employment, and educational ones, due to the pervasive powers that perpetuate inferiority and exploitation. Recent crises around the globe, including shocking invasions, (attempted) coups, and the ensuing systematic assaults against girls and women and other marginalized populations, have served as stark reminders of how readily repression can rear its ugly head, resulting in major setbacks, if and where progress may have already been made.[29]

Consequently, as has been repeatedly expressed across time and space, neither freedom nor equality can ever be taken for granted, as they must constantly be (re)negotiated, defended, and fought for.[30] Constant vigilance must thus be exercised everywhere, and the Roman Catholic Church is certainly no exception. While there may have been some gains in terms of inclusion and accountability, they are nowhere near complete, nor can they be presumed to be permanent, given how we have witnessed often vehement anti-feminist reversals by previous popes in the past (Ruether 2003), and given that the Church's conservative faction remains ever-present and can still regain control in what is still a troubled and unchanged Church (Chittister 2023, 2014; Gutiérrez 2016; Johnson 2014; Romey 2022; Schenk 2021; Schneiders 2021, 2011).

It is in this spirit that we return to the sisters' and former sisters' views on contradictions and controversies shared over a decade earlier, and we bring them into sharper focus in light of current national and international contexts. As we do so, we scrutinize what remains entrenched and what appears to be evolving in terms of the gender (in)equalities and social (in)equities that nuns have sought to address, and we point to ways in which such societal and religious conditions can be informed by sisters' past and ongoing resistance tactics.[31]

SITES OF RESISTANCE

Each amplifying a site of resistance for reflection, the chapters flow through stories of missionary work abroad, to social justice thinking and advocacy across issues of clerical abuse of women and children, to the criminalization of women's ordination, to reproductive injustice, celibacy and sexuality, and homophobia. Staged this way, the chapters forecast the overarching continuum reflective of women religious' complex navigation that involves sustained ambivalence on the one hand, and unwavering conviction on the other.

Chapter 1, "Resisting Repression in Foreign Missions," sheds light on some of the sisters' experiences within oppressive and politically charged contexts in Latin America, Asia, and Africa from the mid-twentieth to the early twenty-first centuries. Particularly, we highlight the innovative ways in which they negotiated their social justice involvement alongside and beyond their proselytic and charitable aims with the impingement of broader structural conditions creating such precarious backdrops. As their practices shifted towards, or at least also involved, resistance tactics along with advocacy-oriented and activist-based engagement, they shared their experiences in controversial and sometimes dangerous encounters involving considerable risks and serious repercussions.

Chapter 2, "Advocating Social Justice," explores how sisters' societal involvement has become more solidarity-based and social justice–oriented in recent decades. Their advocacy work, including public justice, seeks to address broader structural sources of inequalities. In order to shed light on the breadth of sisters' social justice initiatives carried out through empowering approaches "with" people, rather than patronizingly "for" people, this chapter proceeds in four stages. First, we contextualize sisters' path-breaking work in health care, education, and social work. Then, after drawing attention to their earlier forms of activism, we present their contemporary advocacy in the areas of social, environmental, and economic justice. We conclude the chapter by illustrating how sisters manage their identity as "radicals" in their own families, as well as the backlash that they encounter within their own religious communities as a consequence of their inclusive and social justice–oriented approaches.

Chapter 3, "Taking Feminist Positions," presents the women's complicated yet bold feminist positions, drawing on multiple instances of patriarchal oppression by the institutional Church. We draw on women's own descriptions and examples of feminism to demonstrate how widely varied the women's relationships are to the language and aims of feminist activism. Here we underscore a major tension for women religious that threads throughout subsequent chapters: between a passion for gender justice and community service, and the patriarchal constraints of the Catholic Church. We also allude to their creative strategizing around issues of gender equality, planting the seeds for chapters to come.

Chapter 4, "Critiquing the Criminalization of Women's Ordination," applies the feminist lens detailed in chapter 3 to the issue of gendered leadership, spotlighting current and former sisters' responses to the Vatican's canonical criminalization of women's ordination in 2010. In so doing, we relate their feelings of outrage, disregard, and indifference to the range of resistance strategies they employed to challenge the restrictions. While sisters' and former sisters' opinions on women's right to ordination are highlighted, so too are their intentions and actions in response to the Church-based constraints that are leading some to more open spaces and creative rituals beyond those available under the institutional and hierarchical priesthood.

Chapter 5, "Denouncing Clerical Abuse against Children and Women," seeks to shatter the perception that Catholic sisters were either naïvely unaware of or silently acquiescent to the Church-based violence experienced by both women and children. It does so by exploring the sisters' critiques and experiences vis-à-vis the abuse within the Catholic Church, including some cases in which nuns themselves were survivors of clerical abuse. In this chapter, we also shed light on the ways in which Catholic women religious have counselled and empowered survivors of such Church-based violence.

Chapter 6, "Supporting Women's Reproductive Justice," refutes the stereotype that all Catholic nuns are ardent supporters of the anti-abortion movement by attending to the various ways Catholic women religious have defended women's reproductive justice in highly constrained circumstances. Together, the women's stories on issues of abortion provision and contraception establish the tension between feminism and the Catholic Church, particularly given the fraught context of anti-abortion activism in Canada from the 1990s to the present day.

Chapter 7, "(Re)Negotiating Celibacy and (Re)Considering Sexuality," counters assumptions that Catholic nuns are always compliant and chaste by offering a rare glimpse into sisters' reflections on their nuanced and evolving embracing of the vow of celibacy. First, we present and contextualize the sisters' own critiques against the patriarchal control of nuns' sexuality through the habit and the vow of celibacy. Then, we shed light on how women religious struggled, to varying degrees, with celibacy, and in some cases grieved the resulting loss of companionship, children, and grandchildren. We also reveal how some sisters rejected compulsory celibacy through both heterosexual and lesbian relationships and how they made sense of the consequences that often followed. We then explore how sisters now conceive of sexuality and celibacy more broadly by taking into consideration inclusive, compassionate, and non-physical or non-sexual dimensions.

Chapter 8, "Resisting Compulsory Heterosexuality," begins by briefly reviewing the canonical principles and policies of exclusion employed by the Catholic Church that operate to exclude the 2SLGBTQI+ community from religious practice. We then explore not only the outspoken ways in which women religious have expressed frustration and disagreement with the exclusionary practices of the Catholic Church, but also the creative ways in which current and former sisters experience, approach, and advocate for more inclusive and compassionate spiritual and religious communities.

In the "Epilogue," we ruminate on the sisters' courage within patriarchal constraints. We recall compelling examples of the sisters' unwavering commitments to systemic change and consider their calls for change in the context of the intensifying commitments to patriarchal rule by the Roman Catholic Church. The sisters in this study and other women religious scholars and authors cited herein, and those whose voices are not yet appearing in the pages of academic books, have not shied away from calls to action. In this final section, we synthesize their appeals in order to underscore the need for social justice activists and allies to speak up. As we consider the potential of the sisters' inclusivity and the implications of the continuum as women religious (re)vision their future both within and beyond the institutional Church, we wonder about the eventual generational loss of these committed advocates in the inevitably tumultuous years to come.

1

Resisting Repression in Foreign Missions

Christine Gervais and Shanisse Kleuskens

Speak out any place you can.
Judith

INTRODUCTION

Catholic women religious established and maintained foreign missions throughout the world for centuries as part of their religious duties,[1] but relatively little is known about their work and experiences in this transnational history (Grimshaw and Sherlock 2008; O'Brien 2016). As part of their proselytic work to extend colonial ideals and hierarchies, missionaries intervened through educational, evangelical, medical, and other social services. Much of their work reflected assumptions of religious and racial superiority that many of the sisters and their congregations later regretted and revised.[2] As gendered colonialism and racism spurred and sustained missionary intervention,[3] the stories told by sisters in this chapter paint a complicated picture of development work that included their aim to "reform patriarchy at the core of the church" (O'Brien 2016, 1) by working with community.

Similar to their counterparts (Bruno-Jofré et al. 2017; MacDonald 2019), the sisters' stories in this chapter reference their exposure to radical epistemologies of liberation advanced by Latin American activist leaders such as Peruvian philosopher and priest Gustavo Gutiérrez and Brazilian educator and organizer Paulo Freire. Inspired by the tenets of liberation theology of the mid-to-late 1960s, which emphasized the fair distribution of goods and services in a society as well as uplifting the standpoint of impoverished people, they aimed to work in solidarity with communities. They predictably faced various obstacles supporting marginalized populations in this way, particularly as volatile political, social, and economic terrains mired their efforts to intervene in education, health care, and social welfare. As a result, sisters shifted their attention to the broader structural conditions generating such precarious backdrops – ones upon which their charitable efforts would have little impact. Here, the sisters reflect on their controversial roles in development and the personal risk they incurred, unfolding elements of resistance and compliance among insider-outsiders striving to do community work on behalf of a colonial institution.

This chapter sheds light on the experiences of eleven Canadian women religious with missionary experience in nine countries on four continents.[4] Nine sisters and two former sisters were from three distinct Ontario-based religious congregations. Within the one community, Sisters Ella, Edna, Nellie, Noreen, and Penelope embarked on foreign missions in Latin America for various periods beginning in the 1960s; Sister Maureen and former Sister Naomi worked for shorter periods in the late twentieth and early twenty-first centuries in Latin America and in Africa, respectively.[5] From another congregation, Sisters Josephine and Shannon and former Sister Judith worked in Latin America throughout various periods beginning in the 1950s; Sister Shannon also worked in two countries in Asia prior to her time in Latin America. Within a third religious community, Sister Corinne worked in three countries in Africa.

Building on Canadian scholarship that examines the roles played by women religious in advancing Vatican II and liberation theology–based reforms, and by extension in activist or political movements in missions abroad (Bruno-Jofré et al. 2017; Bruno-Jofré and Jofré 2015; Foisy 2012; MacDonald 2019), this chapter brings to light the risks and repercussions associated with both their development efforts and their resistance tactics. In so doing, we illustrate the complex, multiple, and nuanced ways in which resistance occurs (Faulkner and MacDonald 2009; Holtmann 2008; Munn and Bruckert 2010; Ó'Murchú 1997). We illuminate the extent to which the women religious featured herein were willing not only to counter state-based control and conflict, but also to endanger themselves as they worked in community.

BEYOND CHARITY AND TOWARDS SOLIDARITY

Similar to other Canadian sisters' experiences (MacDonald 2019), the women herein recalled that they geared their educational, medical, and social service efforts towards the most vulnerable populations in the most economically impoverished, culturally marginalized, and geographically dislocated areas. Contrary to popular presumptions, women religious now often conduct their feminist and social justice work without evangelization conditions attached, and instead engage in fuller community consultation with the local populations, emphasizing inclusion, dignity, diversity, and citizenship on the part of the sisters, as observed in studies of foreign women religious involved in education projects in mission settings (e.g., Elmúdesi Espaillat 2017, 2024). Through this allyship and solidarity-oriented approach (Ó'Murchú 1997), they have worked to provide education, housing, and employment to children and adults.[6] They have prioritized relief for those who were most in need in the aftermath of natural disasters. They have worked in solidarity with oppressed groups, including Indigenous Peoples, refugees, girls and women, and people living with disabilities. Sister Corinne's work in three countries in Southern Africa for over forty-two years reflected this approach as she prioritized girls' education, orphans, and elderly women affected by the AIDS epidemic; she also contributed to environmental awareness, advocacy efforts, and tree planting.

Given the complex contexts in which they worked, and the fraught conditions of development work more broadly (Mason 2017), it is difficult to determine where their humanitarian efforts ended and their social justice advocacy began, as they melded community work into protest alongside some of the countries' most excluded populations.[7] In such engagement, the sisters appeared to mobilize Eurocentric feminist ideas of liberation in their focus on gender inequality, yet their advocacy with marginalized communities also suggests a deeper feminist understanding that colonial control and heteropatriarchy are intertwined – however fraught, given the intrusion of Western ideas of liberation and equity into Global South communities through their education and advocacy. For example, while in Africa, Sister Corinne witnessed the injustice faced by many diocesan employees, particularly the women, resulting from clerics' command of sexist working conditions and wages; out of concern, she found ways to supplement their pay in the short term and advocated for labour equity over the long term. For Naomi, frontline humanitarian work was a means to an alternative end for the people whom she assisted:

> I went to [Africa] … I was working with … a project to support the women, the widows to become more … self-reliant … and self-sufficient … I felt … I was protesting what had happened by putting myself out to try and create another alternative.[8]

Such a shift towards advocacy was certainly the case in the realm of education where they sought to advance human rights by promoting awareness of (in)justices, aiming to empower marginalized people to defend their communities.[9] As such, their conscientization efforts may be considered broadly as forms of resistance, in which they – from their privileged positions – facilitated the means for others to exert their own agency and challenge complex relations of state, church, societal, and institutional power (Faulkner and MacDonald 2009; Ó'Murchú 1997), including through strategies of subversion, contestation, and even counterforce (Munn and Bruckert 2010, 142).[10] Such education-based efforts are also consistent with the social justice–oriented and solidarity-based approaches that many sisters doing missionary work have embraced, including Gustavo Gutiérrez's ([1971] 1973) *A Theology of Liberation* and Paulo Freire's ([1968] 1970) *Pedagogy of the Oppressed*.[11]

INFLUENCES OF LIBERATION THEOLOGY AND VATICAN II PRIORITIES

The gradual acceptance of liberation theology[12] among some Church leaders along with the foundation laid by Vatican II[13] catalyzed the shift in women religious' meaning of mission into one of solidarity with and for disenfranchised people, rather than one focused solely on evangelizing and charitable assistance (Bruno-Jofré and Jofré 2015; Keeley 2016; MacDonald 2019). Ninety-one-year-old Sister Shannon, who started her decades-long multi-continent mission work in the 1940s, conveyed these influences:

> The documents of Vatican II did stir us up for many who saw need for changes. Added to that were the Documents of Medellín.[14] Many religious felt the call to live more closely

with the poor and a number of members of different communities did so with various reactions from more conservative members.

Many of the women, and particularly Ella, Edna, Corinne, Judith, and Penelope, reflected on how their learning about and embracing of liberation theology manifested in their social justice practices while they worked in their respective mission countries, be it through boycotts of companies deemed corrupt,[15] protests against state repression, or outreach and advocacy for racial and gender equality, all of which constituted various resistance strategies and tactics aimed to subvert, contest, and counter state, corporate, and societal power (Faulkner and MacDonald 2009; Munn and Bruckert 2010). Sister Edna, who served as a teacher in Latin America from 1969 to 1983, fondly recalled her introduction to liberation theology and how its ideals influenced the social justice work in which she and her religious community engaged:

> Oh yes. Oh yes. That was our life ... I remember Gutiérrez, he brought the scripture part ... I went to my first ... liberation theology [class]; it must have been 1970 ... and I brought a teacher with me ... then we bought books and then with the parish priest, we asked for a half day off in our school ... to dialogue once a month on this liberation theology with the teachers. You know it was a reflective way and that was great. And then it was that year that we had a teachers' strike and as a result of that, we looked at it in our gathering and what we would do.

Equally inspired, Sister Ella exclaimed her enthusiasm for practicing liberation theology in her formation work with novices – a duty that she was sent to Latin America to fulfil in the early 1980s: "I lived it in [Latin America]! Oh ... it was so Gospel! It was so right! ... Yes! Yes! ... We fostered it everywhere we could." Sister Noreen, who also served in Latin America in education and formation in the 1970s and 1980s,[16] enthusiastically recalled her more intense engagement in earlier years resulting in part from the philosophy's popularity where she worked: "In [Latin America], this is where I did my best ... social activism."

Although less enthusiastic about the radical and activist aspects of the philosophy than Sisters Edna, Ella, and Noreen, Sister Nellie, who worked as a teacher, local superior, and catechetical director and in parishes for forty years in Latin America, was nevertheless inspired by liberation theology. Sister Nellie coordinated a community breakfast program, modified her primary school teaching, and participated in letter-writing and boycotts, all with a view to addressing various forms of economic injustice including food insecurity, the cost of living, and inadequate wages. As such, she engaged, albeit to varying degrees, in contestation and subversion tactics that sought to improve conditions for the most marginalized members of the local community (Munn and Bruckert 2010).

Among all the women who referred to liberation theology, there were none more outwardly passionate about it than former Sister Judith, who spent twelve years as a teacher and principal in Latin America from 1958 to 1970. Yet, a hurtful rebuff by her religious community as she sought to educate her sister-peers in Canada about the emerging approach dampened her enthusiasm.[17] Her zeal was made evident as she tearfully recalled feeling coldly disregarded after her attempt to render a rights-oriented liberation theology paper accessible to her peers before one of their chapter meetings in the late 1960s:[18]

> At that time too ... I was reading voraciously about Vatican II as it came along! ... But there was nobody to talk to about it ... and that was frustrating for me. Ah! I was in such turmoil! And I took the Medellín document ... I heard Gustavo Gutiérrez ... speak ... It was dangerous ... I was on dangerous ground ... But it was too exciting! ... I couldn't forget that from that time. But the beginning of the document, ah you know, the hopes, the dreams ... it is SO BEAUTIFUL![19] So promising! Maybe that's the way it always is with theory you know and putting it into practice is ALWAYS something harder ... I knew this special chapter was coming up and I wanted the nuns to consider this Medellín thing. I took one of the documents and translated the whole thing and ... had copies made. I said to all of them [travelling back to Canada] "Take it." There were forty-five copies; there were forty-five people. And I sent this begging letter saying "Please read this!" I only got one answer [crying]: "You spelled the word 'reflection' wrong" [crying]. I didn't hear from one single person ... not a comment ... there was nothing. I mean I wanted comments on the document, not on me!

The deep sense of rejection that Judith experienced all those decades ago was still ever-so-present through her tears and pauses during our conversation in 2009. Such an emotional account indicated the extent to which Judith, like many sisters during the Vatican II era, was hopeful about liberation theology because she felt it resonated with and promoted a profound mutuality between the inclusive spirituality and social justice activism that she sought to advance. And yet her attempt to create solidarity among sister-peers quickly failed, indicating both the range of political orientations among sisters and the intimidating climate in which sisters negotiated their positions as insider-outsiders within the Church.

The sisters' practices of liberation theology were not only stalled by varying degrees of acceptance within their religious communities, but also by risks of state-based harm from authoritarian regimes angered by their "interference," as well as by Church-based internal backlash against the sisters' too-public activism (Bruno-Jofré and Jofré 2015; Keeley 2016; Peña 1994). Such risks were prevalent within the mid-to-late-twentieth-century context in which women religious' employment of liberation theology and their activist ethos shook the Catholic Church's identity and authority; this often drew criticism and sexist remarks from Catholic leaders and laypersons who deemed the women's actions to be meddling in political affairs and deviating from their traditional role as the Church's apolitical servants (e.g., Keeley 2016). Importantly, as we show next, women religious have consistently countered such backlash via their ingenuity and resilience.

RISK AND RESISTANCE: SISTERS' COURAGE AND INNOVATION IN THE FACE OF REPRESSION

At various moments over a sixty-year period from the mid-twentieth to the early twenty-first centuries and across multiple continents, sisters encountered repressive state rule that put them at risk of being jailed, deported, or worse. Regarding the context in Latin America, Sister Edna remarked, "Well we had to [be cautious] 'cause we were on the line ... whereas the others they were protesting very militantly and they were being supervised and some of them were never allowed back in the country." Sister Shannon recalled the oppressive constraints under dictatorial rule in the Caribbean, where she served for almost fifty years from 1958 to 2006. As she "observed how people were coping with the reality of the dictatorship" she noted:

> [Y]ou never say in public what you really think; you participate in all the public activities and shout the slogans regardless of recent tragedies in your own family brought on by the ruler. One senses a dark cloud hanging over all. It became a way of life, even children learn very young not to talk to strangers who might question them as to what was being said in their homes.

Sister Shannon's description of the citizens' reactions to the end of the dictatorship in that same country sheds further light on the magnitude of the inherent risks:

> The ringing of the church bells, the dancing in the streets, dancing on every corner six months after the tragic death of the [d]ictator and the last members of the [dictator's] family left the country, were just a slight indication how relieved people were that the [c]loud had finally lifted. There were rough political times ahead but at least they were different.

About a decade later in the 1960s in Africa, Sister Corinne faced a similar context:

> I was always among those who were advocating … more openness … greater equality but … since we were living in … that dictatorship, it seems to influence … even the Church … at a certain time … they kept very quiet.

When asked specifically if she had sought to implement liberation theology, Sister Corinne elaborated that she and other Church representatives exercised caution as they did so:

> A bit yes. But there again … it's a different situation [in Africa] altogether because there, there's the political situation … you have to be careful … It was a dictatorship so … even the bishops were thrown in jail at one time … and one was expelled … an Irish bishop was expelled.

State control challenged their capacity to work in these settings, often due to the muzzling effects such threats had on their religious communities and parishes. All the sisters who served in foreign missions spoke of moments when their safety was jeopardized because of oppressive control. Similar to their counterparts from both Canada and the United States whose mission settings were defined by conflict or war (e.g., Ortiz 2002; see also Bruno-Jofré and Jofré 2015; Coburn 2015; Keeley 2016; MacDonald 2019), some became victims of verbal attacks or physical violence, while others even encountered death threats and were forced to leave the countries in which they were working. Many spoke of the strategic ways in which they either avoided or challenged military personnel following dictatorial orders.

Safety was a concern for all women religious within these settings. Their strategies for handling the threats varied widely, demonstrating their mobilization of a range of innovative strategies and tactics to cope with, as well as resist, the oppressive regimes and conditions in solidarity with the people for whom they advocated (Ó'Murchú 1997). Some sisters were discreet; others directly confronted state agents responsible for government repression through contestation and counterforce (Munn and Bruckert 2010). Along this spectrum, the sisters' and former sisters' resistance included protests against both unjust conditions and the antagonism presented by their church communities towards liberation theology and its revolutionary potential for the Catholic Church (Ó'Murchú 1997). All sisters, regardless of their approach, demonstrated acute awareness of the situations they navigated and courage in standing with the oppressed.

SKILFUL AND STRATEGIC: DISCRETION AND DEFIANCE AGAINST STATE AND CHURCH OPPRESSION

> You don't brandish … any flag.
>
> Sister Noreen

Given the politically contested contexts in which Sisters Ella, Edna, Nellie, Noreen, and Penelope found themselves as missionaries in Latin America from the mid-1960s onward, their work involved navigating competing state, counterstate, and religious entities with caution. Although Sister Nellie, who was much less engaged politically, did not feel at risk of repression, her more activist peers certainly did. For example, while Sister Ella recalled feeling "unsafe … because of … [the insurgents] … the terrorist groups" active in the country at the time, she also pointed out threats from the Church itself as they sought to practice liberation theology: "Oh! [It was] … not so much political as ecclesiastical. It was even worse! You know ... there were pockets of the Church in [that Latin American country] that would be so anti-liberation 'cause they're attached to Rome." Given the power and reach of the Roman Catholic Church locally and internationally, the sisters often had to be discreet as they excitedly embraced the emerging philosophy.

Sister Penelope, who spent twenty-three years as a teacher and formation director in Latin America, did not feel unsafe politically under the repressive state. She did, however, feel the need to exercise caution vis-à-vis the Church's surveillance over religious members' engagement with liberation theology:

> Yes some of them did [lose their lives]. No, in the environment in which I was, no. But in [the capital city] ... through the religious conference centre, we felt [it]. As a formation director, we were often told ... by the cardinal that a certain line of teaching ... wasn't accepted, and so courses would be thrown out that we would have had liked to have programmed for the young people being trained in religious formation.

Living with the knowledge of activist priests and nuns across Latin America who had been tortured and/or assassinated,[20] Sister Penelope qualified her sense of relative safety, and in so doing described the strategies that she and several representatives from other religious communities employed to mitigate risks while exercising their agency to study and pursue liberation theology:

> You had to be careful because we didn't want to lose the religious conference centre and that was the risk ... of bringing in programs that were not approved by the hierarchy ... you could lose [it] altogether ... and to what benefit? ... At least by having the religious conference centre there, you had a framework out of which to be able to work with the youth ... and to lose that framework would have been very [detrimental].

Sister Penelope feared the loss of religious education as a vehicle for sharing liberation theology with youth if the Church or state were to become suspicious of the nuns. She described with a smirk how she and other members of the religious community tactically "worked the system" (Munn and Bruckert 2010):

> Well, the only way we felt safe in rebelling was for the teachers … there to take the courses. Like, if we couldn't bring Gustavo into the formation program … as a speaker to the young students … we [formation directors] could go listen to his courses and bring his train of thought into it.

As Sister Penelope's peer Sister Nellie pointed out, their discreet and cautionary practices yielded positive outcomes, at least for members of their congregation: "We went into courses in [the capital] and with Gutiérrez … we tried to put it into practice, but we didn't die [laughs]."

As Sister Edna echoed her counterpart's concerns and strategies, which were focused primarily on Church-based constraints, she illustrated the risks and intimidation associated with constant surveillance:

> We had to be very careful what we said. In fact, in the parish when we … used to have teachings and go to different parts of the parish … we had to be very careful what we said because it would be reported. And sometimes there'd be one guy sitting back there with a gun in his arm. So you had to be very careful.

Pervasive surveillance from both Church and state demanded innovative strategies from Sister Edna and her peers (Sisters Ella, Nellie, Noreen, and Penelope) to render their liberation theology practices as inconspicuous as possible if they were to avoid repercussion:

> Well, we did in [a rural town in Latin America]. You see in [town], I felt it more. They were really liberation people. They were very, very active and they used to say our parish was not … involved in liberation theology. But we were but in a different way … with the people and working with them in the protests … they recognized we were very much involved but in a different way. We were not … militant and the ones who were … militant, you see … they were on a list and if they left the country they wouldn't be back. And they used to always say, "Are you following liberation theology?" And I said, "Well, come and see." And I resolved from that experience in the parish … they came to recognize that we were involved in liberation theology … We used to go to the classes and learn more about it but it's how you [put it into action].

As Sister Edna illustrated with this memory, her congregation felt pressure from passionate advocates of liberation theology to engage with it more actively, but they knew that doing so might backfire. Evading the question "Are you following liberation theology?" was hardly avoidant; instead, this example demonstrates the shrewdness with which they practised the theology they so fundamentally believed in while avoiding being "listed" and expelled from the country.

Resistance was not always so discreet. Women religious drew upon this same aptitude and that of their communities for organization and preparedness to carry out more overt liberation-informed social justice endeavours.[21] While often in somewhat clandestine gatherings, Sister Edna was also active in risky public protests "in the shanty towns of [the capital where there were] bigger populations, bigger problems closer to the government and the army." Her account testifies to the multiplicity of resistance, including solidarity-oriented and counterforce strategies in which sisters have engaged (Faulkner and MacDonald 2009; Holtmann 2008; Munn and Bruckert 2010; Ó'Murchú 1997). Sister Edna's involvement in "lots" of public marches was underscored when she proudly exclaimed: "Oh yes we protested!" She clarified the issues they were protesting about: "well there it was violence. People were killed innocently and then there was … the repression that the people were feeling in that area. So there was lots of those." When asked if she thought she had risked her life by engaging in political protests, she replied affirmatively: "Oh definitely, definitely." But she felt that the risk was worthwhile given the cause, and was proud of her courageous efforts: "I thought that was pretty brave." When asked if she had feared potential repercussions from participating in long marches, sometimes over 200 kilometres from her mission town to the capital city in the late 1970s, Sister Edna did not recall any major concerns and seemed to have drawn strength from the organizational, informational, and theological preparedness of the community parishioners, fellow sisters, and teachers:

> No, we did it as teachers … I remember in my early years there … oh often … we used to march … from [the town] to [the capital] in protest and ah we had in our parish … in 1978 where there was a national strike and several people were killed. Oh yes, we protested! … [But] I felt we were well prepared. We prepared as Christian communities … several parishes would participate … we had the … facts correct. We had somebody

> from the Catholic university come out and explain to us. Every fifteen days we'd have a debriefing with somebody to explain the facts from a theological point of view. So … we were prepared. So we didn't just make a decision off the top of our head.

Sisters Noreen, Edna, Ella, and Penelope's actions exemplify their capacity to strategize, organize, and generate solidarity amongst their congregations and communities while mitigating the risks associated with a range of defiant approaches to social justice activism. In doing so, they illustrate how resistance is not just actions, but a deliberately considered and employed set of skills, tactics, and strategies (Faulkner and MacDonald 2009; Holtmann 2008; Munn and Bruckert 2010; Ó'Murchú 1997). Though current and former women religious tended to subversively resist institutional oppression from state and religious leaders, they were also willing to directly confront such repression.

INJECTING HUMOUR AS RESISTANCE UNDER COMMUNIST RULE IN ASIA

Sister Shannon served in Asia in the late 1940s. She recalled with delight how she defiantly smirked and giggled at a commander of the new communist regime during a meeting to formalize the sale of the sisters' pigs. This incident occurred after a gun-wielding military guard had marched her and two sisters from her convent to this meeting. Based on her experience growing up on a farm in Canada, she did not understand all the "fuss"; she thought it was ridiculous that the military was forcing her religious community to fill out and sign paperwork for the pigs – a procedure that did not exist before the military began to harass religious foreigners. She resumed her composure only after an elbow nudge from the sister beside her reminded her of the evident seriousness of the meeting. Similar to the comedic relief that women religious have employed as they coped with and resisted constraints elsewhere and across time, including the often pedantic discipline in convent settings (Gervais and Watson 2014), Sister Shannon's small but significant chuckles in response to the perceived ridiculousness of the military's orders demonstrate the potential to use humour and "draw attention to absurdity" as recognizable tactics among a range of subversive strategies of resistance (Munn and Bruckert 2010, 143).

Sister Shannon then explained that this meeting over the pigs was the first of many situations that the military used to intimidate the sisters shortly before they forced them to leave the country – a departure that involved being escorted on foot by four gun-wielding soldiers to the nearby river where they boarded a small boat that led them to a long crossing to a bordering country.[22]

ENGAGING IN DIRECT DEFIANCE DURING POLITICAL UPHEAVAL IN LATIN AMERICA

In the early 1960s, during a time of post-dictatorial political upheaval in a Latin American country, Sister Josephine acted defiantly on numerous occasions through a remarkable range of subversion, contestation, and counterforce tactics (Munn and Bruckert 2010).[23] Importantly, during her tenure as a high school educator and principal, Sister Josephine's own outspokenness in these situations stemmed from her desire to protect her activist students from state harm. In one instance, she disobeyed military police orders explicitly aimed at her, and she defended her stance by effectively reasoning how they were incongruent with local customs; she was thus able to attend the wake of a beloved human and land rights activist who had reportedly been killed. Sister Josephine described the ordeal:

> Mama [T] – a woman in the campo – had been killed … a lot of people were put off their land … she was shot by one of the guards and we [students who insisted on showing their respect] decided that we would go to the funeral which is [customary] and the police chief called me up to the office and said that we were not to go. And I said, "Look, I'm not a [citizen], but I know some of the customs. It is our duty to go. We will go." So we hired a … truck driver … and we went out into the country to the wake – we didn't go to the funeral, we went to the wake – and back.

Although Sister Josephine recognized the risks to both herself (an easily identifiable, fully habited foreign nun) and others in relation to her defiance, her intentional yet revised non-compliance continued as she supported the students' own counterforce activist efforts by helping them find resistance-oriented accessories (Munn and Bruckert 2010; Ó'Murchú 1997):

> Well, just the going out to that [wake], that was considered a protest and what we also did at that point was, I sent uptown for all the black ribbon I could find. And every student who wanted, put a black ribbon on their sleeve, [to symbolize the death of Mama T.,] and one girl, ah, the black ribbon was ripped off her ... when she was going home from school.

Following the woman's death, students at the school where she was principal had planned to stage a protest. Concerned for their safety, she convinced them to instead host a fast on school grounds:

> Then ... the students were up in arms. They were going to go on a riot and I said, "No that's not the way to go. Ah. You'll only get yourself shot and we'll have more funerals." So we agreed with my teachers that we would have a three day fast in the school [for] those who wanted to, and those who didn't, they simply did not come to school ... So we did that ... the women of the town brought us juice ... and then my teachers ... took those three days to ... give them courses ... on a variety of things that would be related to that.

Sister Josephine's efforts to protect her students from potential risks as they engaged in counterforce resistance tactics showed courage and skill. When police stormed the school grounds to arrest the students, she deftly confronted the authorities through a dramatic act of non-compliance (Munn and Bruckert 2010):

> On the last day ... we had all the doors closed. The police came to raid the place and catch all these "bad" students. Ah they [students] went out the back doors and over the fence. And ah I went out directly to the ... head of the police ... and I said to him [emphatically], "You are on school property. You have no right to be here. Take your men and get off here!"

To her surprise, they left, but not without inflicting harm nearby:

> One poor young policeman, who had been a student of mine, had an open canister of tear gas and didn't know what to do with it. He threw it into the grade school yard and the poor little kids got ... tear gas in their eyes ... Sister [Madeline] was not happy. She was principal of the grade school at that time.

Sister Josephine was amazed that the young man had listened to her at all, but others who knew her reputation as a strict teacher may not have been surprised that she could have altered a military intervention the way she seemed to that day. There was also the matter of her relative privilege as a foreigner affiliated with the Church, which contextualizes the resistance efforts and risks of foreign-born women religious relative to those faced by local community members, including children and youth.

On another occasion around the same time in the same country, Sister Josephine was reprimanded by police and warned to stop what was perceived to be counterstate involvement:

> I was up the street and ah I was about to get into my car and a young policeman came down … he said, "Commandante wants to see you." So I went up and he said, "You've been seen going into … homes that are anti-government. You are not to do that again."

Her response to him was emphatic and unequivocal:

> I said, "Listen here. I don't care if they're anti-government, pro-government or no government! I will go into every home where I think I have to go. And I will do that and you're not going to stop me."

Sister Josephine's defiance may have posed significant risks to herself and to her religious community, but it led to government officials backing off. Since she continued to receive arrest threats, she rallied support from the people of the town; when the commander realized how the community supported her, he tracked her down one day while she was visiting a supportive ally and called her to his jeep window to tell her: "Oh Sister, I'm so sorry. I did not know you were so loved in this town … I won't be bothering you anymore." Later when he was being transferred to the border, the commander was reported to have said upon leaving: "I respect no one in this town except Sister Josephine."

While she found the commander's comment and departure to be "a relief," she remained under surveillance, including by other non-military and non-police state agencies: "In fact I was brought into the Department of Education to explain some things." One day, state authorities questioned her about "a note here that was typed" and insinuated that it had been written on the typewriters at the high school where she was principal. Yet, she stood her ground: "I said, 'Well I've checked it and it's not on our typewriters. It's none of [mine].'"

When Sister Josephine defended what many would perceive as risky political behaviour, whether it was through subversion, contestation, or counterforce tactics,[24] the students' safety was foremost on her mind: "I'm not into anything [politically] but when there's necessity, when you're afraid for the lives of your students then, you know, you act!" Nevertheless, Sister Josephine was not the only woman religious and teacher in her community who acted defiantly, risked her personal safety, and faced repercussions as a result.

NAVIGATING REPERCUSSIONS STRATEGICALLY AND PRODUCTIVELY

Former Sister Judith, a fellow educator of Sister Josephine's, reflected nostalgically on her missionary years compared to her counterparts: "It was a great time to be there! Fascination with [the dictator], the invasion, the civil war, all of that [chuckles] ... It was interesting alright!" Although Judith considered resistance in a foreign country to be "interference" because she felt that "politics are up to the [people of the country]," she encouraged activism and shared her enthusiasm for political engagement: "we did like to stimulate the young people ourselves." It is not surprising that she, like Sister Josephine, engaged in counterforce resistance tactics with her students, and was also reprimanded by the state as a result:[25]

> In the '60s ... I took some steps when I was principal in high school and they caught them right away, you know, the Ministry of Education. We had a silent march one time ... there was ... a young Czech boy in 1968 who burned himself alive ... in the Czech uprising in '68 ... our high school kids were ready for all that. I was also ... one of the coordinators of JEC [Spanish acronym], the Young Christian Students ... So I had boys in the JEC ... that was one thing that my superiors let me do. We had a station wagon and I took 10 boys all over the country to meetings of the JEC and it was ... a revolutionary time ...

> So we decided ... the JEC kids and I, to have a silent march ... So we made big posters about human rights and had a silent march with these posters to the church, and ... I was going blissfully on my way and it REALLY was one with the kids. They still remember that. They were REALLY impressed with that ... [But] I got called the very next day into the capital to the Ministry of Education.[26]

The second time Judith was censured by the Ministry of Education, she contested their allegations for the sake of her students by defiantly and cleverly employing the ministry's language against them:

> Another time too, I invited a speaker. He was a wonderful man but he was running for office ... and he was running for another party which I didn't even connect. I knew he was but I asked him to speak at the graduation ... We were all thrilled about ... that speaker ... We just were naïve ... about the politics ... He was a wonderful speaker and he was a lawyer and he was a human rights person, and he gave a wonderful talk. And the very next day, I got the call to go into the capital. It was a woman then who was ... Director of Education ... but I stood up to her that time. I wasn't afraid. Ah she said ... "Sister, how could you get someone from outside the family to speak at a graduation?" And I said, "The family?" And she said, "Well we're the ones who do everything for you." And I said, "Well ... I had sent three letters ... I have students sitting on the floor for school ... I need a whole classroom full of desks. They haven't come." I said, "... do you treat people in your family like that?" The very next day, I hardly got home, when the truck load of desks came in ... So I played my cards right that time.

Nevertheless, despite her outward involvement in activism and the apparent lack of fear she conveyed as she confronted the director of education, the stark reality of the political climate remained a heavy cloud under which she still had to navigate cautiously:

> But ... I wasn't very daring. I mean it was a time of a lot of militarization ... and I remember ... a young teacher in our school, he and I went to see a movie ... I was driving and they [police] pulled us over ... and checked the car ... And then

> after we started up again, I was saying, "I just feel like telling 'em." And he said "I'd be very careful if I were you." He said, "I spent one night in jail and I would not want anything to happen to you."

While Sister Judith's perceived lack of boldness is somewhat ironic given her previous outspokenness against state representatives, it accentuates the degree to which many of the sisters felt that their social justice efforts and ability to freely serve the community were stymied by the political regimes in power. For these sisters, the repercussions they faced from the powerful were not so much deterrents; rather, such threats fuelled their commitment to local movements, as well as their ingenuity and drive to adapt and continue forward, while simultaneously shifting their counterforce tactics of resistance to more subtle subversive forms (Munn and Bruckert 2010). While their enthusiasm and creativity sought to serve the local communities, their peers did not always share this zeal. In the next section, we examine some sisters' feelings of frustration towards their own religious communities that shunned their innovative efforts and minds.

SUFFERING SECONDARY REPERCUSSIONS

Although Sisters Josephine and Judith were relatively safe and successful with their courageous confrontations, they, like other missionary sisters in Latin America (Bruno-Jofré 2019; MacDonald, 2019), struggled with other losses due to their political engagement. In the case of Sister Josephine, she felt disregarded by her religious community because of her efforts, despite the satisfaction she felt in her ability to divert harm away from her own high school students, whose safety was her main priority:

> [It was] the only time I felt that the community did not support me … in the 1960s … But I was principal in the high school … There was a lot of political trouble at that time … I'm pretty sure my students, some of the boys, were into things that they shouldn't have been against the government and so on. But I was protecting them totally. At one point I had been told not to go out at night because they [state authorities] were going to pick me up. Another time … I was told that they were going to take me to the city … I came home. I told the

> sisters that. I did not get any support … for anything. They didn't like what I was doing in the high school … So I did not feel supported then.

While she was perplexed that her religious community did not seem willing to put in place protective measures to ensure her safety, Sister Josephine sympathized with the reasons for their inaction: "they had lived there in [the dictator]'s time when there was a body on the road and the kids would come in and not say anything about it. You know so I mean they had their fears." While Sister Josephine found solace and solidarity elsewhere ("So I went to the people of the town"), her religious community obliged her to return to Canada. Yet since the matter was never discussed, she remained unsure about whether her forced departure was for precautionary reasons, disciplinary reasons, or both.

Like Sister Josephine, Judith also felt unsupported by the same religious community as they faced the same risks within the same political climate in the 1960s. But unlike Sister Josephine, who accepted her religious order's repercussions and remained a nun, Judith took matters into her own hands, and eventually left religious life. In addition to the rejection that she faced when she attempted to enlighten her congregation in Canada about liberation theology, Judith faced other tensions as she sought to remain true to the ideals of liberation theology and Vatican II. For example, Judith admitted to having been an outspoken, and thus controversial, critic against her religious order at the time. But she felt excluded when she became aware, via another sister, that her political activism was a topic of conversation in the motherhouse[27] and in other convents back in Canada. She felt especially hurt that her sister-peers seemed to misunderstand and misrepresent her resistance efforts in these discussions. In her view, she was only trying to implement the Church-informed, and thus Church-sanctioned, practices emerging from Vatican II and liberation theology.

Judith went on to disclose how her unwavering commitment to social justice principles left her feeling profoundly conflicted as her religious community accepted a building from the country's ruthless dictator at the time. The "gift" would have been nearly impossible to refuse given the potential repercussions of doing so. Sister Shannon's description of the building sheds some light on Judith's concern:

> We ourselves were living in a convent built by the [d]ictator's government. [The dictator] liked spectacular constructions. Because of the way it was built, it appeared much more spacious than it actually was within. Much of the space was being used for storage and work in the dispensary.

Since Judith could not reconcile her principles with what she perceived as a problematic scenario, similar to other former sisters in missionary settings elsewhere (Bruno-Jofré 2019), she left her religious community:

> I've had a fundamental argument with the congregation about how we lived in a [developing] country ... even if there was support there at that time ... there was such fear ... and then the politics like [the superior general] had gotten that big convent for us from ... the dictator! ... And ah it just seemed a reflection on her if we moved out you know ... [But] I thought that we could live more like the people ... Ah I think if it wasn't for that [conflict over the large convent "gifted" by the dictator], I think I'd be there yet.

Judith's departure – an ultimate act of protest – can be understood as an escalation of resistance that included subversion in the form of non-engagement. Later, Judith's resistance involved aspects of contestation as she pointed out incongruities, and culminated in a counterforce strategy; her parting served as both a dramatic symbolic act and a gesture of non-compliance with her congregation's orders (Munn and Bruckert 2010).[28]

In line with recognizing her leaving not as a failure to resist, but as resistance in and of itself, Judith's willingness to give up her religious sisterhood and withstand the emotional toll she suffered by leaving her students and teachers without saying goodbye is also a testament to her intense belief in, and unwavering commitment to, her solidarity with the poor and marginalized, a key facet of liberation theology.[29] Her forthright critique against her own religious community was infused with the emerging philosophy's principles: "Where's the community gonna go if it doesn't go forward? ... What's the world's use ... with liberation theology? ... That was my outlook then."

While Judith and Sister Josephine left their mission in Latin America due to political conflict, Sister Noreen left it due in part to political and economic instability. When she recalled how she had entered religious life because she felt that missionary work was the ultimate expression of her faith in God, and was then asked if her missionary work fulfilled her expectations, Sister Noreen's response clarified the circumstances that led to her return to Canada:

> I never dreamt that it was a life commitment. I went down to [Latin America] and … after X number of years I considered taking … citizenship because I thought I was there for life you know. And fatigue, I went through a stretch … [I] became discouraged … that was the time of the [insurgent groups]; things were being blown up. You know we worked so hard to get people established with electricity, with a house … I worked for the Church but I was very involved in how people managed their everyday lives and I think at some point I lost hope and the moment I did that, all the fatigue … that had been accumulating and the stress and you can't be there if you lost hope. These people live by hope and so I came home and I just came to realize, "Well, this is not where I'm meant to be anymore." I no longer had … whatever you have to have in your heart to be among these people [who live by hope].[30]

Sister Noreen's fatigue and return to Canada are telling. In one way, they speak to the substantial contributions of women religious in mission settings, the burden and risks that each of the women took on, and the damage inflicted upon them on many levels. In another, they speak to the lingering inequalities (colonial and otherwise) in missionary work and the relative privilege of foreign women religious in these settings, given their ability to be selective in their subversion. For example, despite often fostering a rights-based sense of citizenship with the communities in which they worked (Elmúdesi Espaillat 2017, 2024; McPhillips and McEwan 2022), they could leave political turmoil, while the people – the countries' citizens – with whom they struggled remained under various forces of oppression without the option to flee. Thus, while the sisters' courage herein is worthy of acknowledgment, it must also be understood more critically within the context of their privileges, including white privilege, citizenship status, and Church affiliation, which ultimately afforded them additional protection and freedom of mobility – including the option to pack up and slip away (Payne 2021).

CONCLUSION

When recalling their earlier work, both in mission countries and after returning to Canada, the sisters' reflections were diverse. While some of their experiences *looking back* indicated feelings of frustration and rejection, as well as memories of risks in relation to their resistance, their recollections exposed how the ripples of their past work extended into both their own futures and those of the people they served.

In reflections on their missionary years abroad, several sisters and former sisters demonstrated their solidarity with the socially and economically marginalized, not just in struggling alongside them and using their privilege to counter the oppressive actions of political leaders, but also in reciprocally learning from the communities they served (Ó'Murchú 1997). It was an approach infused with the philosophy of liberation theology (Gutiérrez 1973) – something that went beyond traditional missionary goals. Such openness to mutual learning and understanding point to the inclusive, and arguably feminist, approach that the sisters and former sisters had embraced and modelled when they worked abroad (Gervais 2018; Gervais and Kleuskens 2019). Such evolving attitudes are also indicative of a desire to shift away from the white-saviour ideals that had undeniably infused their original missionary work, and towards a culture of "respect for the agency of the people" (Cole 2012).[31]

Judith took such a stance. As she did, her ongoing engagement in contestation strategies and in facilitating counterforce tactics among those with whom she remains in solidarity was evident (Munn and Bruckert 2010). While she remarked that her experience working with people in Latin America "[m]akes you want to speak out any place you can" when it came to advancing human rights, social justice, and equality, she viewed her social justice engagement as complementary to the efforts undertaken by local activists, and emphasized the capacity of the local community that she worked alongside, particularly while *looking forward* to the future of their country. Having left the second site of her social justice work in 1980 in Latin America *after* leaving her religious community in 1970, she reflected on the impetus behind the departure from this site: "That was one of the reasons I think we left too 'cause they were ... moving more politically, the women, and we weren't the ones who could do that. They had to do that themselves. Choose their political paths."

Interestingly, Judith's account implies that she was ahead of her time as she applied liberation theology and decentralized leadership practices in the women's empowerment groups that she facilitated post–religious life. Yet, as Judith observed, although it occurred only after she left religious life (and after her congregation had originally disregarded her promotion of the philosophy), her religious community did move forward with many of the progressive ideas generated through liberation theology in their missionary contexts. In fact, they were also part of a wider group of Canadian women religious that called on Canadian bishops in the early 2000s to reconsider missionary approaches: "We hope that the term 'mission' and the 'mission mentality' will be changed in the Canadian church."[32] This recommendation further reflects the sisters' eventual awareness of the importance of a model of global citizenship, service, and solidarity instead of one of religious colonization – and it was upon such a collective realization that they sought to contest yet another institutional imposition. As one who is now closely and positively associated with her former community, Judith has been impressed with the advancements that have been made, however late they were: "Oh I think it's beautiful what they're doing ... Oh! I'm so proud of them! And their mission statement is S O beautiful!"

We cannot underestimate the significance of these sisters' and former sisters' reflections on the reverberations of their resistance strategies and social justice endeavours abroad. They provide counternarratives to the public history of Catholic women religious' contributions to their congregations' work, and of understandings of the female praxis of Catholicism, particularly in international settings. They also diverge, at least in part, from a history of Eurocentric, imperialistic, colonial, racist, sexist, and at times abusive missionary work that conditioned their predecessors,[33] in favour of an idea of engagement that centres on and serves in solidarity with marginalized communities and their cultural wisdom and political desires (Ó'Murchú 1997). Their strategic, insightful, courageous, and often self-sacrificing endeavours to stand and protest alongside marginalized or vocal activists are understood as an ultimate demonstration of their willingness and commitment to resist both for, and with the people they have felt called to serve. Importantly, this work often reflected their forward-thinking objectives despite, in some cases, intimidating opposition from political officials seeking to suppress social justice efforts, and from religious authorities determined to maintain traditional theological praxis. Despite such volatile situations and potentially fatal outcomes, they often manoeuvred outside of their Church-sanctioned charitable work as they advocated social, gender, and economic justice in solidarity with people across borders.

2

Advocating Social Justice

Christine Gervais and Shanisse Kleuskens

I prefer to see the Church and all congregations concerned with the care of each other and of all people.

Sister Shannon

INTRODUCTION

Sister Shannon's emphasis on "all people" reflects the inclusive approach through which women religious have been advancing their humanitarian projects, particularly over the past several decades. As was evident with their evolving endeavours abroad, sisters have always responded to the needs of society's marginalized populations (Chittister 1995, 6). Yet in recent decades, their societal involvement overall has become more social justice–oriented, while remaining benevolent in many regards (McGuinness 2013; Murphy 2017).[1] Sister Agnes proudly affirmed her community's approach: "We try to do it in a solidarity way and ... I think we did it more as charity in the past." They have also been engaged in advocacy work, including public justice, that has sought to address the broader structural sources of gender-based, racial, and socio-economic inequalities and the resulting human suffering (Bonavoglia 2006; Koehlinger 2007; McGuinness 2013; Ó'Murchú 1997; Wexler 2016). Consequently, in their local initiatives, echoing the observations in foreign settings from the previous chapter, they have increasingly embraced an empowering approach "with" people, rather than one patronizingly "for" people.

To shed light on the breadth of sisters' social justice initiatives in Ontario, this chapter proceeds in three parts. First, we highlight sisters' path-breaking work in health care, education, and social work, including the gendered barriers they negotiated while pursuing progress in these fields. Subsequently, we explore the earlier forms of social justice engagement undertaken by sisters, as well as their more contemporary action, advocacy, and activism, particularly in the areas of ecological justice and peace. Lastly, we explore how sisters have managed their identities as radicals in their own families, as well as the backlash that they have encountered within their own religious communities.

ADVANCING EDUCATION, HEALTH CARE, AND SOCIAL WORK

> Sisters built the education system! They built the hospitals! … The country![2]
>
> Sister Kelly

Sister Kelly made this remark as she expressed her frustration about the lack of recognition and appreciation of women religious' contributions by the Church hierarchy.[3] While Sister Kelly's claim remains relevant to the gender injustice that the patriarchal institutional Church still perpetuates well into its third millennium, it also has broader significance outside the Church context, particularly given sisters' pivotal involvement in wider Canadian society over the past several centuries. Since the institutional Roman Catholic Church both "minimally acknowledge[s] and more frequently ignore[s] the contributions of women religious," the crucial roles that sisters have played in the development of Canada's social infrastructure are less known among Canadians today (Smyth 2007, 10); this reality is aggravated by women religious' declining visible presence within both religious and secular settings.[4]

Throughout their trailblazing endeavours to establish Canada's education, health care, and social service systems, women religious were foundresses, owners, managers, and financial operators (D'Allaire 1983; Dumont 1995; Smyth 2007). The sisters themselves were proud of and grateful for these achievements:

> We were administrators in the health care institutions, and principals, and all that. (Sister Joelle)

> I have deep appreciation for what we, as a community, have been able to realize in the fields of health care and education. (Sister Shannon)

The sisters' fulfilment in their foundational role in education also came to light as Sister Noreen joyfully recalled an event hosted in the early 2010s by one of the Ontario school boards in which women religious were honoured for their past contributions to schools. She delighted in retelling the reason that the organizer planned the celebration: "Her point was that the story needs to be told so it won't be forgotten. That was the line ... that was her point to tell the story of people who had built the education system, you know at great cost and we did ... we worked under great, great odds."

Within their enterprising roles, women religious are counted among many "female firsts" in Canada – "the first teachers, nurses, school principals, superintendents of schools, university presidents and chief executive officers of hospitals" (Smyth 2007, 7).[5] Like their counterparts elsewhere (McGuinness 2013; Thompson 2021), the sisters and the religious communities represented herein have certainly held esteemed leadership positions and have developed innovative projects in the education, health care, and social service fields (D'Allaire 1983; Dumont 1995). As subsequent examples show, sometimes the sisters took unconventional action to further their service to the vulnerable people they supported.

While bridging the fields of both social service and health care, Sister Mabel co-founded a treatment centre for adolescents back in the 1960s; the centre has been dedicated to providing a range of support services to youth who struggle with emotional, behavioural, psychological, and addiction-related challenges.[6] Though the public health benefit of this centre is admirable, the backdrop of its founding is also intriguing. Contrary to the expectations of obedience, particularly in the 1960s, Sister Mabel opened the treatment program with neither the knowledge nor the permission of her community's general superior or council. Sister Mabel firmly and enthusiastically believed in the potential of the project, but she assumed that the council would not support her initiative. Thus, she established the centre by somewhat subversively "working the system" (Munn and Bruckert 2010, 143), specifically taking advantage of her remote location to conceal her preparation. This plan also meant that Sister Mabel changed her own housing arrangements to live at the residence itself, for which she, again, did not obtain permission. She later informed her religious community by inviting the superior general at the time to visit her; upon the superior's arrival, in an after-the-fact "look what I've done" moment, Sister Mabel brought her to the residence to show her the project and her new home first-hand. While the superior general was surprised at her "disobedience," Sister Mabel was relieved and grateful for her "openness" when she reportedly responded: "I understand why you did it this way." Both Sister Mabel's ingenuity and her superior general's flexibility are indicative of their willingness to resist the status quo via what Ó'Murchú (1997, 115) referred to as alternative modes or communities that allow for diverse spaces and creative changes through which hope-filled futures can thrive.

In the mid-1970s, within another community of women religious, Sister Benita initiated a project through somewhat subversive tactics similar to those employed by Sister Mabel. After leaving a teaching career on short notice, which in itself created a stir both within her religious community and at the school where she taught, she immediately began to lay the groundwork for a community house in an impoverished area of her city dedicated to supporting people struggling with homelessness and as refugees. It was only in the final stages of the preparation, and after she had already rented a house, that Sister Benita "appealed to higher loyalties" (Munn and Bruckert 2010, 143) by negotiating permission from her religious community's council – the same day that the final rental agreement had to be signed by 4 p.m. Thanks to what she referred to as a "miracle," the council granted her permission in the final hour. As she looked back on how the project plans unfolded, for the sake of the marginalized people who benefited from her courage and enthusiasm, she was grateful for what her religious community granted her, which she felt was "the freedom of going ahead."

Similar to Sister Mabel, Sister Benita was thankful for the understanding that her religious community upheld in the spirit of the social care and equity of marginalized groups. As we show next, however, sisters' (innovative) endeavours in the fields of health care, education, and social work had to contend with the Church hierarchy's disdain, disrespect, and denial of their fundamental role within the institution.

PATRIARCHAL CONTROL OF SISTERS' EARLIER SOCIETAL CONTRIBUTIONS

We did the social work of the Church and the Church controlled that.

Former Sister Darlene

The sisters faced various forms of gender discrimination resulting from the patriarchal control that has been prevalent within both the Roman Catholic Church and the wider secular society in Canada and elsewhere (Bonavoglia 2006; Briggs 2006; Chittister 1995, 2004; Gervais 2018;

Manning 1999; McGuinness 2013; Wexler 2016). Their earlier innovative contributions were affected by patriarchal influences in at least three ways, including (1) socially ascribed gender roles; (2) interference by clerics; and (3) labour exploitation.

Although they had founded, owned, and managed institutions, the fields in which women religious worked were consistent with gender roles that women have historically been socially ascribed when they have worked beyond the domestic sphere: teaching, nursing, and social work – all of which imply caregiving service that is commonly and presumptuously associated with women's work (Mangion 2008; Schneiders 2013; Thompson 2021; Wittberg 1994). Thus, despite their exemplary societal contributions, traditional gender barriers limited the spheres through which they could share their innovations (Chittister 1995). By extension, despite their relative autonomy over the social service, health care, and educational institutions that they administered, sisters still had to contend with interference by both Church (priests and bishops) and secular authorities (boards of directors) – positions all held by men (Coburn and Smith 1999; McGuinness 2013; Thompson 2021, 2022a, 2022b). Such control – an unavoidable feature of the Church's unremitting domestication of women's religious life (Chittister 1995, 28) – was problematic in at least two ways.

On the one hand, women's religious congregations inevitably became "the foot soldiers of Rome" as they were ordered, and often relocated by bishops, to address "the practical needs of the Church" primarily in social welfare sectors over extended periods (Lux-Sterritt and Mangion 2011, 10; Ruether 2003; Titley 2017). On the other hand, and somewhat ironically given the aforementioned appointing of their services, many of the sisters' original organizations were considered "radical institutions" in their day and were "barely tolerated" by the men-led establishment in both religious and societal spheres because they catered to those among the "useless levels of society" for whom patriarchal authorities did not provide public services (Chittister 1995, 12, 28–9). To add insult to injury, in some instances, sisters' programs that had previously been disregarded, yet excessively controlled by the ecclesiastical hierarchy, later became conveniently identified as "diocesan" initiatives (Chittister 1995, 165). Yet regardless of the Church's resistance, control, or appropriation of nuns' initiatives, the sisters always "forged ahead" by prioritizing existing and evolving needs (Chittister 1995, 164–5).

Patriarchal influences also impacted women religious' employment experiences. For many years in their own institutions, sisters served intentionally without salaries as nurses, teachers, and social workers (Gervais 2018; McGuinness 2013).[7] Yet, as their schools, hospitals, and social service offices became public institutions, they were often expected to continue their unpaid service.[8] Such was especially the case with separate Catholic schools in Ontario. Many sisters recalled how until Catholic high school education in Ontario received full funding in 1984, they were expected to teach without pay, while their lay counterparts received a salary. In addition, like lay women within the context of salaried employment, women religious were often underpaid compared to their men counterparts, including religious ones. Sister Adele recalled an incident when she personally felt the patriarchal presumptions of clerics when she worked as a paid staff member of a parish:

> The patriarchal part of it was … in operation when I was a part of a group who really challenged the salaries of pastoral associates in our diocese where I was working … and that came out of my own experience in the parish, and it woke the priest up in the parish because I got mad! Because the secretary said to me, "Ah, am I supposed to raise your salary too?" and I said, "What do you mean?" And she said, "Well you know the priests' salaries have increased."

Sister Adele contested this disconcerting news by drawing attention to the problematic incongruities related to patriarchal policies and practices (Faulkner and MacDonald 2009; Holtmann 2008; Kaylin 2000; Munn and Bruckert 2010; Ó'Murchú 1997; Schneiders 2013):

> So I went to the pastor and I said, "What's this?" … So he was just kinda embarrassed. He wasn't going to tell me though … I said "You know that I'm working full time, over time here as much as you are, if not more. [chuckles] And … I just find that really insulting you know." … So anyway … he thought about it and he came back and he said "I realize your community is subsidizing you." And I said "This community is not subsidizing me; it's subsidizing this parish and this parish doesn't need to be subsidized by the [name] Sisters." And he said, "Yeah you're right." It was like the light really went on.

Sister Adele's experience was consistent with the challenges encountered by other women religious in Canada and the United States who have, in some cases, received less than half the salaries of men religious and/or were deprived of similar educational or employment opportunities (Coburn and Smith 1999; Leonard 2008). Yet, similar to other instances where resistance is employed in the interest of a wider collective or broader community (Faulkner and MacDonald 2009; Holtmann 2008; Munn and Bruckert 2010; Murphy 2022; Ó'Murchú 1997), what is especially impressive with Sister Adele's handling of the situation is how she transformed her own experience of discrimination into an opportunity to address equity issues and to effect positive change for others' wages within the Church, including those of other lay women:

> First it went on personally … Then it went on … bigger than that. We're asking the [Name] Sisters to subsidize a parish by having someone work for less than a living salary and our sisters had been doing that or had been willing to, well the previous one, but I wasn't. And I said, "… I mean we're not going to be here forever. How are you going to hire lay women or lay men and how are they going to live if the tradition is that the salary of the pastoral associate isn't something a person can live on you know, even simply?" Yeah, so. I was part [of that] … movement … so we ended up with a committee … to draw up some guidelines … We changed the name from the pastoral assistant to associate then too because we thought it was more accurate [chuckles] and it also invited more of a collegiality. So we changed the name and we did get some movement in terms of a more just salary.

Despite the gendered obstacles that hindered their endeavours, the sisters' work in education, health care, and social work served communities beyond the Church. It is also important to recognize, as we do next, that women religious were also involved in agitating for social justice.

PAST SOCIAL JUSTICE ACTIVISM

Despite the above-mentioned gendered concerns, numerous sisters' societal engagement in past years transcended traditional, socially ascribed careers for women (Bonavoglia 2006; McGuinness 2013;

Wexler 2016). In fact, it would be misleading to suggest that only in very recent decades have sisters been engaging in social justice activism. Many sisters were very involved in counterinstitutional efforts, sometimes "disobediently" through counterforce strategies of resistance, as they sought to oppose various forms of injustice (Bonavoglia 2006; Faulkner and MacDonald 2009; Holtmann 2008; McGuinness 2013; Munn and Bruckert 2010; Ó'Murchú 1997). Former Sister Naomi, who self-identifies as "mild mannered," proudly recalled her public activism:

> Oh, I marched for everything, you know, [in] the '70s; I was looking at my buttons. Oh ya ... I was a student, I was a sister ... Cesar Chavez,[9] I can remember him coming; it was when I was in university; but oh ya, those were great years; we just protested everything ... Cesar Chavez was the lettuce [boycott], oh and the wars ... well I have always been a big protester ... like every time there was an [issue].

Former Sister Darlene shared Naomi's concerns about war and was publicly active about it decades earlier: "Well I was activist in many ways, like during the Vietnam War for example, in full habit – this is a funny story – in full habit I dumped garbage on the American consulate lawn in [city]. So ... you know I was activist there." While some may be impressed by Darlene's counterforce and protest-like resistance strategy involving a rather dramatic symbolic act (Munn and Bruckert 2010; Ó'Murchú 1997), she herself, while still maintaining an anti-war stance, acknowledged that her past behaviour was inconsistent with her current approach of non-violence – a reflection that points to sisters' sometimes ambiguous, or at least evolving, attitudes. Nevertheless, the image of a habited nun engaging in civil disobedience conjures up a paradoxical yet myth-busting image of the religious sister.[10] While some members of activist nuns' religious communities may not personally agree with such public protesting against 'the establishment,' the majority of them still do; and in fact, like many of their counterparts in the United States, including the *Nuns on the Bus*,[11] and elsewhere, like the famous "kneeling nun" in Myanmar,[12] they applaud their fellow sisters' activism, particularly that which is anti-oppression, anti-war,[13] and pro-peace in orientation, and, in some cases, join them in these struggles (Reed 2004, 122; UCA *News* 2022).

CONTEMPORARY SOCIETAL CONTRIBUTIONS

The best people in the church are the nuns! By far! I mean they're doing serious work.

Judith

While many people tend to assume that the primary social issue concerning Catholic nuns is abortion, sisters and former sisters are both individually and collectively focused on a wide range of issues, especially those pertaining to social, economic, and ecological injustices.[14] The matters include, but are not limited to, inequality more broadly,[15] and, more specifically, child poverty, human trafficking and modern-day slavery, inaccessible education, and the closing of Canadian prison farms, as well as climate change and the related human and environmental devastation resulting from mining, oil extraction, and other extractive industries.

Today, women religious continue to respond to these issues while also engaging in awareness-oriented initiatives, a form of resistance that Ó'Murchú (1997) refers to as "conscientization"; these include sensitizing others to issues of inequity and engaging in solidarity-based activism intended to propel broader structural transformations (McGuinness 2013). As Sister Ella proclaimed, "We've become more educated. We teach each other and we incite each other to greater commitment to those [social justice] sorts of things. We take them on together."

In the sections that follow, we explore how women religious' contemporary contributions have evolved into wider action, advocacy, and activism that promote social justice across a range of spheres. As Holtmann (2011b) clarifies, the subtleties and intersections of the three approaches can be understood within the modern Catholic approach to social action that many women's religious communities adopted based on the Second Vatican Council's primary document on Catholic social teachings, *Gaudium et Spes*.[16] While there may be subtle differences among, as well as intertwining across, advocacy, action, and activism, we distinguish them to illustrate the breadth of sisters' endeavours.

ACTION

While sisters' involvement in advocacy and activism has increased in recent decades, they continue to respond to the immediate needs of the individuals for whom they advocate in a variety of ways

(McGuinness 2013); as such, they have been feeding the hungry and addressing the structural sources of hunger simultaneously (Weaver 1985). Various congregations have engaged in the frontline work at soup kitchens, food banks, women's shelters, hospices for the homeless, residences for the elderly, temporary residences and furnishings for refugees, winter clothing programs, drop-in centres, street outreach, life skills training – a myriad of activities aimed at providing support to society's most marginalized, all with an emphasis on welcoming everyone without distinction.

Sister Loretta recounted proudly how her religious community had partnered with another group of sisters located in the same city to address child poverty – an issue that was identified as a priority by the Canadian Religious Conference. To this end, in the early 2000s, the two religious communities established a drop-in centre that supports low-income single mothers through the provision of resources in the areas of health, nutrition, education, and recreation.[17] The sisters' commitment to families affected by poverty is enduring. While the staff and volunteers have been resourceful in obtaining grants,[18] the women religious assume the expenses that are not covered by external funding and consistently pay the centre's rent and the salary of one employee. However, as yet another testament to the sisters' principle of humble service, their involvement with this centre is not known to the general public.

While continuing their immediate actions in education, social service, and health care, many sisters have also invested their human and economic resources towards addressing the structural impediments to human and Earth justice, targeting broader political, economic, social, and environmental contexts that they consider oppressive and detrimental, in line with a "structural transformation of society" (Chittister 1995, 12). We explore the advocacy and activism that they undertake toward such a transformation in the following sections.

ADVOCACY

> I want to do something to make the world a better place …
> [F]or the global family of God.
>
> Sister Clara

With a view to identifying and challenging oppressive arrangements, women religious have been engaging extensively in advocacy work intended to heighten awareness about a wide range of social issues associated with an "endangered planet" and "global injustice."[19] They draw attention to these concerns through various educational efforts (Ó'Murchú 1997), including via promotional material on their websites, in email correspondence, on posters in their retreat centres, in discussion points in their bulletins, and by word of mouth.

In addition to promoting the events that they themselves organize, women religious often advertise other groups' social justice initiatives; they do so either in their own private emails or by way of their communities' official websites or emails. Through these means, they have been known to both endorse and encourage campaigns calling for Indigenous rights, corporate accountability, non-violence, a national housing strategy, a poverty reduction strategy, the global day of peaceful action, new human-Earth relations, sustainable agriculture, and local food security projects, among others.

While social justice–oriented sisters often engaged in advocacy work within their local neighbourhoods, they also actively contested through their own religious communities vis-à-vis their church. Notably, midway through the first decade of the twenty-first century, some congregations of women religious represented herein put forward a formal message to Canadian bishops via a Canadian Religious Conference survey, calling for greater leadership from Church officials on a range of matters. Together, they exercised resistance agency as they engaged simultaneously in conscientization and contestation forms of resistance, along with loyal disobedience (Munn and Bruckert 2010; Murphy 2022; Ó'Murchú 1997), by pointing out various incongruities as they articulated their critiques of the Church's problematic policies and put forth recommendations, some of which focused on social justice issues, including ecological stewardship, and solidarity with efforts both in congregations and on the public stage that took a countercultural stance against injustices (Holtmann 2008; Ó'Murchú 1997). The following excerpts reflect the overall concerns and expectations that one of the congregations raised in that message on matters of peace, ecology, and justice:[20]

REALIZATIONS

We recognize that social justice and the transformation of society is integral to the call of the Gospel. Religious communities, especially those of women, have been and are courageously responding to this call.

> We know that many Catholics are walking away from their parishes because they do not find the messages they hear anything that really challenges them to be active, responsible citizens of the world.
>
> CRITIQUES
>
> We deplore that while the people of the world suffer immense injustices, some of our bishops focus on insignificant details around liturgical practices.
>
> We deplore ... the disrespect for the intelligence of the Catholic community shown by some of our Catholic Bishops who, for example, refuse to allow certain Catholic publications ... to be distributed in parishes.[21]
>
> We deplore the opportunities missed by the official Church to stand with others in peace walks and other events organized to show solidarity with those who suffer most.
>
> We deplore the fact that Church teachings on social justice and ecology are rarely referred to in homilies.
>
> We deplore the Church's lack of leadership in promoting a right relationship with all of God's creation, especially in the face of ongoing damage to our ecology, world-wide.
>
> ASPIRATIONS
>
> We hope for a Church that challenges its people to seek justice for all creation.
>
> We hope that religious communities who take counter-cultural stands on issues will be supported by the Church.
>
> We hope to be able to bring critical thinking, wonder, questions, speculation, evaluation and criticism to all issues.

Such perceptive statements are indeed indicative of nuns' profound opposition to the Church's inflexibility on certain social issues. Yet, rather than standing by and simply hoping "that the official Church will speak with more urgency and courage to the issues of time" – a desire identified in the letter to Canadian bishops[22] – many women's religious orders themselves have established advocacy-based and awareness-oriented initiatives that are often situated within their spirituality centres, and include bulletins and workshops, as well as entire offices dedicated to the goals of peace and justice. Similar to that of their counterparts elsewhere (McGuinness 2013), the sisters' advocacy has been rooted in a systemic approach to justice that is research-based and transformation-oriented and takes into account the various intersecting sources of political, social, economic, cultural, gendered, and environmental barriers to human and ecological justice. Sister Edna proudly summarized the processes and benefits of what her congregation refers to as their systemic justice committee: "it feeds to us so we can participate ... and ... groundwork has been done so that's ... dealing with the problem at the root of it ... and on a wider range."

In this context, sisters offer retreats and workshops to promote awareness through critical reflections on spirituality that are infused with ecological mindfulness and social responsibility. Such conscientization practices are intended to develop and enhance an integrated worldview and to encourage all to identify and challenge oppressive arrangements (Ó'Murchú 1997), as well as to inspire alternatives and engage in informed actions that lead to progress in the areas of social, cultural, and Earth justice. For example, several religious communities represented herein have organized what some refer to as "assembly days" to promote Indigenous justice. Within these workshops, often led by women religious of Indigenous descent and by Indigenous elders or activists, they have not only explored Indigenous spiritualities,[23] but they have also examined the political and economic sources of racial injustice, as well as the actions required to ensure that Indigenous rights are upheld.[24] Similar awareness-oriented initiatives regarding many other cultural groups have been organized within their retreat centres so that the sisters can both benefit from and contribute to a greater understanding of multicultural inclusivity. Many women religious' profound concerns regarding culturally based division and discrimination were conveyed by Sister Clara: "It's so impossible to imagine that racism even exists because of the global family of God."[25]

Language is another vehicle through which progressive sisters deliberately model their inclusivity and sensitivity. In so doing, they engage in educational efforts to counter marginalizing tactics tainted by status quo (mis)interpretations (Ó'Murchú 1997). For example, whether it be through private conversations or public dissemination, when they identify their meeting locations, they often refer to "gathering spaces," and when they identify the target audiences for their events, they frequently note that "all are welcome." Furthermore, in the context of the challenges faced by refugees and immigrants, they use terms that tend to be more empowering and inviting; for example, they refer to the individuals as "new Canadians" and to their experience as "resettlement." Their critical orientations are evident in their use of terms such as "xenophobia" or "racialized persons," drawing attention to the broader societal challenges impacting marginalized people's experiences. While such intentional terminology may not appear all that consequential to an already critical eye, it is nevertheless indicative of significant shifts in sisters' communications and actions, which have historically been exclusionary on social, cultural, and religious levels.

ACTIVISM

In addition to voicing their solidarity with marginalized populations, women religious have been politically engaged in activist efforts that seek to contest the "unjust structures" (Sister Adele) that both generate and exacerbate inequalities and exclusions. To this end, and to varying degrees, the sisters have initiated and participated in a broad range of both contestation and counterforce resistance tactics (Munn and Bruckert 2010, 143) of the active protest variety (Ó'Murchú 1997), including marches, vigils, petitions, letter-writing, lobbying, and boycotts to transform marginalizing conditions within their local, national, and global communities. Sister Benita's own examples reflect the multiple and concrete ways in which many women religious engage politically through a social justice lens, including letters to Canadian prime ministers and Ontario premiers:

> I've written to Harper; I've written to McGuinty; I've written to … Paul Martin; I've written to … Chrétien … The issues were … funding for housing … we fought for public housing. I marched … downtown for the march for subsidized housing.

Others, including Sisters Agnes and Adele, have promoted and participated in national and global days of action or major marches in support of health care for refugees, climate justice, and Indigenous sovereignty,[26] among others. While they have signed petitions, including many addressed to members of Parliament on a variety of social matters, Sister Mabel recalled that her community also "sent a lot of letters" regarding the Monsanto case against Percy Schmeiser of Saskatchewan, Canada.[27]

While many sisters have participated in activist initiatives organized by other societal groups, some sisters, as well as entire communities of sisters, have established advocacy groups dedicated to eradicating issues such as human trafficking. Sister Joelle relayed how her community had been inspired by presentations on human trafficking at a meeting held in Rome by the International Union of Superiors General:[28] "Human trafficking … I hadn't been aware of that issue until then. And we came home and decided we'd educate our people … I think sisters were in the forefront of that." Sisters Sarah and Adele both responded to a similar call to action and had been directly involved in the founding of a community-based non-religious advocacy organization that engages in both awareness and activist efforts aimed at preventing human trafficking in Canada and throughout the world.

To illustrate the extent to which current and former sisters have been involved in activism, we highlight some of their engagements on the issues of *ecological justice* and *peace* – both of which were prominently discussed in our interview conversations.

ECOLOGICAL JUSTICE

The sisters' and former sisters' social justice orientation has been both enhanced and informed by their enthusiastic emphasis on the environment. Like their counterparts elsewhere (McFarland Taylor 2007), they have been drawing attention to a shared responsibility to the "Earth community" by promoting Earth Hour and Earth Day and by engaging in activist endeavours "seeking to address the issues of climate change" (Sister Adele), among others. Sisters like Clara who were not afraid to "speak truth to power" have also raised awareness about, and inspired others to challenge, resource extraction, mining-related conflict, and agrofuel production that result in extensive ecological and human devastation. As a further testament to their commitment to advocacy, numerous communities of women religious within the province of Ontario, including all but one of those represented by the participants in this study, have been involved in sponsoring, organizing, and/or attending conferences, workshops, and other awareness-oriented events on Earth justice.

In recent years, as women religious have engaged in activist efforts, they have shed light on the wider context in which people are situated by making reference to, and offering understandings of, bioregionalism, the "sacred universe," and the cosmos.[29] Sister Kelly explained how her community emphasized the broader picture:

> I think we have a tremendous charism. It's at the heart of the Gospel ... that all may be one ... bringing about union ... Union of ourselves and our neighbour and now we've extended that to the universe, you know, and the planet.

The sisters' reverence for sacredness, which has encompassed a profound respect and gratitude for creation and the Earth, is evidenced in the sisters' promotion of ecological justice. Eco-friendly approaches to life were not only something that they raised awareness about, but also practices that they themselves carried out. Sister Penelope explained her group's approach:

> Our cluster[30] has been looking at the whole issue of cosmology and our whole relationship with the universe and all the creatures of the universe including my little animal here [referring to her pet dog] ... and, you know, appreciation for my responsibility in what the universe is going to be in the future ... Trying to just be more green ... recycling, it's very much in [the] foreground of living now, trying to live ... and preserving water and conserving water and not using Styrofoam and not using plastic and that sort of thing.

As Sister Penelope underscored by her reference to cosmology, women religious have engaged in spiritually informed ecological justice that they attempt to live out on a daily basis. Some women's religious communities have also constructed new buildings that are certified "green" or have retrofitted their existing buildings to be as eco-friendly as possible.[31] Their other less structural, yet commendable, efforts are rendered visible by the notices and signs that we have seen around retreat centres that are encouraging and facilitating recycling, composting, and energy conservation as "environmentally responsible" gestures undertaken out of respect for "our lovely universe."[32]

In moments of participant-observation, the primary author also observed first-hand how some sisters uphold their firm eco-friendly beliefs in spaces outside of their own residences and centres when they decline the water bottles they are offered in private or public settings because they disagree with the environmental exploitation associated with both the production of plastic and the extraction of water – an example of the many ways in which some sisters live their activism for ecological justice through small but significant gestures throughout the course of their day. Both their individual and collective gestures reveal how the women religious herein have been part of a long-standing and still growing global movement of "green sisters" who have been raising awareness, embracing ecofeminist-spirituality, effecting eco-friendly changes, modelling sustainability, and practising conservation (McFarland Taylor 2007). The extent to which the sisters saw their eco-spirituality and eco-justice endeavours as intertwined was a further reflection of how their advocacy work was an integral and evolving part of their religious practice (Gebara 1999; Holtmann 2008; Ruether 1992).

WORKING FOR PEACE, AND DOING IT PEACEFULLY

There's a demonstration on the [Parliament] Hill and we missed it! How come?

Sister Adele

This comment was often said jokingly, yet disappointedly, by Sister Adele's social justice partner, who is also an activist nun, when they would hear about a protest after the fact. Since Sister Adele took part in "many, many, many demonstrations," it was rare that they missed them. She also clarified that not only were they involved in pro-peace protests, but they always ensured that whatever demonstration they took part in, they "were peaceful and only peaceful and we wouldn't be there otherwise." When they educated themselves and their religious congregation about peaceful initiatives, Sister Adele was adamant that they were mindful of both thought and action and that they focused on institutional inequalities rather than individual errors:

> When we speak, we really are non-violent; when we act … we are clear about our stance and I hope that we'll be really careful, and careful with people … [W]hat we're challenging in those instances are institutions, not people. We're not attacking people. I mean … it would be easy to get into attacking people. But

> that's not what I want to do ... and that's not what it's really about. If you're trying to change structures, it's structures that you address. And you don't tear down people ... They're a person to be treated with dignity.

As noted earlier, many women religious have been engaged in anti-war initiatives over several decades. Sister Clara is a tireless proponent of peace, whose stance is unapologetically critical and anti-state,[33] and she, like many of her peers, has engaged in a range of conscientization, subversion, contestation, and counterforce resistance strategies over the years (Munn and Bruckert 2010; Ó'Murchú 1997).[34] She proudly recounted that through her social justice advocacy, she has openly cautioned others not to be deceived by governments that try to convince the public that weapons are essential to either personal or national security.

More recently, and particularly since September 11, 2001, several sisters, including Adele, Agnes, and Corinne, have been involved in pro-peace demonstrations. As Sister Adele recalled her activist efforts, she realized that most of them were peace-oriented: "A lot of them are around war ... we've been on the Hill lots with other people, with other groups ... we often went as a group to take part in the anti-war things particularly." The group to which Sister Adele referred is an inter-faith pro-peace women's alliance that she helped to establish and that gathered weekly around the peace flame on Parliament Hill for over a three-year period "to support ... the anti-war movement, to keep us out of the Iraq war." When the primary author praised Sister Adele for her involvement in founding the group, she humbly yet insistently clarified the non-hierarchical approach through which the group originated: "But we started them together with others." Sister Adele elaborated on the informal and inclusive way in which the group developed – a testament to the sisters' circular models of leadership, organization, and governance:

> It was after 9/11 and seeing the response of violence, of meeting violence with violence ... it was ... a small group of women religious here ... from different communities who met, and it was just at the end of that meeting, we were talking about how we just might do things together to support each other in social justice ministry. And one of them said, "What are we going to

> do as women as a response to 9/11?" And we said, "That's important. Let's meet again." We met again and then said, "Let's widen the circle" ... and then we said, "Let's really widen the circle" and it became interfaith ... so we continue to be actually ... lay women ... with women religious of different communities and also ... a Jewish woman ... a Muslim woman ... sometimes there are some young women that she'll bring along or sometimes some of her friends her own age too ... So we're small but we haven't quit![35]

In addition to their public demonstrations, as well as their congregations' peace and justice offices, other sisters have focused on promoting peace at the micro level within their own individual realm, all the while being mindful of the wider connection to peace on a global scale. For example, as Naomi elaborated on the inspirational influences in her life, she clarified the link between her own personal peace and Earth-wide peace:

> Thích Nhất Hạnh ... would maintain that peace does have to begin in each heart because ... if we carry the seeds for war, war will happen. So ... on a personal level, I'm committed to looking at, you know, watering my seeds for peace and addressing my seeds for war and then I'm working actively ... to live in greater harmony with all of creation.

Sister Shannon shared a similar view as she recognized how a personal mindset may limit the potential for peace on a broader scale: "One of the obstacles to peace is clinging to our own opinion and being closed to respecting another's point of view." Such critical and thoughtful reflections are indicative of how current and former women religious have been increasingly emphasizing societal accountability on broader scales that involve both the micro and macro dimensions of the human experience, including the promotion of both inner and global peace.

As we have already seen, sisters' concern for human and ecological rights has often extended beyond community, provincial, and even national issues, with their persistence and passion propelling their voices and the effects of their efforts into forums and countries beyond their immediate circles. Perhaps ironically, however, their tenacity has been tested in the most intimate of environments – their families and religious communities. As we explore in the last part of this chapter, sisters have had to contend with challenges both to their identities as activists and to their social justice initiatives. In turn, they have embraced these challenges as opportunities to practice patience, discipline, and empathy.

SISTERS AS "RADICALS IN THE FAMILY"

> I think we need to be more radical witnesses ... I think we are called to be countercultural and sometimes I'm not sure how countercultural we are, but I think we're called to be that.
>
> Sister Clara

Sister Clara shared this statement as she proudly reflected on how her activism helps to challenge the stereotypical perceptions of women religious as passive citizens. Her specific reference to *radical witnessing* resonates with many sisters' engagement as advocates and activists. As a result of their "countercultural" stances, their compassionate and inclusive approaches, and their corresponding conscientization efforts (Ó'Murchú 1997), sisters and former sisters related that they were often considered the "radical" in the family when it came to social justice issues.

One of the most emphatic examples of relatives' perceptions of sisters' radicalism involved the sister whose childhood story we recounted at the outset of the book. When she was six years old, she had made her brothers feel uncomfortable in church when she stood up and openly criticized a visiting priest because he was conveying a "hell, fire and brimstone" message in his homily. Her refusal to listen to the homily and to the priest's command for her to sit down and be quiet, along with her subsequent exit from the church in protest, generated sentiments of discomfort and disapproval on the part of her siblings: "My brothers thought I was totally off the wall. I just embarrassed them all in church. I didn't care." To this day, she remains a strong and unapologetic resister of all things discriminatory and unjust.

As Sister Maureen reflected on how sisters are often viewed as radicals by their relatives, she laughingly admitted: "They all often say that about me!" She, along with other nuns, recalled how they tended to hold alternative views, while their siblings, and particularly their brothers, tended to have more traditional opinions:

> My family ... well maybe it's because I am a sister, they're challenging me all the time. And I have a brother that ... Honest to God, no matter what I say, he doesn't agree with it. Like he was for Bush and [laughs] ... I honestly think he brings [conservative] things up ... to challenge me. (Sister Maureen)

> It's funny, eh, in the same family, my brother, he's a year and a half younger than I am ... and when we changed from a complete habit into a partial habit and then into slacks, "You're going too far too fast." This is my own brother, brought up the same ... he's just of a conservative bent, you know. (Sister Theresa)

> It's been interesting with my family. My brother's seven years older than I am and ... I find he's a challenge sometimes, not with the Church that much, but with ... racism and ... things like that we have disagreements about. But it's interesting like I've always been able to ... point out different things that make them [relatives] think too. (Sister Loretta)

As Sister Loretta reflected on how she has debated and dialogued with many of her relatives, all the while encouraging them to be more open minded about social justice issues, she also clarified, with much consideration yet again, how and why some women religious may have a broader and more compassionate approach compared to some of their family members who may have "narrow-minded" views: "Well just because they don't know! ... We've had more opportunities to be out there though and to hear ... and to really understand and I think they haven't had that." Sister Maureen had the same understanding regarding why she and her conservative-oriented brother held differing opinions: "But ... we have to remember that here's somebody speaking from a different place, you know." Sisters Loretta and Maureen were referring to the ways in which women religious have been exposed to the complex contexts of various forms of marginalization, either through retreat-based awareness-oriented initiatives that their religious communities have facilitated for their members, or through direct experience with oppressed individuals and groups in local and foreign social justice projects. As such, through their own educational efforts and active protests (Ó'Murchú 1997), they have learned the importance of compassionate approaches and life-giving advocacy (Faulkner and MacDonald 2009). That said, sisters' religious communities are not always fully facilitative of social justice initiatives, as we explore next.

NEGOTIATING PUSHBACK AGAINST THEIR HUMAN RIGHTS APPROACH

In addition to having encountered pushback within their own families, women religious also faced challenges within their religious orders and in the wider church communities. The sisters' commitment to human rights was undeniably impassioned and they felt the same as Sister Corinne about how human rights were significant in their religious life (Holtmann 2008): "I mean it's primordial … I think … as a Gospel itself, it's human rights; Jesus came … to bring that out, you know." Comparably, Sister Maureen proudly asserted that her human rights focus has "always been strong." However, similar to other nuns' experiences, it was the strength of her convictions that earned her a negative reputation among some of her fellow sisters, whose reactions sometimes discouraged her:

> I was into that quite a bit and … I remember I was at some meeting and somebody was saying, "Maureen, Maureen, what do you want anyway? You're always looking for something!" [laughs] … And … I find that stayed with me because it really hit me [laughs].

While Sister Maureen faced rejection by fellow women religious in earlier decades, Sister Sarah recalled the compromises that she continued to make as she negotiated domestic decisions among sister-peers who did not share her social justice convictions. Here she referred specifically to the difficult choices related to boycotting certain products in favour of purchasing those that are fair trade:

> I … definitely buy what I can fair trade. I'm actually the person in the house who does the shopping so I like to buy fair trade, local … environmentally that goes with kind of the screens that I like to use although … if someone puts lemons on the list, well I kind of cringe but … in the interest of community

> sometimes I can't be [always buying fair trade]. I would be a lot harder on myself than, like ... there are things I would not buy for myself that I will buy for the community because I feel that everybody's got their ... personal responsibility.

Contrary to Sister Sarah's internal struggle, Sister Rita recounted her early-twenty-first-century efforts to counter a setback by a new parish priest. Given how Sister Rita considered Sister Clara to be "a prophetess if there was ever one walking around," Sister Rita and a progressively minded priest had been promoting Sister Clara's social justice writings amongst the parishioners in the rural parish in which they both served. However, when both Sister Rita and the pastor left the parish to work elsewhere, the new priest questioned the political nature of Sister Clara's social justice newsletter and refused to allow its continued distribution among parishioners. Sister Rita was frustrated when the new priest insisted on obtaining approval from the bishop and the chancery office: "That sent me around the bend." When she intentionally went out of her way to return to the parish to call out the new priest about his refusal, she defended Sister Clara's social justice bulletin by pointing to its impact: "I know it's sometimes difficult to read Sister Clara's papers but it's because my conscience has really been pushed ... [It] is marvellous ... it perks[36] everyone's conscience." Taken together, Sisters Rita, Sarah, and Maureen's accounts are indicative of how many women religious are rights-informed in an institution that is not rights-respecting.[37] Relatedly, their testimonies also reveal how, despite the dissonance they experience due to their religious congregations' and parishes' attempts to mute their orientations, humble service can coexist with courageous resistance, spirited personalities, and passionate practices of human rights–based faith (Holtmann 2008; Murphy 2022).

CONCLUSION

The women religious interviewed have clearly continued to work for those on the social and economic margins, as they have been doing for centuries (Bruno-Jofré et al. 2017; Smyth 2007). That said, their contemporary contributions, which remain considerable, are noticeably more social justice–oriented and solidarity-based, and are in many ways indicative of their genuine realizations of the wrongness of discriminatory religious doctrines and harmful societal divisions

(Ó'Murchú 1997). Consequently, these women have often been at the forefront of resistance-oriented activist efforts "to challenge unjust structures in society and in the Church" (Sister Adele) through their advocacy and service work (Holtmann 2008; Murphy 2022). By extension, while their past charitable works were saturated with an evangelization agenda, and arguably colonizing and conditioning ones too, their current eclectic spiritual base has enabled them to be of service to others without imposing their religious tradition. As such, like their contemporary counterparts across the globe,[38] the sisters herein can be recognized as spiritual women who have been facilitating social progress, with a view towards wider societal reconstruction and ecological renewal. In turn, women religious' more recent prophetic visions and practical quests have been forward-looking, compassionate, and reflexive: seeking the pacification and humanization of all people and of all creation, developing a dialogue of diversity, and promoting not sameness, but oneness (Chittister 1995, 2004).

3

Taking Feminist Positions

Christine Gervais and Amanda Watson

> But if you are a woman, who wants to hear your story? The garden is called quicksand, the place you should not go, the people you should not talk to, the books you should not read, if you are going to be a "nice" woman. The planting of it is called "dissent," "heresy." But till it we must.
>
> Chittister (2004, 165)

INTRODUCTION

For women religious in a patriarchal Church, identifying as feminist is a bold move. Advancing feminist perspectives, particularly in the decades before the language of gender empowerment became common in North American popular and commercial media,[1] is a fight on many fronts against a powerful hierarchical organization (Bonavoglia 2006; Osiek 1986; Wexler 2016). Given this context, we interpret the work of feminism here to include acts of resistance and expressions of feminist opinion – both of which open the sisters to scrutiny and reprimand by institutional Church authorities who perceive such positions as dissent and even heresy (Chittister 2013; Faulkner and MacDonald 2009; Fisher 2012; Elliott 2004; Holtmann 2008; Kristof 2012; Manning 1999; Murphy 2022; Ó'Murchú 1997; Osiek 1986; Romey 2022; Schneiders 2011, 2013).[2] While subsequent chapters shed light on the ways in which the sisters have enacted feminist resistance in subtle ways, this one explores the extent to which women religious have dared to utter their feminist views in contentious circumstances. The sisters report a range of strategies that they felt compelled to employ in order to resist patriarchal norms – from tempering their tones to choosing their audiences and settings – and some reflected emotionally on the challenges they faced, including the obstacle of their own socialization and loyalty within the Church (Chittister 2004; Holtmann 2008; Huygens 2023; Murphy 2022; Schneiders 2004, 2013; Wexler 2016).

Whether the sisters were variously inclined to keep their feminist values under the radar or express them confidently with clear intentions of disrupting clerical and institutional norms, their collective positions reflected diverse strategies toward the same ends. Taken together, the sisters' range of expressions of feminism gives a sense of the complexity of advancing gender equality in a community of varied support and hostility (Barr Ebest 2003; Dumont 1995; Gebara 1999, 2002; Holtmann 2008; Howard Ecklund 2003; Hunt 2024; Huygens 2023; Kalven 2003; Osiek 1986; Romey 2022).[3] The following sections show the sisters' feminist articulations as strategic, contextual, and unwavering.

"I CHOOSE MY MOMENTS"

As the sisters navigated oppressive attitudes, they were sometimes less forthcoming with feminist assertions since they expected to be met with backlash, including from some sister-peers who did not take kindly to challenges to the status quo organization of patriarchal power in the Church – a testament to how women themselves were conditioned to be complicit in churchmen's clerical constraint sustained by fear-instilling tactics (Elliott 2004; Ó'Murchú 1997). Their caution also implies hesitancy to be seen as a feminist killjoy (Ahmed 2010), or as someone who deliberately spoils the enjoyment of others with what are perceived as disrespectful or outlandish views or behaviour. They reported strategically maintaining a passive or feminine tone to appear nonthreatening to potentially sneak their points across to skeptical audiences. Responding to whether she felt comfortable expressing opinions on gender equality, Naomi reported how she proceeded with caution:

> Oh I do! I feel very comfortable but I also choose my moments ... there's still people ... I have close [male and female] friends that I have to be careful with ... who either don't relate to the issue, which totally amazes me, or feel threatened ... so I mean to this day I'm careful ... in my circle, either people are with me or they're not, and I'm respectful.

In response to the same question about comfort level, Sister Corinne echoed the importance of tone, supporting the idea that the style of expression is key for its efficacy as well as her comfort level: "Quite yeah. But it depends what you say … and how loud you say it. [chuckles] Yeah." And, in line with familiar experiences of exclusion and degradation by feminists who speak up against various forms of injustice (Chittister 2004; Ó'Murchú 1997; Osiek 1986; Wexler 2016), some sisters recognized that not only would their messages not have been understood if they did not strike the right, nonthreatening tone, they might have actually made matters worse for themselves and others. Their political convictions were tempered by the reality of being considered too disruptive. On expressing gender equality within her congregation and the broader church, Sister Clara claimed that she always felt comfortable, but clarified how communication is sometimes (re)considered:

> It depended when that issue ever got raised but I find … the way you do it is so important. Some of us … turn people off … you can't … you know … sometimes I just think, oh don't say that. I know that they're angry and I know that they have a reason to be angry, but it doesn't do anything for the troops kind of, it makes it worse.

When asked if she felt safe to express opinions on gender equality, Sister Clara shared how while she has softened her own tone in the hope of inspiring people who seem hard to reach, others were influenced by her formerly unhesitant and sharp approach:

> Oh yes … I try to be … a little more gentle … [but] some are getting wild instead though. It's getting to be hilarious … one said to me, she said, "I don't know what's getting into me. I've never been like this in my life" … that's how … you have to inspire. That's why when you come up angry … you don't inspire people. I try very much to inspire people.

Her amusement is intriguing, perhaps a way of coping with the steady sexism surrounding the sisters' positions in the Church. Even in tense and frustrating circumstances, she derived humour from the willingness of her colleagues to unapologetically ruffle the feathers of people in power. Sister Clara did not let us forget that the sisters are powerful and dynamic even in positions of subordination by a patriarchal organization and broader societal misogyny (Chittister 2004; Elliott 2004). Taking a less vocal but direct approach, Sister Penelope was also discerning about the way in which she communicated her opinions. She never felt silenced by Church clerics, "because I don't think I ever spoke out strongly and I still don't ever speak out strongly; it's only my actions; I speak by my actions." She indicated that she would only have felt safe to express feminist ideas in certain spaces and among certain people.

Some of the sisters who exercised caution when expressing their desires for gender equality recalled how their articulations evolved as feminist ideas became more accepted, or at least less shocking, over time: "Oh now I can … yeah" (Sister Benita). Reporting on previous decades, Sister Ella was fearful of repercussions if she spoke out about gender equality: "Fearful you know that it would be misunderstood. You'd NEVER be heard. You'd never be heard or understood … just a gut feeling that was right and ah hang on to it if you can't express it yet, hang on to it and it'll be your place." When asked if she felt comfortable to express feminist thoughts more recently, Sister Ella replied, "Mhmm. Pretty much." She added, "I guess I expressed these kinds of things more around people to whom I pretty well know that they think the same … even a bishop or two [who are] quite accepting." Rather than painting women religious with a feminist brush, Sister Ella reminded us that openness to gender equality and the potential for solidarity appears in unexpected places and does not neatly align with gender or institutional rank.

On the contrary, Sister Jeanette seemed comfortable discussing gender equality among other women, even if they disagreed with her, perhaps reflecting a less threatening environment among a group considered peers in terms of rank, or perhaps because the group did not include men:

> I'm not afraid to express it … Even in our community there are some sisters who are against women priests and that. Well, I'm not afraid to express myself with my own sisters. I just say this is my viewpoint; I respect yours so now you respect mine. And I'm just saying what I feel and that's it.

Yet, although Sister Jeanette claimed that she was not worried about potential repercussions by priests and that such negative reactions "never entered [her] mind," she was nevertheless cautious about whom she confided in outside of her community. She indicated that she would never discuss gender equality with a priest or bishop because "I don't think I'd feel comfortable. I don't think they're at that space."

Even sisters who reported feeling more comfortable identifying with and expressing their feminist values did so with an eye on the end goal. Sister Agnes explained that she "definitely" felt comfortable to express feminist ideas within her religious community, but she was both cautious and strategic when she conveyed the ideas among Church officials:

> Well I'm a little more guarded because … I try to do it positively. Like as I did with … Bishop [name] … I tried to say that this is so beautiful, it's scriptural. We're using our voices to praise God you know. I'm pointing out as well as I can and I think very well … why we think this is good celebration at liturgy and he tells me why it's not. But I still don't [back down]; I still continue to say why I think it's good liturgy.

Her characterization of women using their voices in scriptural ways also calls to mind how praising what are seen as essentially feminine traits (Elliott 2004), in this case associated with beauty and celebration, reinforces what Glick and Fiske (2018) refer to as ambivalent sexism. Clearly, the atmosphere that sisters were navigating was undoubtedly variously hostile to ideas about gender equality, and the sisters showed acute awareness of the need to package messages so that they would be better received, and even to harness sexist attitudes in service of improving that reception. Similarly, Sister Joelle, who reported feeling safe to express feminist thoughts and concerns about gender equality, was somewhat more hesitant after experiencing opposition, particularly from priests. As was evident by her statement "If the occasion would present itself," she would not necessarily seek out or initiate conversations, nor would she remain silent.

"WE JUST HAVE TO BE CAREFUL SOMETIMES"

The sisters' strategy – to strike relatively unthreatening and calm tones and to choose their moments and audiences strategically when it came to raising issues of gender inequality in the Church – aligns with what others have described with respect to how they positioned themselves politically. Similar to Catholic women elsewhere (Huygens 2023), Canadian women religious have tended to be less publicly vocal than their US counterparts in their contestation against gender discrimination within the Roman Catholic Church and in society at large (Gervais 2018; Reed 2004). There were important reasons for their caution. The sisters in this study were commenting at a time when women religious in the United States were being investigated by the Vatican for so-called radical feminist manoeuvres that allegedly undermined the moral teaching of the Church – a standoff that reflected the Roman Catholic Church's persistence in controlling women's contributions, and particularly their leadership (Chittister 2014; Schneiders 2013, 2014; Schenk 2014; Wexler 2016), and one that Canadian sisters understandably wanted to avoid. When Sister Mabel referred to her open expression of feminist opinions, she immediately clarified how the geographic location in which her activism occurred had a bearing on her public participation: "But that was in [a US city], the [American] sisters … they do a lot of that a lot more … Oh! No [in Canada] we're much more … conservative and much more placid and much more … Canadian!" Sister Mabel went on to share how the lack of feminist critique on the part of Canadian women religious regarding the patriarchal dimensions of the Church frustrated her: "When I first came back, I thought 'everyone's dead around here.' You know when I came back from the States after 20 years, like I couldn't fit in. It was a totally different culture."

Sister Mabel was not alone in her perception of Canadian congregations as being subdued when it came to vocalizing calls for gender equality. Sister Loretta admitted, "I talked to a lot of people … but no, I have not [spoken openly about inequality] publicly." On why not, she explained:

> Well, a few years ago, we were very vociferous about things and … we got into trouble. I'm talking "we" as a congregation … and it was like you're hitting your head against a stone wall. So we didn't seem to be accomplishing anything by that. All they did say was "They're just angry women" … and that's not true. So we kind of pulled back, I think … I think we kind of gave up on that and said it's not worth it.
>
> BUT… I'm speaking personally … if I had an occasion to say something if somebody was [inappropriate], I would say it. I'm not afraid to say it. But … I'm not going to go out looking for it.

> Well, we just have to be careful sometimes … I think we do speak our minds when we have an opportunity to, and people know where we stand but … we're older too … if we were … a young congregation, I think we'd certainly be out there.

Sister Loretta clearly spoke about the past with hindsight, reflecting on what she thought may have been a general, deflating sense of unease and dejection among sisters after that specific experience of rejection by Church leaders in her congregation. Sister Maureen similarly recalled the context of past initiatives, underscoring a kind of uncertainty about her own potential to act based on the widespread feelings of the time:

> I don't know for myself why I didn't … I wouldn't have done it without getting permission like letting them know what I was doing. I don't think I would. Maybe I would too, you never know. I could; sometimes I respond spontaneously at the moment and then you know think about it after. BUT sometimes we're not conditioned to think that way somehow … which is not good. It's a very sad situation for us.

Echoing countless women and women religious across time and space (Bonavoglia 2006; Elliott 2004; Wexler 2016), Sister Maureen's reflections were emotional, as she pondered aloud the way she internalized her own sexist socialization and how this self-discipline likely impeded her ability to act with conviction in response to specific events. She referred to the circumstances as simply sad, invoking a picture of sisters in conflict with themselves. Sister Sarah's impressions were similar, as she also admitted feeling frustrated by the question of whether her congregation of women religious would ever reject Church authority if pushed too far. Explaining how a new archbishop imposed historical ideas and rules on a variety of issues, not specifically pertaining to gender, Sister Sarah revealed,

> Oh definitely … definitely, definitely, it frustrates me and it causes me to ask the question like, "How far can somebody push a group of people until they really revolt?" … I often ask the same question about my religious congregation … "Why don't we sometimes as women's religious congregations, why don't we just stand up and say no?"

> … Yeah it's a question that I think about all the time with the Church and … I don't understand what we have to lose. And … I think of Hildegard who she and her sisters buried a soldier … they took a stand against the position of the Church and buried the enemy kind of and were excommunicated for it. The … foundress of … the Institute of the Blessed Virgin Mary, the IBVM's was excommunicated for a period of time …
>
> Like to me… right now there's … a visit going on from the Vatican to the sisters in the United States. To me it's like "Oh! We're doing our job" in a sense when those kinds of things happen because I think that's part of who we are is … to make sure that … power is not abused, that there is a role I think for women religious to hold the hierarchy accountable.

Here Sister Sarah was speaking in the context of the Vatican investigation of the sisters in the United States who were explicitly reprimanded for their feminist views and activism (Murphy 2022; Schneiders 2013; Wexler 2016). Thus, when asked if a group of sisters could indeed revolt, she qualified her affirmative response by noting a potentially significant risk:

> Yeah I think we could. Yeah! … I think … it causes a lot of conflict because … there's a lot of … good that's done under the wire that in some ways we would be jeopardizing that by becoming so public … I think that's part of it.

Though her desire to disrupt status quo hierarchies of power in the Church is unambiguous, Sister Sarah articulated a sense of doubt over how publicly to hold power to account. Asking if they would "go our own way," she seemed to answer by wondering if some hills should be climbed covertly. Reflecting a sense of contingency, Sister Maureen's sense of courage to express feminist thought was not always consistent, and she also linked this actuality to how sisters were socialized:

> I'd like to say that's what I want to do but I don't know whether I do that all the time. You know sometimes we're conditioned to "don't rock the boat," you know? I'd like to say I do. I know I do it sometimes but … I don't know that … I'm at the stage yet where I can do it at all times.

Being careful, for these sisters, included strategizing around their particular goals, reflecting on their trained complicity, and considering the risks involved in speaking out, both to themselves and to the feminist project at stake.

FREEDOM "ON THE EDGE"

Some sisters did not mince words when it came to identifying with feminist values of gender equality, but they remained strategic. When asked if she felt safe to express her feminist thoughts as a woman religious, Sister Adele replied, "Oh yeah!" without hesitation, but she clarified her comfort level within the broader Catholic Church, speaking of the need to be tactical:

> Well … I do … but … I choose the circles I travel in the Church … I choose to be where there's the freedom to go ahead and do [what I feel called to do].

Sister Adele was referring to the way in which she has been selective about the parish she was a part of because it is very progressive with its social justice and gender-inclusive approaches. Similarly, Darlene has also been strategic in her selection of workspaces. When asked if she felt safe to express feminist thought, she replied:

> Yes, because I'm on the edge of the Church anyways and I'm not [as visible] publicly; this is a kind of private ministry in a sense; it's not part of the officialdom, you know, even though I work here in a ministry that is supported by the sisters here. They have a pretty open, justice-oriented kind of a thing anyway and I fit very well here but I am on the fringe and I'm not very involved in the official Church out there. I don't go to parishes. I don't do any of that.

Rather than tempering her tone, Darlene's strategizing has involved working in liminal spaces where she was less likely to be met with hostility (Murphy 2022).

Somewhat ironically, Sister Mabel's reflection on the perceived limitations of her leadership role emphasized the relative independence of sisters on the edge of the Church, and the limitations of those with institutional visibility, even if they are in positions of relative power.

On why Canadian women religious have not openly expressed their anger and frustration against the patriarchal Roman Catholic Church, Sister Mabel commented on her perceived responsibility as a leader:

> See, one of the things as general superior, I can't just speak out ... as a religious sister, whatever you do, it affects the congregation and so over half of the congregation would be scandalized at the way we feel about the Church ... and ... it comes up in discussions. But you always have to be careful, I feel, in speaking out because of the whole congregation ... I am very conscious of ... there's a real bind there. I'd speak out much more except that I am a representative of the leadership of the congregation ... If you had a deliberate confrontation, they would be very upset.

Her consideration of context was not limited to her own personal consequences, but on the potentially negative impact on her congregation which looked to her for leadership. On how the sisters could inspire or at the very least affirm other (lay) women who struggle with gender inequality, Sister Mabel revealed the sisters' awareness and discernment in that regard: "There's a lot of conversations ... in our area ... about ... how the Church isn't [inclusive]."

Echoing Sister Adele's desire for freedom above, and Darlene's sense of being on the "edge of the Church," Sister Noreen reflected on the liminal space within. As she revealed her willingness to express feminist thoughts, she referred to her mother's inspiration which she interpreted through a nuanced lens of autonomy and agency:[4]

> I need to say something about my mom. I think ... my mom ... was a fighter; my mom was ... confined to being a mother ... and in Quebec having many children in many ways, and she loved every one of us, but she had them because the Church said women should do it and boy I knew that ... my mom ... did her bit, but ... then my mom wanted to go to work ... and you know have some independence. My dad wouldn't hear of it because ... the man of the house, he's supposed to be the breadwinner and all of this. I think ... even though she was pretty shackled by what was expected from the outside, my mother was a free person inside; she was a free person inside and really inspired ... me to retain my personal freedom in an oppressive situation and there is a way to do that ... My father resisted my mom ... I think my

> mom tried the boundaries, she tried to push them; she never sat back and started to feel sorry for herself or started to criticize.

Even as the sisters' experiences and views overlap, their comments repeatedly show that there is not one template for articulating feminist values in or on the fringes of their church communities (Chittister 2004; Huygens 2023; Osiek 1986; Schneiders 2004; Wexler 2016). Sister Noreen's "personal freedom," inspired by her mother's internal power, calls up Virginia Woolf's (1929) famous notion that freedom of mind cannot be shackled or locked. When compared to reflections on how they were conditioned to keep the peace, though, and modify their tones, the sisters were, and remain, intricately tangled in strands of power and subordination (Brock 2010; Chittister 2023; Elliott 2004; Manning 1999; Ó'Murchú 1997; Osiek 1986; Romey 2022; Schneiders 2004; Wexler 2016).

OVERCOMING "THE INERTIA"

> The women's movement has brought strain to women's communities themselves between those who see the questions as dangerous to the faith and those who do not.
>
> Chittister (1995, 13)

As Chittister's words underscore, congregations of women religious are far from homogenous, and fear over pursuing feminist questions can derive from the dynamic ways in which sisters position themselves and their responsibilities within or with respect to the institutional Church. The sisters' views and feelings were not static in this regard, and some reported struggling with what they perceived as the inertia of the institutional Church and of their own collectives; Sister Mabel clarified the context:

> Across … congregations … you don't rock the boat. [With the] LCWR [in the United States, they put] … placards out there and there's something that goes out to everybody. We don't do that. I don't know what the inertia [is] … I think it's a very conservative kind of culture.[5]

Still, sisters have found avenues to exercise power, sometimes with mixed feelings (Brock 2010; Chittister 1995, 2004; Huygens 2023;

Murphy 2022; Osiek 1986; Schneiders 2004; Wexler 2016). Sister Maureen depicted how the struggle against others' traditionalist views could be challenging and fulfilling simultaneously:

> I know that we have a couple of sisters here that are ... very anxious that we belong to the Church, the Church doctrines and that kind of thing. And I don't mind disturbing them. I don't know what it is that sometimes I'm conscious about. Maybe ... not so much recently but I have been, and you know that's something I'll have to work on.

Yet, at other moments, Sister Maureen was content and confident in standing her ground. For example, when she reflected on openly criticizing the presence of a priest as the only celebrant of the Eucharist, Sister Maureen explained that other sisters "just kind of accept it" but she questioned it, and when the "flak" was directed towards her, she did not get upset. "It didn't bother me," she said. Sister Maureen went on to say that when she "ruffles feathers" among both patriarchally oriented women religious and men clerics, "sometimes that's a good feeling."

While she acknowledged that she had a strong temperament, Sister Marian admitted that on some issues, she may have "given up opinions" when she spoke with priests. When asked specifically if she felt safe to express feminist ideas, Sister Marian was initially more definite: "Yes I do, yes ... given the opportunity to I would, yeah." Yet later she identified a potential barrier: "You see we have a corporate image too, you know, and I think I'm spooked by that sometimes." It is not always easy to be a dissenting voice in a powerful institution, even if one has clarity of convictions (Brock 2010; Chittister 2004, 2023; Holtmann 2008; Huygens 2023; Ó'Murchú 1997; Osiek 1986; Romey 2022; Schneiders 2004; Wexler 2016). Sister Edith nuances the idea of the institution representing hierarchy and oppression exclusively and she explains her sense of loyalty: "I think ... that as a member of a community you feel a certain loyalty towards the members. You don't just provoke them unnecessarily [chuckles], but I think there's a growing consciousness too of the inequalities and the need for social justice which includes ... gender equality." Still, she does not confuse her loyalty to certain community members with her social justice aims, simply reminding us that the need for social justice and gender equality is still provocative to members who she respects.

Feeling clear about her own sense of gender equality, Sister Noreen seemed to discern the sense of inertia as well, not wanting to spend time trying to convince those with entrenched views:

> Oh yes, again, in certain situations I wouldn't even go there, okay, I'm more discerning where I put my energy because sometimes you do more harm than good you know, if people who are closed minded, you know some of them, I think sometimes, I'm not going to be the one to open their minds. God will do it; but not through me.

In contrast to the sisters' personal navigation of the internal institutional inertia over the years, in the mid-2000s, some congregations of women religious sent an extensive set of insightful messages regarding gender (in)equality in the Church to the Canadian Catholic bishops. Some of the many incisive statements about gender (in)equality that one congregation proposed to include in the collective message via the aforementioned Canadian Religious Conference survey included but were not limited to:[6]

> REALIZATIONS
>
> We recognize the involvement of many people of our Church: cleric and lay, women and men in these organizations, schools, spirituality centres and institutions and in diocesan and parish programs.
>
> CRITIQUES
>
> We deplore the real exclusion of women in the Church and the lack of a venue for true dialogue with the institutional Church.
>
> We deplore the rigidity of leaders regarding issues such as … [the] inclusion of women.
>
> ASPIRATIONS
>
> We hope that the Church leaders will recognize the training and gifts of women, and their desire to serve God's people and that new opportunities will be created for women to exercise real authority in the Church restoring the full equality that Jesus envisioned in a Church that models itself on Acts 2.
>
> We hope that the power of women with fresh ideas, hope and willingness to risk will attract younger women (and men) to the Church as leaders.

> We hope for a venue for open dialogue with the Church where the experience of many women in the Church will be heard.

Such discerning declarations reveal how, as Dumont (1995, 184) predicted more than a quarter-century ago, the patriarchal stronghold of the Roman Catholic Church has indeed triggered rigorous feminist opposition by the sisters. They are also illustrative of how women religious have refused to be silent when they felt compelled to continually denounce institutional inertia on matters related to gender (in) equality (Holtmann 2008; Murphy 2022; Ó'Murchú 1997) – an effort that is particularly noteworthy given how their power has been persistently denied and demeaned for centuries (Elliott 2004; Romey 2022). While most sisters were buoyed by their congregations' shared stance and collective endeavours, as we show next, others were independently assertive in their views on gender equality.

"SHE DIDN'T BACK DOWN FROM ANYBODY"

> She was very much a feminist. Very much! ... She didn't hesitate. She didn't back down from anybody!
>
> Sister Loretta

That is how Sister Loretta praised another sister for her strong feminist stance. Her description sheds light on the unyielding commitment that many women religious have asserted as they faced gendered challenges courageously.[7] Sister Loretta herself seemed fearless in her willingness to express feminist thought: "Yeah, I do feel safe ... you know, let the ... chips fall! [chuckles] They don't like me, so what! When ... you get to be this age, I don't care anyways! [chuckles]."

In response to the question of whether they felt comfortable, confident, and safe to express feminist ideas, numerous other sisters and former sisters responded emphatically, decisively, and eagerly: "Absolutely, absolutely" (Carol); "Anywhere, any place!" (Sister Carmen); "Yes of course and some don't receive it but that's okay" (Sister Kelly); "Very!" (Sister Mabel); and "Definitely" (Sister Agnes).

Judith, who answered, "Yes! Yeah!," was always eager to discuss gender equality within the broader context of political and economic conditions. Sister Sophie echoed a comparable conviction: "Oh yes, I wouldn't hesitate you know. I don't think any of us would really; we're not afraid of our bishop. We're not afraid because he can't tell us what to do you know." The sense of solidarity is clear in these comments. Sister Theresa felt safe to express feminist ideas due to the support of her religious congregation: "I had my whole community behind me." When asked whether or not she was concerned about potential repercussions from Church officials, she replied quite readily and confidently: "No, I'd look forward to it! ... I'd take it on!"

In contrast to Sister Theresa's sense of community support, Sister Rita drew her comfort to express pro-equality views from outside of her congregation and among what some may view as unlikely supporters: parish priests who encouraged gender inclusivity. While some sisters have been sidelined by parish priests, Sister Rita felt that she was given and respected for a prominent parish role by the pastor whose approach was intentionally non-hierarchical:

> Well, I think right in the parish ... I had such a good experience in the past twelve years ... [priest's name] did change rules or regulations ... [so] I was always eager and able to stand out in front you know and take my place ... I always had the right to speak about what I wanted to speak about you know, things to do with liturgy and ... I was always there to do whatever I wanted to do ... And I led particular prayer sessions and that kind of thing which weren't old fashioned.

The reflections of Sisters Mabel, Theresa, and Rita, as well as Judith, are indicative not only of their own inner strength that gave them the confidence to speak out, but also of the courage derived from the external supports of their religious communities, and in the case of Sister Rita, of equality-oriented priests.

Comparatively, while some sisters were less outspoken about their feminist views, they were prepared to defend their opinions when they deemed it necessary. For example, although Sister Josephine admitted to not being very vocal about gender equality, she did feel safe to do so and was prepared to challenge discriminatory comments: "if somebody says to me 'well a woman doesn't do that,' I might say, 'Why not?' You know."

While some sisters have felt confident to vocalize their feminist opinions since they discovered and embraced feminism decades ago, others needed more time to build up the necessary courage. For example, while at the time of her interview, Sister Sarah felt comfortable to express feminist thought, her confidence was also a result of extended personal development: "I think that as I grow and mature as a person that it becomes easier. Like I don't think the situations necessarily become easier, just as I grow more confident in myself is where that … kind of assurance and courage to [stand up comes from], cause essentially, I think it's just courage to be myself."

CONCLUSION

Feminism has concentrated the voice of contemporary religious life.

Chittister (1995, 4)

The relative restraint shown by women religious in Canada compared to their US counterparts should not be dismissed as lack of interest in or identification with feminist aims; rather it should be recognized as strategic, and thus, as an intentional form of resistance. The sisters' comments herein have also shown that there are many factors impeding or facilitating the comfort and confidence of women religious to express dissenting views against the power of the institutional Church (Barr Ebest 2003; Brock 2010; Chittister 2004; Elliott 2004; Huygens 2023; Murphy 2022; Ó'Murchú 1997; Osiek 1986; Romey 2022; Schneiders 2004; Wexler 2016). These contextual influences range from potential conflicts to the sisters' stage of life, to their reported sense of freedom within. In reflecting on their willingness and capacity to strategize and resist, many sisters refer to a sense of support from someone, whether outside of their own congregation, on the fringes of the Church, or from Church officials and community members who offer a validating voice (Faulkner and MacDonald 2009; Holtmann 2008). As we illustrate in the chapters that follow, regardless of the extent of their confidence or its source, the sisters' courageous questioning of controversial Church doctrines and their life-giving forms of renewal and resistance were undoubtedly, and unapologetically, informed by feminist leanings (Barr Ebest 2003; Chittister 1995, 2004; Faulkner and MacDonald 2009; Holtmann 2008; Manning 1999; Murphy 2022; Ó'Murchú 1997; Wexler 2016).

4

Critiquing the Criminalization of Women's Ordination

Christine Gervais and Shanisse Kleuskens

> [I]nstitutions silence and suppress thought …
> churches excommunicate dissenters.
>
> Chittister (2004, 7)

INTRODUCTION

There is no doubt that progress has been made towards the greater inclusion of girls and women in Catholic churches in the decades since Vatican II.[1] Then, in early 2021, Pope Francis signed a decree that formally permitted women to serve in roles near the altar and in the sanctuary during Mass (*Vatican News* 2021). He demonstrated openness towards women deacons – ordained ministers whose duties can include assisting priests and bishops in the liturgy – by establishing two commissions to study the matter in 2016 and 2020 (Giangravé 2023; Glatz 2022; Zagano 2021a).

But such gains now look like window dressing as Pope Francis's recent actions undermine progress for women in the Church. The work of the second commission announced in 2020 has not been reported (Giangravé 2023; Wexler 2016; Zagano 2021b); the deliberations seem to have stalled (Barlow 2022), and several of the commission's ten members have appeared to be opposed to women deacons (McElwee 2020; Schenk 2021). In 2024, Pope Francis betrayed his position when he emphatically affirmed a "closed door" stance on ordained women deacons during a media interview (Hertzler-McCain 2024; Hunt 2024; White 2024a).

According to Kate McElwee, executive director of the Women's Ordination Conference, the official inclusion of women at the altar and in the sanctuary, as of 2021, did not actually reflect "a radical shift" because they had already been serving in such roles for decades (Davidson 2021; Women's Ordination Conference 2021b). Neither would it amount to progress for women or broader society without consequential changes in Church teachings and practices (Bruni 2015; Chittister 2023; Wexler 2016). Still, opposition to ordaining women deacons reflects the deeply sexist anxieties of the Church and the desire to shore up patriarchal authority amidst societal change, efforts that are truly bizarre as women's roles in the Church expand in minor ways. One cannot overlook, for example, "the deep irony that women may now aid in selecting bishops, [yet it is] a role they themselves are prohibited from holding on account of their gender" (Women's Ordination Conference 2022b). While changes in papal tones regarding women's participation may have seemed uplifting several years ago, Pope Francis continues to undermine meaningful inclusion.

The inherent irony was even more pronounced in 2021 when Pope Francis *renewed* the Vatican's 2010 decree[2] that reinforced the criminalization of women's ordination under Pope Benedict XVI (Holy See Press Office 2021; Women's Ordination Conference 2021a; Zagano 2021b).[3] The implication is that "the attempted sacred ordination of a woman" to the priesthood remains classified as a "grave delict" against canon law that can result in excommunication from the Roman Catholic Church (Vatican 2010, Article 5). The recent re-codification of the ban is yet another example of how patriarchy in the Roman Catholic Church has been written and re-written in religious law and literature for over two millennia at least (Daly 1973; Elliott 2004, 2012; Roll 2015a; Stone 1976).[4] It is also further indicative of what some (e.g., Cavanagh 2010) consider the example *par excellence* of the intensification of patriarchal power within the Church in the twenty-first century.

While Pope Benedict's decree is now more than a decade old, its recent interpretation by Pope Francis brings the sisters' interviews and Chittister's reflection hauntingly close to the present. Here we explore the sisters' frustrations, rejections, and transcendence of the criminalization of women's ordination and, in effect, their presumed religious identities within the Church, situating these responses within broader legal, cultural, and religious contexts of ongoing gender discrimination. In the context of the Roman Catholic Church's nascent and reluctant consideration of the diaconate for women, their comments ring truer than ever.

SITUATING THE LONGSTANDING EXCLUSION OF WOMEN FROM THE ALTAR

I just said to myself, "What am I doing in a place that doesn't want us to start with?"

Judith

Within the deep-rooted patriarchal structure of the Roman Catholic Church, women have been marginalized, degraded, and oppressed by hierarchical authorities, as well as systemically excluded from leadership, decision-making, and the sacramental system (Leonard 2007, 235; Schneiders 2004, 33; Wexler 2016).[5] This gendered exclusion has been particularly prominent at and around Church altars. For example, according to Canon 813, Section 2 in the 1917 Code of Canon Law, women were prohibited from even approaching the altar.[6] As Roll (2015b, 470–1) has duly pointed out, the instruction *Quam plurimum* in *Actae Apostolicae Sedis* of 1949 stated that "all the authors teach unanimously that it is forbidden under pain of mortal sin for women, even nuns, to serve *at the altar*" (italics in original). As per Section 70 of the 1975 General Instruction of the Roman Missal, the appointment of women to ministries performed "outside of the sanctuary" as well as the designation of the "suitable place" for women to carry out the duty (e.g., reading) remained at the discretion of men clerics (Hoffman 1991).

Even more recent revisions were not fully inclusive (Morrill and Roll 2007; Roll 2015b). Based on an interpretation of Canon 230, Section 2 of the 1983 Code of Canon Law, Church authorities permitted girls and women to serve at the altar in 1994. However, until Pope Francis's 2021 decree (*Vatican News* 2021) such permission remained at the discretion of men. With men's continued contempt for women's and girls' participation at or around the altar, it comes as no surprise that their gendered exclusion from the priesthood remains codified in canon law under Canon 1024, which states that "[a] baptized male alone receives sacred ordination validly" (Vatican 2016). By way of its catechism, the Catholic Church abdicates responsibility for this sexist discrimination by referring to the alleged choice of Jesus Christ as documented in scripture, placing this decision conveniently outside of the papal hierarchy:

> [t]he Lord Jesus chose men (viri) to form the college of the twelve apostles, and the apostles did the same when they chose collaborators to succeed them in their ministry. The college of bishops, with whom the priests are united in the priesthood, makes the college of the twelve an ever-present and ever-active reality until Christ's return. The Church recognizes herself to be bound by this choice made by the Lord himself. For this reason the ordination of women is not possible. (Catholic Church 2000, par. 1577)

Though the exclusion of girls and women from both participant and leadership roles is not unique to the Catholic Church, relative to recent developments outside the Church, and within Canada particularly, its stubborn commitment to gender inequality within its ranks indicates not only a lack of progress, but also regressive control within the first decade of the new millennium. In the last century, various regulations, proclamations, and agreements, such as the United Nations' (UN) *Universal Declaration of Human Rights* (1948), the UN *Convention on the Elimination of All Forms of Discrimination against Women* (1979), and the UN *Declaration on the Elimination of Violence against Women* (1993), as well as, domestically, the *Canadian Charter of Rights and Freedoms* (1982) and the *Ontario Human Rights Code* (1962),[7] have sought to end the systemic discrimination against women in their personal and professional lives.[8]

Some Christian denominations have kept pace with women's social and economic progress. The Pentecostal Assemblies of Canada (2018) has maintained "an egalitarian position that celebrates the unrestricted leadership capacity of women in the church" (4), and has ordained women since 1984 (1). Eleven years after its inauguration, the United Church of Canada (2023) ordained its first woman minister in 1936. The Anglican Church of Canada has, in the last century, enabled women to participate in all levels of church leadership, including ordination as deacons, priests, and bishops (The Anglican Church of Canada 2022).[9] In contrast, much like the Roman Catholic Church, other denominations such as the Orthodox Church in America (2023)[10] have maintained the discrimination of women from priesthood on doctrinal grounds.

FACING REJECTION FROM THE ALTAR

Despite the shared disenfranchisement of Catholic women with their Christian sisters, the Catholic Church's long-time prohibition of women's leadership generally and ordination[11] specifically has left women angry and dejected (Bonavoglia 2006; Dugan and Owens 2009; Dumont 1995, 177; Holtmann 2008; Kaylin 2000, 135; Manning 1999; Murphy 2014; Osiek 1986; Wexler 2016; Women's Ordination Conference 2021a).[12] While a few nuns, such as Sister Rita, felt "equal" to, and recalled having had a "really great experience" with, certain priests who respected their parish activities, the manifest exclusion of women specifically from church altars has been deeply troubling for the majority of sisters interviewed. The altar remains one of the Catholic Church's most masculinized places.

For the four current and former sisters who recalled aspiring to the priesthood as children and young adults, their longing has lasted a lifetime. For example, Sister Kelly explained: "My desire to be a priest from the time I was little – I used to say mass on the stairs' steps you know – has never died in me." Two of the four women spoke of having grieved over the prohibited opportunity. Eighty-four-year-old Sister Carmen wanted to become a priest. She recounted her lasting emotional struggle to grieve the possibility: "I went through a grieving process ... I was shocked a bit, then I became angry ... there was some frustration but now I feel very, very sad ... I'm still in the sad mode, but it's very much like a grieving process."

Like Naomi, who also felt anger and grief for the sake of "the wider community," Sister Joelle felt a similar disappointment for herself and others:

> I worked through a discernment and came to terms with the fact that I do have a call to ordination. But ... I can't ... I got in touch with that ... but it's not possible. But wouldn't it be great! Wouldn't it? Because there are so many needs ... I really resent the fact that so many people are being deprived, not only of the Eucharist, but of ministry, because of the limitation of ... ordination to ... women.

Parallel to Sister Joelle's resentment, many sisters also felt that both women religious and lay people have been cheated out of the potential benefits of women's organizational and liturgical capacities because of the barrier:

> Sisters are missing out, but also that the lay people are missing out ... Yeah, that is a great [loss]. Like to see that happening in the Church and nothing done about it! (Sister Maureen)

> They go on putting down women, not letting us use our gifts in the Church ... it amazes me that bishops go on not using women's gifts in the Church ... I'm still very angry about the gifts of women [not being used], I guess especially in my case with all the courses we've had, all the experience we've had, all the workshops we've taken, all the praying we have done, and all the dialoguing and so on. So yes, I feel that, I feel that very much. (Sister Agnes)

Sister Penelope pointed to the deprivation derived from the Church's hierarchical and patriarchal structures, as well as to the way in which women religious have been relegated to the laity, and thus not to the leadership level (Bruni 2015; Chittister 2023; Ganim 2013; Manning 1999; Wexler 2016), as a means of ensuring their subservience:

> We're a threat to the clergy at this point, therefore our leadership roles are never called upon much within the church setting, more our roles of service, as servants, but never our leadership roles.

For many sisters, this denial of women's leadership was particularly frustrating in light of the sexual abuse scandals that were becoming more known at the time of their interviews at the start of the 2010s. For example, Sister Agnes expressed how the continuation of men dominating altars was even more insulting when women were not only prohibited from leading liturgies and presiding over the Mass themselves, but they were also expected to accept as their pastors some of the priests who were banned from parishes due to their sexual abuse against children,[13] yet were allowed to celebrate Mass in nuns' motherhouses and retirement homes:

> So here's this person [who has sexually abused] up there [on the altar] and we're down here [in the pews]. We're very gifted women who could be celebrating Eucharist, who could be doing wonderful reflections you know [spoken louder] and I guess that's when it really, really bothers me especially.

Such experiences had clearly impacted the sisters' sense of belonging in their own church. The second-class status that they have endured

(Briggs 2006; Daly 1968; Fisher 2012; Ganim 2013; McPhillips and McEwan 2002; Wexler 2016), as well as the alienation that they have experienced as a result of patriarchal governance, have undoubtedly been demoralizing throughout their entire lives as sisters (Chittister 2023; Romey 2022).[14] However, as we explore next, when sisters sought to collectively counter such exclusion, their efforts were met with silence locally and enormous backlash internationally.

VOICING THEIR OPPOSITION

Canadian sisters have historically been cautious in questioning the Church's hierarchy outright on this matter, not only out of fear of repercussions by "the local bishops" (Sister Joelle), but also in part due to some sisters' own adherence to the Church's patriarchal position on ordination – a complex situation that inevitably presented challenges for feminist-leaning general superiors such as Sister Joelle:

> When I was in leadership, I was very conscious that ... a number of the sisters ... would not have agreed [with public statements or protests against the Church's stance] ... So congregations aren't uniform in this ... And there are a number of sisters ... who are quite happy with the hierarchal Church, the status quo and so on. So as a leader representing the congregation, I didn't ... feel that was [appropriate to speak publicly in favour of women's ordination].

Nevertheless, one congregation represented herein took the courageous step in the mid-2000s to convey their critiques of gender discrimination in the Church to the Canadian bishops via the aforementioned survey. The community of sisters wrote about gendered exclusion generally and about women's ordination particularly, including the following persuasive lines of argument:[15]

> REALIZATIONS
> We recognize that nothing in Scripture or theology prevents the ordination of women.
>
> We recognize that although it is presently a requirement that priests be celibate, married men are being ordained but not celibate women.

CRITIQUES
We deplore male domination of the Church because of the exclusion of women from ordination and thus from a role in decision-making at leadership levels of the Canadian Church.

We deplore that the Church continues its myopic and patriarchal obsession with celibate, male clergy only.

We deplore the refusal by the Vatican even to be open to the question of a married clergy or the ordination of women.

We deplore male dominance around the altar and in the sanctuary and lack of involvement of women in various liturgical ministries.

ASPIRATIONS
We hope that the Canadian Bishops will be given permission to ordain women.

We hope for more openness to use the gifts of the laity, especially women, and to place them in positions of decision-making.

Such sagacious statements are certainly a testament to women religious' capacity and willingness to engage in rigorous feminist conscientization and opposition to contest power and effect change within the Roman Catholic Church (Faulkner and MacDonald 2009; Holtmann 2008; Murphy 2022; Ó'Murchú 1997).[16] The declarations are further revealing of sisters' comprehensive attempts to counter their presumed religious identities that imply acquiescence (Ammerman 2003), redraw the submissive roles that had been assigned to them as women, and prepare to face the consequences (Avishai 2008; Burke 2012; Kaylin 2000, 12). Not surprisingly, there were repercussions to this rare, openly pointed resistance against the Church hierarchy; apparently, the process "created a stir" (Sister Edna) and "oh the bishops were wild with that, but no response" (Sister Mabel). While the sisters were frustrated by the clergy's backlash locally, what was particularly troubling was how, rather than the Church hierarchy considering gender equality more seriously, the Vatican instead launched a broad-scale counterattack against women religious' and lay women's worldwide advocacy towards women's rights in the Church generally and for women's ordination specifically.

Swift and disproportionate reprisal by the Church was intended to further silence and marginalize women religious from daring to speak out against Church doctrine. The sisters were accused of engaging in "radical feminism" in their daily activities and during annual conferences; they were also censured for "protesting the Holy See's actions regarding the question of women's ordination," especially the Leadership Conference of Women Religious (LCWR) (Congregation for the Doctrine of the Faith 2012; Murphy 2014). The scrutiny of sisters in the United States began approximately two years after the Canadian Religious Conference's report was sent. The backlash was four-pronged: (1) the 2009 to 2015 investigation and doctrinal assessment[17] of the LCWR, (2) the 2008 to 2012 apostolic visitation of religious orders in the United States, [18] (3) the 2008 retrenchment of the prohibition of women's ordination, and (4) the exacerbation of gendered exclusion in 2010, when women's ordination shifted from being prohibited to being criminalized, as we discuss next.

FROM PROHIBITION TO CRIMINALIZATION: DOUBLING DOWN ON THE SUPPRESSION OF WOMEN

The canonical criminalization of women's ordination and the corresponding sanction of *latae sententiae* excommunication apply to both the person who confers the ordination on a woman and she who receives it (Vatican 2010, Article 5).[19] As a result, Catholics, at least ones in "good standing," can neither debate, nor request, nor advocate women's ordination, at least not without risking punishment by their Church (Cavanagh 2010, 18).

While the Church has prohibited women's ordination for centuries,[20] and the clerical hierarchy has disciplined nuns' behaviours and pursuits outside of traditional gender roles (Chittister 2014; Johnson 2014; Schenk 2014; Schneiders 2011, 2013, 2014), controversy flared in 2010 when the institution included women's ordination on the same list of the "most serious crimes" as clerical sexual abuse and heresy.[21] Through this decree, the Roman Catholic Church "made it clear that in their view, the thought of women fulfilling their calling to the priesthood was as reprehensible as the sexual abuse of a child" (Cavanagh 2010, 14). Along with Cavanagh (2010, 14), many felt compelled to ask: "In what twisted world could the empowerment of women be equated with the abuse of children [by men priests]?"

As the latest of countless tactics by Church authorities to exclude women from leadership, criminalization – reinforced yet again through a decree in 2021 (Women's Ordination Conference 2021a; Zagano

2021a) – further weakened women's already unequal position in the Roman Catholic Church. Criminalizing women's leadership at the end of the first decade of the twenty-first century seemed outrageous, and undoubtedly set back gains made in prior decades (Cavanagh 2010). While sexism in the institutional Roman Catholic Church is deeply rooted (Bruni 2015; Chittister 2004; Johnson 2002a; Manning 1999; Ó'Murchú 1997), the move to criminalize women's leadership relegated women to the extreme social, political, and economic margins of the Church. The reinforcement of that criminalization through revisions to Canon 1379, paragraph 3, in 2021 is further testament to "the consistency of the Vatican's misogyny" (Women's Ordination Conference 2021a; Zagano 2021a).

As we explore in the following sections, some sisters reported feeling personally alienated and offended by the criminalization in 2010, which for them represented the institution's inertia toward sexism. Others mourned the inevitable impact of the decision on the membership of the Church community and its loss of the enrichment that women role models and leaders would have provided to its ranks. Others redirected their energy toward alternative theological, spiritual, community-building, and life-giving initiatives in non-hierarchical settings (Dunne 2008; Faulkner and MacDonald 2009; Leonard 2007, 2008; Murphy 2022; Ó'Murchú 1997). Still others were fuelled by the edict to continue the fight for their right to become priests.

SISTERS' EXASPERATION OVER THE 2010 CRIMINALIZATION OF WOMEN'S ORDINATION

As one might expect, the sisters and former sisters were appalled by the reinforced restrictions against women's ordination. For example, Sister Agnes's exclamation revealed the intensity of her disgust with the decree: "'The criminalization of women's ordination!' ... Don't these words almost sicken you?!" As Naomi elaborated on how she felt about the new legislation, she demonstrated how the retrenchment of women's rights was not lost on the current or former women religious:

> Well, I just think it's appalling; I mean it's so alienating. I have no aspirations [to become a priest], but it further alienates me; I think that's where it hit me. I mean oh good grief, it alienated me ... again, it just confirms the exclusion of women as equal, as people.

Still other sisters were concerned about the losses resulting from the decree and its incoherence with cultural norms and institutional needs. For example, Sister Edith found that "the statement was offensive" and expressed concern for the collective health of the community, "the future of the Catholic Church," because "young women may be hesitant to commit to an organization which is blatantly sexist." Sister Kelly echoed the concern when she stated that "the church is 'bleeding its women,'"[22] and many other participants maintained that the decree was exacerbating the systemic problem. Similarly, as she reacted to the decree, ninety-one-year-old Sister Shannon recognized that as the Church was concentrating on the intensification of its anti-woman regulations yet again – just as it has so often done throughout the centuries (Elliott 2004, 2012; Wexler 2016) – it was unavoidably stifling other more inclusive relational opportunities: "The Church authorities seem to have put more emphasis on the observance of rules than that of living with concern for each other in a community spirit with all peoples … I find it difficult to believe that authority can state how God would punish failures to fulfill some 'man-made' law." Responding to the decree, the sisters simultaneously shed light on the ensuing losses and the desirability of women's leadership and ordination. Sister Corinne conveyed both: "Concerning the statement from the Vatican on the ordination of women, I think it is sad since some women feel called to the priesthood and would have a beautiful ministry."

SISTERS' DISREGARD OF THE CRIMINALIZATION OF WOMEN'S ORDINATION

I ignored it.
Naomi

While the sisters were frustrated by the criminalization of women's ordination, their overall stance on the issue was one of disregard, based in part on their past experiences within the Church. Although the criminalization tactic was shocking to many Catholics and non-Catholics (Cavanagh 2010), most women religious interviewed defiantly dismissed it, in part because they felt comfortably detached from the decree and the institutional Church that set it. For example, Sister Theresa explained how she remained decidedly removed from the decree: "As an elderly woman religious, I no longer take very seriously such a male-oriented, man-made decree. I feel that such a decree only further reveals the desperation of the Vatican in the face of the beliefs and actions of intelligent and educated lay people." Similarly, Mildred rejected the decree because she perceived it to be outdated: "I feel it's like anything else that comes from Rome, mostly it's behind where the people are already at." Sister Noreen, who herself did not advocate for women's ordination due to her frustration with the Church's clerical hierarchy, took a somewhat removed approach by opting to become informed by the source (the Vatican papers): "I had read it in the original. I waited to see how long it would take for it to hit the paper, and when it hit the paper, I was able to talk about the original document."

Comparatively, amongst all the participants' reactions to the decree, none were more resolutely resistant than Judith's critique of the Catholic Church as an institution waning in legitimacy due to its patriarchal power and pernicious decision-making. To this, she advocated avoidance:

> I am so far removed from the machinations of the Catholic Church that I hadn't even heard of their latest edict against women! I continue to be astounded that there are women who still want to join the club of the ordained in an institution that is hierarchical, patriarchal, and dictatorial. My instinct would be what Hafiz proposes in his poem, We Have Not Come Here to Take Prisoners:[23] "Run like hell, my dear, from anyone likely to put a sharp knife into the sacred and tender vision of your beautiful heart."
>
> The affronts to women religious, and by extension to all women, by the official Church, are every day more blatant and crude. To mount a huge investigation of U.S. nuns and at the same time declare this [2010] the year of the priest as dozens more of them go to jail for their [sex] crimes calls into question the sanity or clarity of purpose of the decision-makers in that institution.[24] And now to drag out a decree, to speak about "crimes" with regard to women's ordination indicates desperation and panic. It seems there is a clear and noticeable narrowing of the doors to membership in the Roman Catholic Church. The windows, opened by John XXIII, are long shut and locked! How can anyone sustain their loyalty and allegiance to an institution that appears misogynous, cruel, and vindictive, and that can only rule by decree, law, sanctions, and threats of hell?

> The world's major organized religions are patriarchal and hierarchical and women continue to struggle for a place in the ranks. For many women, change from within seems possible and they believe they can help to achieve it. Others of us believe that organized religion has turned in on itself and its goal now is to preserve power at any cost. If there is a God, a Loving Spirit who cherishes life, I can't find Her/Him/It hovering near any of these institutions, least of all the Catholic Church.

While perhaps less piercing than Judith's *cri de coeur*, Sister Joelle's interpretation of the decree emphasized similar concerns regarding the pervasive persistence of the Vatican's control:

> There is such … a protectiveness … I'm appalled that that language could be used, and it indicates to me … how bureaucratic a structure it is … I mean I think that that little clause was within a much broader clause in canon law. And it was a matter of the bureaucrat saying, "Well, we have to tighten this up," and they just were not paying attention to the language, the concept … you know? … But … it's just appalling to think that they would … but it's the Curia … not even realizing the impact of that [pause]. Incredible! … So … the whole abuse question and this ordination example indicate that it's time that women were involved in administration in the Church!

Naomi's response to the decree shed similar light on its domineering dimension. Initially she noted:

> Well, I think it's just indicative of the absurdity to which people who are you know holding onto power … would choose to criminalize an act that is, to me, so self-evidently one that should be open to [all]. So … I've always taken it as an indication of the dysfunction, and almost the desperateness.

Naomi also explained how the decree affected her pre-existing concerns with the Church:

> Well, it just confirms for me … first of all the impossibility of change; and secondly, for me anyway, it just confirms … the inevitable decline of an institution that refuses inclusiveness. Inclusiveness, I mean, it's the way everything is going.

The intransigence to which Naomi referred resonated with all the sisters. As such, several of them interpreted the decree as one example among countless manifestations of the Vatican's constant reminders of women's inferior position within the Roman Catholic Church (Chittister 2023; Romey 2022; Schneiders 2021). For example, as Sister Joelle reflected on her reaction to the decree as a woman, she explained her lack of surprise at its release in light of her ongoing feeling of victimization within the Church: "Well, it's just more of the same in one way. Do you know what I mean? I'm so used to being marginalized and victimized that you think, 'Here we go again.'" Darlene echoed Sister Joelle's emphasis on the consistency of the Vatican's position on women as it was made even more evident through the decree: "I wasn't as mad as I thought I'd be. [laughs] I was saying, 'Oh yeah, here we go again' [laughs]." Similarly, through a sarcastic rejoinder, Sister Noreen showed how the decree was indicative of the continuity of the Church's stance on women: "Why are you surprised? Right? There's a consistency here to be admired [laughs]!" Nevertheless, despite the laughter through which she expressed her previous interpretation, Sister Noreen conveyed her serious concern about the decree's impact on women worldwide when she shared: "I just think, oh my God, the Church, did you have to? Really? Was it necessary? It's part of the grieving ... I grieve and with everything ... as if we needed anything else." Thus, Sister Noreen's reaction emblematized the sting of discrimination among women religious, even when many have become numb to the Church's repeated attacks.

Similar to other Canadian Catholic women who draw on their faith's origins when they express dissenting views against the institutional Church (Holtmann 2008), Sister Maureen dismissed the 2010 decree that criminalized women's ordination because it "is not in line with Jesus's teaching and his way of life."[25] Yet she went further with her rebuff to point out the irony of the matter: "I feel that the Vatican's statement is the most serious crime against the Catholic Church." Sister Maureen captured the sentiment of many of the women interviewed regarding their views of the criminalization of women's ordination: that deeming the presence of women in a priest's role as criminal has crossed some sort of line into the absurd, even for an institution which maintains its misogynist traditions (Holtmann 2008; Manning 1999; Women's Ordination Conference 2021a).

BEYOND THE DECREE: SISTERS' NEGOTIATION OF WOMEN'S RIGHT TO ORDINATION TO THE PRIESTHOOD

While women's ordination represented an issue upon which many current and former sisters sidestepped the hierarchical Church, all sisters interviewed still viewed it as a woman's right. Not all sisters, however, were active advocates. Many, such as Sisters Rita, Benita, and Edna, believed firmly in the right, but neither sought it for themselves, nor engaged in activism for others:

> I'm not looking at my age or I don't know if I ever would've looked to have become a priest but … many sisters could become priests. (Sister Rita)

> I'm not fighting for ordination … I don't think I'd like to be a priest, not at this stage anyway … [although] I see one eighty years old was just ordained! (Sister Benita)

In particular, Sister Edna perceived the confines of the Catholic Church's hierarchy as inevitable and therefore pacifying, which reflected her stance on pursuing the right:

> We will never be able to do what the priests do under the present condition so there was no use to fight for it. It was better to remain part of it, to participate … talk about women's ordination. I say to women, "There's a lot we can do. Let's do what we can to work towards the next step." … I never had a big aspiration because I knew it wouldn't happen. But … if the Church said yes, I'd have no problem … 'cause I'd felt, I was at home.

Yet, others remained strong proponents. Sister Carmen had been outspoken on the issue for years and she recalled critiquing a priest publicly at a women's church group many decades earlier:[26]

> One priest I remember said a woman's place is in the kitchen and I got up at the same Catholic Women's League meeting and I told them … there are all these women … "What do you want to say when your granddaughter comes to you and says,

> 'I wanna be a priest?'" [By the time change happens, if ever] it's going to be great-granddaughters, I should have said, but I said granddaughters [chuckles].

Many women, like Sister Carmen, have openly promoted women's ordination through consciousness-raising efforts and protest-based activism (Holtmann 2008; Ó'Murchú 1997). While three were actively involved in organized movements that advocated for women's ordination and have been members of the Catholic Network for Women's Equality (CNWE),[27] some women religious, such as Sister Benita, have attended Women's Ordination Worldwide (WOW) conferences. As an unwavering supporter of women's ordination, Darlene engaged in direct and intentional resistance against Canon 1024 by attending the ordination of both Canadian and American women priests who were part of the Roman Catholic Women Priest (RCWP) group.[28] Her pride was evident when she claimed to have encouraged some of the current Canadian women priests to seek ordination, and when she mentioned that she had met one of the bishops from the RCWP. At a progressive conference promoting gender equality in the Roman Catholic Church that she attended years earlier, Darlene recalled being inspired by an elderly attendee who demonstrated both fearlessness and humour as she identified the Church-imposed consequence she was subjected to as a result of her activism in favour of women's right to ordination:

> At Call to Action[29] one time I was walking along with this old lady, in fact I helped her over the steps, so she was probably … well into her eighties. So because it was an international conference, I just, you know, looked at her name tag and said, "Oh, you're from … Nebraska," and she said, "yes, I'm one of the excommunicated ones." I said, "Oh my … you're the first one I ever met in the flesh." So we started to chat and she said, "You know, when I was a girl going to Catholic school, I thought excommunication was the worst possible thing, that you were going straight to hell." And she said, "I have to tell you, I'm enjoying the experience" [laughs loudly].

While Sister Shannon was not involved in formal activism like Darlene, she did express her concern about the 2010 decree and she shared her belief in women's right to ordination by emphasizing the presence of women around Jesus: "Regarding the priesthood for women, my thoughts are these: I believe there were women at the Last Supper when Jesus said: 'Do this in memory of Me.'"[30] Sister Shannon went on to explain that "[i]t is a woman's role to serve at table, to prepare food for 'the journey of life.'" While such a statement may be perceived as one that reinforced traditional gender roles, Sister Shannon actually pointed to a blatant contradiction in relation to gendered divisions of labour between the domestic and religious institutional spheres: while women have been expected to prepare and serve food within their private homes, they have been denied the "opportunity" of doing so at Catholic Masses[31] – public spaces and spectacles where such visible acts have been highly revered, and as such have been controlled and protected by the patriarchal hierarchy of the Roman Catholic Church.[32] Sister Shannon's final message conveyed optimism for inclusive ordination and thus for the upholding of women's right to the vocation while still recognizing the exceptionality of the call – one that is not inherently gendered: "Not all are called to the vocation of the priesthood, neither male nor female, but I hope for the day when women who are called will have the opportunity of living their vocation to the full."

A WOMAN'S *RIGHT*, BUT NOT A *WOMAN'S RITE*: TRANSCENDING CHURCH-BASED ORDINATION

> I accept it, but I myself, would I ever want to go that route?
> No … I wouldn't want to see us entering into the hierarchy,
> definitely not the Church the way it is right now.
>
> Sister Penelope

While all the sisters and former sisters viewed ordination as a woman's right, many had reservations about the institutional role for both themselves personally and for others collectively. As Sister Penelope illustrated in the quote above, the support for women's ordination by the women interviewed was balanced with their desire to build a church community that reflected values of equality, inclusion, and spiritual creativity, values which they felt could not be realized through their ordination within the Church's current patriarchal and hierarchical structure (Hunt 2009; Ruether 2003; Schneiders 2004; Schüssler Fiorenza 2001). It was the exclusiveness of the Church that led many sisters, despite their firm rights-based beliefs, to resist this treatment by raising critiques against the priesthood, and moving beyond it, rather than advocating for it (Hunt 2005, 2009; Ruether 2003, 2005; Schüssler Fiorenza 2001, 2005, 2016; Wexler 2016).[33] Sister Ella agreed that it was essential to support a woman's vocation to the priesthood, but she cautioned against the replication of the exclusionary practices typical of the hierarchical church: "There are some women who feel called to the priesthood and we can't ... but honour a call you know ... as long as they wouldn't you know stand on their dignity in ... an exclusive way." In doing so, Sister Ella added nuance that is sorely missing from the framing of vocations under patriarchal leadership.

Reflecting commonplace group dynamics where some, but not all, are called to serve in leadership roles, not all sisters would have been called to the priesthood if the vocation had been open to them. When asked if she would want to be a priest, for example, Mildred replied laughingly and emphatically: "Never! In the least!" Such was the position of all the participants, who, at the time of their interviews, desired neither to be priests nor to be affiliated with the institutional Church, because they refused to imitate men or to participate on men's terms (Schneiders 2004, 36). All preferred their current positions as laity-based women religious supported by an inclusive community of forward-thinking women. As Sister Theresa reflected, "I'd never want to be a priest ... there are clergy and then there are the faithful ... the laity and I belong to the laity ... I'd rather be where I am." Sister Maureen was similarly disinterested but echoed the critique of status quo hierarchies and inequalities as shaping her lack of enthusiasm for the priesthood: "I wouldn't want to be a priest the way things are now ... it's hard, hard, hard to be part of the hierarchy."

Sister Maureen's mention of the hierarchy as an obstacle was significant because for numerous current and former women religious, the place of the clergy within the sexist hierarchy of the Roman Catholic Church constituted one of the main reasons that they had moved beyond the vocation of the priesthood for women. The concern over the hierarchical position surfaced with Mildred, who counselled various Christian and non-Christian religious leaders:

> I think women ... could make very good ministers of the church ... I've worked here with women ministers in my practice and I have attended church services; I was at a funeral just last week with a woman minister, just excellent and so if they can keep it at that level, great ... but I would not want to see women

> ordained and become men … part of the hierarchy and I'm afraid sometimes that happens.

While Darlene, who was also involved in counselling, was supportive, she too was aware of the constraints created by the patriarchal hierarchy:

> Yes, I believe there is a value in … women being ordained who proclaim themselves to be Catholic … I'm also very conscious of the struggle of other ordained women in the other Christian churches, and I have helped six of those when I came here, so I'm even more conscious of how difficult it is for them in their churches.

Given her strong critique against the hierarchical power, Sister Noreen was emphatic and incisive about her lack of interest in, or support for, pursuing women's ordination:

> I don't think we should bother … I don't think we should reduce ourselves to want to join a line up like that … Why would we want that for? Really? Can we be as effective? Because then we get trapped. Do we want the power too? Is this a power thing? Uh? If we are convinced we can, you know, be a mission, being church to each other, we need leaders … but why would I want to be a part of that?[34]

Sister Noreen was also frank about her lack of desire to become a priest: "No, and I would not encourage any woman to go for that, not presently … Why!? I would say why!?" While Sister Noreen grieved when a sermon "goes to a place that is limited," and while she firmly believed that ordination to the priesthood is a woman's right, she elaborated upon her serious concerns about the potential impact of the hierarchy:

> Oh, women have the right to everything, but … I wouldn't fight for that and I would question women who fight for it … Why?! Is it also to have equal power? Be careful there. Or is it to be more effective with the community? Right? Is your ministry going to be enhanced by being the priest or are you going to have more power because you're the priest and you're wearing the Roman collar? I would have a discernment going on between

> those two things ... So to me, that's what it's about you know, so I'm not getting excited about women['s ordination], you know as I said when I see one coming along with the Roman collar ... my first response is, what did you have to do that for?

Sister Noreen's concern over the risk of being corrupted by the power within a hierarchical structure was echoed by Sister Clara, who, at the mention of women priests, said excitedly: "Oh, I love it! I love it! Yeah." When she was asked if she wanted to be a priest herself, however, she replied emphatically "No!" and gave the following reason, consistent with many others: "Well because ... when I see women as priests, I think they get transformed by it, you see ... priesthood inside of what we have [within the hierarchy] ... I didn't want that [for women]." Likewise, Naomi explained why she did not personally want to be a priest, drawing attention to what she perceived to be negative conditioning effects:

> When I was studying in [a US city], I was studying with some Anglican women actually who were priests, and we happened to have ... a ritual in class, and one of the women who was taking part, and she put on this voice, she put on "the voice," "and as God said" and I thought it was really strange, and I thought I could not get into that.

As such, while Naomi perceived the role of "playing" a priest as limiting and somewhat peculiar, even within other Christian denominations, she also found that their traditions provided for more creative freedom. Yet, while she remained loyal to the Catholic faith, she dismissed the Catholic priesthood because of its constraints:

> I would not have the patience nor could I function within the dysfunction of clericalism, and ... this is a typically Catholic response ... priests are always like almost confined to like parish leaders ... and I never wanted to be that. I must say, I was studying and rooming once with some Anglican women who were studying for the ministry and they were involved in all sorts of pastoral things, you know like they were in hospitals, and I thought to myself, oh isn't this so restrictive. I never wanted to be a Catholic priest because I didn't want to be a parish priest ... But in these other traditions, they are so much

> more creative; I think it would have actually been fulfilling to be a priest in that, but I am Catholic; I'm not Anglican and so I've just, I've not been interested in it.

Nevertheless, Naomi's quest for more creativity as a spiritual model was fulfilled in other ways within Catholic ministry, and, as a result, made her dismissal of the priesthood easier. While she believed in the right to women's ordination, she did not officially engage in advocacy for it because she found a safe and supportive space within a progressive and inclusive Catholic parish that welcomes women's leadership in a variety of ways, including in the delivery of homilies: "I never joined the women's ordination movement, not because I didn't believe in it, but I never wanted to be ordained … you see, I've always been at [a progressive parish]." Given her involvement at that parish – a space that offered an ideal alternative community prioritizing diverse, creative, and mutually engaging spirituality (Ó'Murchú 1997) – she did not feel compelled to advocate for women's ordination. She went on to explain the background of her strategic approach:

> I was at [US College] … and I took a great course from Rosemary Radford Ruether that was wonderful and Rosemary had us taking the bible and … we would go through some of these particular verses and say "this is not God's word and work" … So I tended to put my energies, and this is typical for my life … I learned from Rosemary at that time; she said, "I work in the open spaces and I always tithe my anger." And that has always suited me.

Sister Corinne, who was involved in a variety of feminist and social justice initiatives in her city, held a similar view. She clarified how she was content beyond the priesthood:

> Well, I've been asked that by … members of my own family … with the question of ordination, well I'm for it of course … I approve that women should be ordained one day as deacons, deaconesses and priests, but for me no, I don't feel it's for me. It's not my call. And I'm quite happy with what I'm doing and I don't feel I'm restrained in any way in whatever I'm doing and I can be creative.

The open spaces and creativity that Naomi and Sister Corinne prioritized were precisely what Sister Kelly was drawing upon as she moved much farther beyond the official priesthood. Sister Kelly described herself as "a very passionate advocate for women in the Church," which in the past included her quest for women's right to ordination. However, in 2010, in response to a post-interview questionnaire specifically on the topic of the criminalizing decree, Sister Kelly noted a marked shift in her opinion regarding women's ordination compared to the advocacy-oriented outlook that she had shared in her original in-person interview in 2009. What she suggested resembled a decentralized and inclusive approach that was far beyond any institutionally based ordination for either women or men:

> I have moved in my thinking re[garding] the need for women priests or an ordained priesthood at all. I am convinced that ... Jesus's words at the Last Supper were for all of us – we are all called to "do this in memory of me." The priesthood of the laity would revive Eucharist as Jesus lived it – in self-emptying loving relationships. The self-giving of the bread and wine are the symbols for that Eucharist celebrated wherever we gather for prayer and communion of hearts however we do that – over a meal or/and sharing. I believe that every loving relationship in which we engage is Eucharistic living. I am not so sure of only a male priest being able to enact "transubstantiation." I am trying to hold both the belief of Eucharistic Presence enacted through the power of the Holy Spirit – not the male priest – and the belief that every Christian has the permission from Jesus to share Eucharist with others.

What Sister Kelly was advocating resonated with what feminist theologians and activists have been promoting for decades, which is a "discipleship of equals" rather than ordination, in order to bypass or transcend the intransigent authoritarianism of the hierarchical Church in favour of autonomous spiritual gatherings (Hunt 2005, 2009; Ruether 2003, 2005; Schüssler Fiorenza 2001, 2005).[35] Sister Kelly's shift in thinking in response to the Vatican's criminalization of women's ordination reflects her willingness to evolve her own motivations and interpretations of resistance in pursuit of greater inclusion and a loving faith (Holtmann 2008; Ó'Murchú 1997).

While some sisters and former sisters may not have been prepared to abandon the goal of women's ordination completely, moving more confidently and comfortably beyond the institutional parameters seemed both essential and enriching for many of the women interviewed. Such was certainly the case for Darlene, who has facilitated many women-led spiritual celebrations over the years, but who was also content to participate in some of the traditional church rituals in the chapel of the religious community where she worked as a spiritual advisor because they were feminized and women-centred: "I've done that lots too. I don't do it anymore because I don't have the need of it myself personally anymore because I do go here; as I say, this is a lovely chapel ... it's very feminine." True to the proverb that necessity is the mother of invention, and like their counterparts from earlier centuries who countered clerical constraints with creativity, the women religious interviewed continued to demonstrate collective and individual ingenuity in the face of institutional inflexibility by patiently, and with integrity, enacting women's rights (Elliott 2004; Faulkner and MacDonald 2009; Holtmann 2008; Mangion 2008; Ó'Murchú 1997).[36] In a way, their renouncement of the rite of priesthood, which constituted a form of resistance agency (Avishai 2008; Burke 2012; Murphy 2022), neutralized the very control that the authors of the criminalizing decree sought to exercise.

CONCLUSION

The criminalization of women's ordination and continued patriarchal practices at Church altars had forced many former and current sisters to (re)negotiate their own perspectives, identities, and roles as women while simultaneously being members of a religious community. This has been emotional work, as the women herein expressed sadness, alienation, frustration, and outrage over the longstanding patriarchal domination of Catholic Church altars and the explicit denial of cultural gains through the criminalization of women's ordination in 2010. Sister Carmen described her negotiation of this dynamic: "Twice I've been asked by the United Church and the Anglican Church would I consider leaving ... So I could be a minister. Twice! ... And I said I wasn't ready to leave my church yet." Like Sister Carmen, many of the women, despite the discrimination they faced, resisted the stigma of the obedient and quiet woman religious (Brock 2010; Murphy 2022). For some, this meant working within the structure of the Church to push for the representation of women in the institution's leadership (Holtmann 2008). Others, such as Carol, opted for loyal disobedience and more life-giving alternative communities as they expressed the need to take their skills, their gifts, or their efforts elsewhere (Faulkner and MacDonald 2009; Ó'Murchú 1997), and disregard the Church's edict as a reflection of the Church's outdated approach to follow in the footsteps of Christ: "I'm not willing to … financially support an organization that will not ordain women or recognize the whole feminist theology. I will NOT support an organization that will not change its language – that's such a simple thing to do! – [I] will not."

Especially with Pope Francis's May 2024 outright refusal of a future with women deacons (Hertzler-McCain 2024), it is difficult to predict if the Roman Catholic Church will progress in its position (or at least move beyond its "medieval mind[set]" [Chittister 2023]) regarding women's ordination and participation in Church leadership more broadly. It is likewise unclear if any of these possible advances would reflect a structure for which Sister Kelly, among several of the women interviewed, would advocate. That said, and having already lived through decades of Church sexism, some sisters remained optimistic. For example, despite her disappointment, Sister Corinne remained hopeful for progress: "I believe that … the wind of change may blow … It happened in the history of the Church."[37] Sister Theresa held a similarly sanguine view. While she did not expect gains in the short term, her optimism for the ultimate realization of women's ordination stemmed from her faith in an almost certain attainment of gender equality:

> While I don't believe that Women's Ordination will receive official recognition in my lifetime, or in Pope Benedict's, I feel certain that it will eventually happen, driven by the gradual recognition throughout the world of the equality of women and men.[38]

By contrast, several of the women provided more apocalyptic views for the future. While Mildred hoped that "people become conscious enough" to see the injustice of it all, she actually viewed the decree and the negative reaction against it as leading to what she considered to be the desirable downfall of the Roman Catholic Church: "I think it will help the demise, which should be a good thing." Similarly, albeit in varying ways, both Darlene and Naomi related women's ordination to the demise of the institutional Church:

> I have an inclination … that this patriarchal Church has to crumble a bit more before there's room for women, otherwise they're going to be just persecuted and killed. (Darlene)

> I totally support women's ordination, but … I've just disassociated myself from it. I really don't pay much attention. I feel [the Church] it's going to kind of self-implode. (Naomi)

The premonitions of the women religious interviewed are as pertinent today as they were when vocalized over a decade ago, especially in reflecting on the most recent positions of the Roman Catholic Church regarding women in leadership roles. In 2016, the Vatican came to an externally induced "epiphany" to explore the possibility of women deacons, reluctantly (if not disingenuously) signalling its intent to bring the Catholic Church into the twentieth (but not yet into the twenty-first) century in response to the demands of women religious.[39] Echoing the optimistic visions of Sisters Corinne and Theresa, this announcement appeared to have indicated a shift in the winds, building on previous changes such as the Vatican's allowance of married men into the deaconate in 1968 (Gautier 2018).

Other signals, however, bear out Naomi, Darlene, and Mildred's prediction of the Catholic Church's potential implosion. A May 2018 essay prepared by the Vatican's doctrinal prefect stressed the fixed nature of the Church's ban against and criminalization of women's ordination, noting that "it is a matter of serious concern to see the emergence in some countries of voices that question the definitiveness of this doctrine" (see McElwee 2018). Additionally, nearly three years after its establishment in 2016, the first commission responsible for the study of the issue of women deacons had failed to reach a consensus on the question, instead deciding that its members would each conduct an individual study on the question (McElwee 2019b), while the second commission set up in 2020 seems to have stalled (Barlow 2022; Giangravé 2023; Zagano 2021b). When pressed on the topic of women deacons in light of the commission's ambiguity on the issue in 2019, Pope Francis ultimately underscored the Vatican's exclusionary position when he responded that the issue required a historical and dogmatic basis rooted in Catholicism, otherwise, "[i]f someone wants to make another church, they are free to do so" (McElwee 2019a). Upon reflection, what is remarkable about the pope's 10 May 2019 meeting with the International Union of Superiors

General is not that he spoke of the Church's refusal to change with the times, but rather that a sister in the crowd, faced with millennia of women's discrimination within the Roman Catholic Church, still chose to directly address Pope Francis and inform him that she, among others, sought to participate as the equal of men in her vocation (McElwee 2019a).

The synopsis report of the October 2023 Synod on Synodality offered no further insights on the question of women's ordination; it reviewed the varying views on allowing women into the diaconate, and simply stated that "[t]heological and pastoral research on the access of women to the diaconate should be continued" (XVI Ordinary General Assembly of the Synod of Bishops 2023, 21). The Vatican then announced in March 2024 that the October 2024 Synod would no longer include discussion of women in the diaconate, deferring this topic to June 2025 along with other issues deemed controversial (Giangravé 2024; Wooden 2024). That same spring, Pope Francis ironically placated women in a rare media interview (CBS News 2024), admitting that "[w]omen are the ones who move changes forward." In the same breath, he cemented his stance that "[w]omen are of great service as women, [but] not as ministers ... within the Holy Orders" (White 2024a). Despite recognizing women's contributions – and fundamentally depending on them for the Church's continuation – the Catholic hierarchy is clearly not prepared to "move forward" by giving them a full leadership platform (Hertzler-McCain 2024; White 2024a).

Even though the institutional Church reiterates threats to women for seeking equality, the legacies of resistance of the women religious interviewed live on – as both laywomen and women religious continue to challenge the Church for the good of future generations, even to the pope directly.[40] Some women religious have resisted sexist attacks by transcending or distancing themselves from the Church's offensive rules, but others have chosen to demand change from the institutional hierarchy. Through a spectrum of approaches, they have employed a dynamic form of women's resistance (Faulkner and MacDonald 2009; Holtmann 2008; Murphy 2022; Ó'Murchú 1997), one with the ability to ebb and flow with the tides of time, and to persist in advancing women's role in the Roman Catholic Church. As voiced by the women religious herein, and as echoed by prominent sisters and women's rights activists over a decade later (Chittister 2022a, 2022b, 2024; Giangravé 2023; Hertzler-McCain 2024; Schenk 2021), this progression must and will occur, whether the Vatican accepts it or not.[41]

5

Denouncing Clerical Abuse against Children and Women

Christine Gervais and Amanda Watson

We deplore the continuing horror stories of past abuse.[1]

INTRODUCTION

Clerical abuse by the Catholic Church has elicited exceedingly difficult emotions among nuns. As devoted yet critical members of a rigidly hierarchical Church, the women religious we interviewed were deeply shaken by the revelations of clerical sexual abuse that surfaced publicly in Canada and elsewhere from the late 1980s onward.[2] Not one woman with whom we spoke reacted dismissively to our interview questions on this matter. The sisters herein were ashamed of the abuses; genuinely concerned for the well-being of the victims, including their sister-peers; sincerely interested in holding perpetrators accountable; and vehemently critical of the Church's widespread cover-up that suppressed harms and continued to place both children and women at risk (Bonavoglia 2006; Manning 2002; Wagner 2018; Wexler 2016). And yet, reflecting the complexity of their positions discussed thus far, some were simultaneously compassionate towards offending priests.

While media reports of sexual abuses by the Catholic Church are not new, journalists and victim advocacy groups have maintained pressure both in Canada and abroad by continually scrutinizing and publicizing cases. There remains a lack of full accountability on the part of both the institutional Church and many individual offending priests, not to mention that evidence of the Church's extensive cover-up, deflection of responsibility, and intimidation through "legal hardball" keeps surfacing (Butler 2022; Cooke 2022; Ormsby 2010).[3] Prominent among the more recent and most absurd deflection tactics was the then retired, and now deceased, Pope Benedict XVI's 2019 letter. Rather than addressing the Church's cover-up, he blamed "the continuing Catholic clergy abuse crisis on the sexual revolution, developments in theology following the Second Vatican Council, and modern society's aversion to speaking about God" (McElwee 2019c).

While not as explicit as public criticism from outside the Church, the sisters were highly critical of the ways in which Church officials "time and again chose self-preservation over the protection of the most vulnerable people entrusted to their care" (Sprows Cummings 2018), and, by extension, failed to support victims and appropriately address abuses (Elliott 2020; Heyder 2022; Manning 2002). As they expressed their disgust and disapproval over a decade ago, several sisters speculated on why clerical abuses occurred and persisted. Their initial suppositions emerged through a range of feminist, psychological, and institutional interpretations:

> Well … it's power … the old boys' club, number one. (Sister Kelly)

> We're not whole without … human contact and … I think we're seeing the results of that … and … the teaching is harsh … there was … no promotion of … you know, to reach out and love … is who we are … and it's normal, you know. But there was something in the screwy teaching we had … It didn't solve anything … It drove it underground. (Sister Marian)

> I'm not blaming the celibacy strictly, but … I do think the … fortress mentality has a lot to do with it because basically it was protecting the image. (Sister Joelle)

While such considerations of the source of abuses may be important for prevention and rectification purposes, we emphasize the sisters' reactions to the cases, cover-ups, and consequences to understand how they made sense of their complex positions as insider-outsiders in an abusive institution. The following sections pertain mostly to the sisters' responses to clerical abuse of children, but we close with a section on priests' abuse of women – a widespread and systematically overlooked problem globally.

CRITIQUING THE COVER-UP

Contrary to the complacency that some might imagine on the part of Canadian nuns when it comes to problematic matters associated with the institutional Church, the sisters herein were critical of the ways in which Church leadership addressed, or rather failed to address, allegations of abuse. Similar to how most Catholic and non-Catholic onlookers felt when the sexual abuse scandal(s) surfaced publicly, the sisters reacted to the revelations with a sense of revulsion (Bonavoglia 2006; Dugan and Owens 2009; Manning 2002; Wexler 2016). While they were shocked and repulsed by the abuses themselves, like their counterparts elsewhere (see Rimer 2002), they felt particularly betrayed by, and ashamed of, the Church's systematic cover-up:

> It's appalling. (Sister Joelle)
>
> Makes me sick. (Sister Kelly)
>
> Dreadful. (Naomi)
>
> It's horrendous … the way that it was handled. (Sister Loretta)
>
> Certainly … I think it's terrible for any of us to abuse anybody. (Sister Carmen)
>
> Well, there's … anger … there's disappointment … and shame. (Sister Corinne)
>
> Absolutely sinful. Ridiculous. (Carol)

As others shared their feelings, their awareness of the Church's tactics used for the cover-up became apparent:

> I get frustrated with the hiding of the abuse of children by priests … Oh. Diocese after diocese after diocese. (Sister Nellie)
>
> Well … I feel like many people. It's too bad that … they didn't face the issue earlier. They let it go on and they just covered up … the priests. (Sister Corinne)

> I find it sad that our church was not able to do things differently ... rather than being the example, they hid it, they moved it places but never dealt with it and that is sad and we're suffering the consequences. (Sister Edna)

> I get angry when I think of any cardinals or any bishops who have protected or [were] pushing priests from this place to that place to the other place. (Sister Rita)

As Sister Marian expressed her dismay at both the initial occurrence and the systematic suppression of the abuses, she highlighted a frustrating irony:

> It was let go for so long and so many in authority knew about it and ... didn't do anything about it ... [It is] SO contrary [to Gospel teachings] ... absolutely contrary and I abhor it ... I just find it horrifying.

Other sisters were troubled not only by the Church's systematic cover-up, but also by some individual clergy's problematic reactions following media exposure of the abuse. Sister Maureen, who was deeply concerned that "so much was hidden," recalled observing a priest "FUMING" following a journalist's report on CBC's *The National*. This priest allegedly expressed his anger not out of concern for the harm inflicted against the victims, but rather because the public was becoming aware of the abuse – to which Sister Maureen thought, "My god! ... That's continually" their response to it surfacing after their extensive efforts to keep it "hidden."

Many sisters also negotiated competing feelings of critique and sympathy as they reflected on the cover-up. Darlene conveyed concern for those who were harmed and contempt for those who degraded and denied them: "Absolute sympathy [for the victims]! And rage at the Church. It's sinfulness and it's like the culture of protection of the sin as it were and again not taking care of the children."

Darlene was certainly not alone in her consideration of victims. In fact, some sisters had much closer encounters with the cover-up's implications for survivors and for those who remained at risk. Sister Agnes recalled a worrisome situation she faced first-hand in the late 1980s and early 1990s that stemmed from yet another instance in which the clergy hid potential risks to children. As a high school chaplain, one of her annual duties was to recruit several priests to hear students' confessions. One year, one of the priests informed her that another priest who had been responding reliably to her request for several years was "not to be on school property" because he had been convicted of sexual abuse and had served time in prison in another Canadian province. As Sister Agnes remembered the revelation, not only did she remain concerned for the youth at risk decades later, but she also criticized the multiple levels within the Church hierarchy that perpetrated the cover-up:

> So [the divulging priest] came in and he closed the door and he says, "Agnes, I have something … that I'm going to say to you and if you ever say that I said it, I will deny it." So he said, "You can't have Father [Name] for … the sacrament of reconciliation" … My God! So … I found that very interesting. "If you say I said it, I will deny it." So I had to go to my principal and tell him this. He was … shocked and ah mad as hell! [whispering] That for four years we've had [this priest here] and he's in charge of altar servers! But [the archbishop] must have known. He would have known … And that was covered up. So … the deception … the protection [of] their own, thinking they're protecting the Church, and why they haven't wisened up to that? They think they're above because they've been taught you know it's all God … it comes from above.

For Sister Mabel, the implications of such protection were even more personal and painful. She condemned the cover-up that went on for "years" involving her nephew, who was "abused by this priest over and over again" from the time he was seven years old until he was about twelve. Sister Mabel explained that her nephew only told his family about the abuses when he was an adult after overhearing a family conversation about his own much younger nephew becoming an altar server. Mabel reported that her nephew "just absolutely lost it and he told the whole story." Following her nephew's disclosure, Mabel's sister and brother-in-law went to their diocesan bishop, who allegedly "listened to them and did nothing. Absolutely nothing!" Instead of addressing the abuses and holding the offending priest accountable, the Church moved him "from place to place … he was a freelancer I guess because he used to come to different parishes to fill in on Sundays and stay for a week when the other guys were on holidays." Mabel was not only furious over how the Church "just swept the whole [thing under the rug]" but she was also upset over the lack of closure for the numerous victims: "He used to make visits up here ... And there were so many boys affected; none of them would tell. So it never went public."

While the individual impacts on those directly affected by clerical abuse remain the sisters' primary concern, their critiques of the cover-up's institutional implications are also instructive. The Roman Catholic Church has undoubtedly long sought to entrench itself as both a beacon and an enforcer of morality worldwide. Yet its institutional image has been severely tarnished by its own hierarchy's inability to uphold its values through a serial cycle of actions, reactions, and inactions. Judith pointed to the absurdity of it all as she fittingly illustrated the contradiction inherent within the cover-up:

> Oh! Well, I mean, I don't think they have anything to say anymore ... about ethics or morals ... They have so devalued themselves that ... they're a laughingstock besides. Honest to God!

Such a fall from grace is particularly striking against the backdrop of trust in a religious occupation that claims to promote the highest moral and ethical standards of personal and spiritual conduct. Yet this perfectionist idea of clerical life was a standard that men as clerics had set themselves (Elliott 2004; Manning 2002). As we show next, it is an ethical standard to which they have still not been held fully accountable.

HOLDING EVERYONE ACCOUNTABLE

The sisters' overall sense of responsibility in the context of clerical sexual abuse appeared evident in three distinct ways: first, in their own individual sense of shame and their awareness of their role in what they considered a collective responsibility; second, in their insistence that the Church's institutional obligations to survivors be fully and transparently realized; and third, in their expectation that perpetrators be held publicly accountable.

FEELING THEIR OWN SENSE OF ACCOUNTABILITY

You share the shame because you're there; you're a member of it, you share it.

Sister Corinne

While none of the sisters interviewed disclosed that they, or anyone in their congregations, had sexually abused children, many of them genuinely felt the same collective responsibility conveyed by Sister Corinne. Compared to the institutional Church's countless cover-up tactics (suppressing suspicions, dismissing allegations, intimidating victims, exploiting legal avenues to their advantage, and hiding assets), the sisters herein have expressed a shared sense of accountability indicative of their deep-rooted and authentic concern for the well-being of others.

While some dwelled on the shame as an emotional manifestation of responsibility, others focused on the relational aspects as part of their rationale for their collective concern. For example, Sister Jeanette felt that "if the person is the victim, we are the ones that are the offender," and thus for her, "it's all our responsibility. We are all part of the church."[4] Similarly, Sister Sophie reported that while she did not have any direct involvement, she shared in a collective sense of shame "among religious": "[I] just feel so badly that so many sisters and so many priests have been involved in that." Interestingly, unlike the Church hierarchy that has long denied allegations, Sister Sophie, along with Sisters Corinne, Sarah, and Theresa, readily referred to not only priests' but also nuns' roles in the abuses, including those perpetrated against "children in residential schools" (Sister Theresa).[5] While such admissions may seem belated and negligible to some observers, they remain significant given how many sisters were intimidated and silenced, or were the targets of severe backlash, when they did try to expose clerical abuses against children (Bonavoglia 2006, 102; Condon 2000).[6] Sisters' subordinate position under the clergy, and the forced and harmful labour practices they faced in residential schools as a result (Gresko 2007), have been recognized, even among those who were justifiably critical of Church members' controlling involvement in such settings (Rastello 2023c); for example, in reference to Kuper Island Residential School, Duncan McCue (2022, 22:30) pointed out how "the Oblates ruled the school, relentlessly cowing the children, even the nuns, into meek obedience."[7]

EXPECTING INSTITUTIONAL ACCOUNTABILITY FOR SURVIVORS

The sisters' overall sense of accountability consisted of both critiques against the Church's blatant lack of consideration for the well-being of victims, and their insistence that the Church both set and meet its organizational obligations in support of survivors (Manning 2002). Such sentiments were variously conveyed by several sisters:

> Such a lack of ... concern for the victims. (Sister Joelle)

> I would say the Church itself is an impediment to people's human rights ... and the Church's whole loyalty ... to the institution rather than ... to the individual, the victim ... the person. (Sister Kelly)

> I don't agree with some ways the Church ... is responding to it ... and I just feel sad ... that we haven't stepped up to really ... say we're sorry and make ... some way of ... allowing ... more education and more freedom for people to be able to claim ... what's rightfully theirs ... and what rightfully happened to them ... it's one of the things that I really, really find very difficult to accept. (Sister Jeanette)

In echoing how little the Church hierarchy did to support the victims of perpetrating priests (Sprows Cummings 2018), Sister Mabel recalled how some victims, including her nephew whose story we recounted earlier, have had to seek out their own sources of healing:

> He's not had healing [from the Church] but he has himself healed ... He's had therapy for years and years ... They [Church authorities] offered nothing.

While many sisters focused on how the Church should have done much more to foster greater accountability for the sake of the survivors, and she certainly agreed, Carol also directed her attention toward the seemingly targeted approach that the Church took in laying blame on a particular group – gay priests. Carol was emphatic both in her expectation of authentic accountability and in her critique of the Church's misguided shifting of blame away from the institution and onto a few "bad apples":

> Let's own it! Let's sit down and study human sexuality … [but] you know, they will not deal with it … On so many levels! I mean this whole abuse thing! Instead of dealing with some of these people … they're promoting … and supporting the notion that … priests who are involved in abusive situations … are homosexuals … And it's not true! But … they continue to promote that… which really pisses me off! … That it's the gays! … And therefore, let's have a witch hunt and make sure we don't have any gays into the seminary. I mean it's such bullshit! That's happening! Now they're having these great big long psychological tests to make sure that there's no homosexuals getting in!

Carol's frustration was not only with the Church's vile homophobia, including the pathologizing discourse aimed to strategically associate, and thus problematically conflate, being gay with paedophilia and sexual abuse by priests (Donadio 2010; Marcel 2013; Voices of Faith 2018), but also with the Church leaders' unwillingness to consider how its absurd and misogynist treatment of human sexuality has fostered a climate where child abuse by clerics, including against girls, was possible for so long (Demasure 2021; Manning 2002; McPhillips and McEwan 2022).[8] While certainly not the same as Carol's expectation of an authentic study on human sexuality, yet still aimed at addressing the broader context and ensuring greater accountability, Sister Edna was actively engaged in educational efforts intended to guide Church representatives on how to deal truthfully and supportively with victims' disclosures:

> Now … I did organize for the conference of religious … workshops so that religious, men and women, could come and prepare the steps. Get … professionals in … and to prepare their policy, and that was something!

While the initiatives with which Sister Edna was involved may be indicative of preliminary efforts on the part of the Catholic Church in Canada to at least begin to support survivors and to end the cover-up at an institutional level, as we show next, such steps were not yet satisfactory for some sisters, who sought stronger accountability measures.

SEEKING CRIMINALIZATION AND RETRIBUTION

As part of their call for collective responsibility, many sisters were adamant that abusive priests be held accountable publicly, and in some instances, retributively. For some, such as Sister Joelle – a member of her congregation's leadership team – that meant a new motto for all to follow: "Transparency! Transparency! Transparency!" Unfortunately, the institution has not yet practised what it preached (Cooke 2022). For others, such as Sisters Rita and Ella, it went beyond denouncing the cover-ups; it also involved acknowledging the benefits of public disclosure:

> I've always felt very badly about all that kind of thing that happened throughout the years; there's no doubt about it ... the sexual abuse ... has been ... very, very difficult ... It's just terrible that bishops to have protected priests ... it was all wrong ... But the fact that it's all coming out is great, hard to bear but [necessary]. (Sister Rita)

> [They assumed that] nobody is ever going to know. It's going to be kept under wraps. Well! It's so healthy that it's aired out. And may it always be to the fore. (Sister Ella)

For still others, such as Sister Jeanette, while they felt that rehabilitative support for both victims and offenders must be prioritized, they insisted that perpetrators "be brought to justice, the same as everyone else." Many others also echoed that criminalization was both warranted and desirable regardless of the religiously impelled benefits of reconciliation:

> Well, all I can say is ... sin has a social consequence and ... once you confess, sure, you are forgiven. But my thought is, oh I feel very strongly ... oh my god, I feel strongly ... that, in many ways, this is a terrible thing to say, I'm happy the abuses are catching up with the abusers. I am very happy for that. There's justice for everybody, and the priests are not exempted. (Sister Noreen)

> I do think ... the criminal prosecution ... going to the police is the definite first step ... It's a criminal offence, and so why not? (Sister Joelle)

The desire for retribution was stronger for certain women religious than for others, out of concern for the vulnerable populations most often affected; such was the case for Sister Mabel, who was also particularly outraged given the sexual abuse perpetrated against her "little seven-year-old" nephew:

> They should be strangled ... I don't understand it. I just cannot get my head around it. Why? ... I get enraged because there's two kinds of people, well there's three really, the elderly, children, and animals, that I could kill if anybody abuses them.

Similarly, as Sister Penelope criticized the institutional Church for failing to create the conditions required to hold perpetrating priests accountable, she shared her preference for retributive and carceral forms of accountability, and her awareness of the collateral costs of the cover-up:

> I don't think our church handles well ... the issues in order to make people responsible for their actions ... I think it's been curtailed ... that whole justice issue around that because we have priests here and I find that very difficult, you know ... they have been cut from doing priestly duties but yet ... they live a good life. They are walking around freely, they can take a vacation two and three times a year ... What punishment is that, you know? What makes them really stop and think about what they've done? Now it's different if a person is put in jail, like we do have one in jail, but at least he's paying the consequences of his actions. But there's others that have just been hushed up. And so by hushing them up, they are living the life of a free man ... with privileges ... because who's paying for these? ... It's the lay people because the money has to be coming into the diocese to be able to give these people the stipend to live on, to feed them ... So ... no I don't like what's happening.[9]

With a similarly retributive leaning, Sister Josephine felt that a process of justice was certainly warranted across multiple and much "higher" realms, especially for members of the hierarchy who orchestrated the cover-up:

> I think that … if any priest is … accused of abuse for instance, sexual abuse of boys or of girls, that priest should be taken out of service immediately and it should be investigated … But to move a priest who is a paedophile from one place to another is absolutely wrong and I think the bishops that do that are looking at a hard judge when they get to Heaven.

SUPPORTING VICTIMS OF CHILDHOOD ABUSE

Sisters' sympathetic support for the survivors of clerical abuse took many forms; concerned for their healing, sisters provided personal counselling, and cooperated with criminal investigations. Several sisters, including Ella, Loretta, Kelly, Clara, Mabel, and Sarah, were actively involved in supporting victims of clerical abuse, most commonly through counselling or spiritual direction. When asked if they had ever helped in the healing journeys of individuals who had been sexually violated by Church authorities, their responses were unequivocal:

> In this very room! Lots of it … Oh my gosh! You wouldn't believe … what some of them are living. (Sister Ella)

> Yes, I have. Yes, I have. It's a LONG process, let me tell you. It's a very long process. But … it's … very life giving too for people. (Sister Loretta)

> I have … and also … the mothers of boys who have been. [Interviewer: So you've picked up the pieces?]: [softly] Tried to. It's hard. It's very, very hard. (Sister Kelly)

> Two girls [who] were abused by a priest who also abused the boy, along with the boy's mother. Yeah. Oh no, it's an awful case. I can hardly talk about it. It was so awful. (Sister Clara)

Among those who were not trained to offer therapy, the feelings of helplessness were wearying. For example, Sister Nellie worried about the plight of victims as "broken, broken down people" yet she would "get frustrated trying to think of how you can help them ... I'm not a psychologist so ... it's just horrible." For others who specialized in mental health therapy, the counselling support they provided survivors sometimes involved their own relatives. For example, to support his healing, Sister Mabel carried on "long [phone] conversations" with her abuse-affected nephew because "the Church did absolutely nothing for him."[10] While Sister Mabel "really encouraged him to sue," her nephew opted not to because "all he wanted was the guy to admit" – a desperate plea that was never answered, even after the young man confronted his abuser directly, and as a result, the priest was never held accountable.

Sister Sarah was similarly involved in therapeutic care, but as she served a population whose exploitation by the Church was extensive and multi-generational, her support was sometimes justifiably rebuffed:

> [Sigh] Well ... my closest experience to it would be my experience working with First Nations Peoples and ... I was a healer of some of the victimization and that's a very painful place to be because you kind of stand there for the Church and you sometimes ... are the person who is taking the anger or the rejection or whatever it is. It can be also a very privileged place of meeting people in their very woundedness ... and I have experienced that.

Like other women religious across Canada, Sister Sarah articulated the complicated position of insider-outsider as settler and member of the Church not only bearing witness to, but also trying to mitigate, harms generated and exacerbated by her very institution (Rastello 2023a, 2023b, 2023c). Whereas Sister Sarah's association with the Church was inescapable in that setting and she empathized with the residential school and sexual abuse survivors' frustration directed towards her, Sister Ella intentionally looked beyond her Church affiliation, and instead drew on her spirit-led outlook to focus on the needs of individuals harmed by that same institution:[11]

> Well I don't ... think of myself as a representative of the Church so much as I am just this woman here with the opportunity to listen and I just pray, "God, use me, just use me as an avenue for your goodness or grace ... for healing. And if you can use me for this person, wonderful." That's my stance.

Some sisters' support toward victims and their families also consisted of reporting instances of abuse to authorities, efforts that often did not yield an appropriate survivor-centred outcome due to the extent of the cover-up. Sister Benita, a former teacher, recalled her involvement in a case in which an abusive priest from Canada dodged criminal responsibility for decades in part through being assigned from "one high job to the next in the Catholic Church ... [including when] they brought him to Rome" after she had reported an allegation against him:

> One of the girls in my classroom from [a rural town] came and told me. She said, "Can I speak with you, sister?" And I said, "sure," and she told me that her brother had been [abused]. He [the priest] had this little cabin in the hills, and her brother had gone to the cabin, and had really wanted to be a priest ... And ... so he ... tried to, um, abuse him ... the boy came home and told the family, and the father and mother almost wouldn't believe him. Like, the priest would not do this ... but that was ... when I was in [a rural area] ... in the late '70s ... and so they're just doing something now.

After advising the "shocked" sibling "not to worry" and reassuring her "that it would be taken care of," Sister Benita claimed that she told her immediate authority – the school principal who also happened to be her superior within her religious congregation.

It was only around the time of her interview for this study, decades later, that the matter had been investigated because the family "wanted to go to court and they wanted to do something about it." While the case drew media attention and the priest was eventually convicted and imprisoned, Sister Benita remained disillusioned not only by the delay, but also by what appeared to be a continuation of the cover-up. Shortly before our conversation, she had been contacted by criminal justice personnel because "the police wanted to follow up to find if there was anyone in the diocese that knew about it and didn't do anything." She alleged that she had been subsequently contacted by a priest who claimed that "we can't see any record of it [her original reporting]." Such denial exacerbated her frustration with the Church hierarchy because "they knew," yet they deprived the victim and his sister of the attention, assistance, and accountability they deserved all those years ago.

While Sister Benita's concern for the sibling may have been genuine – "I listened to her that night" – it is not surprising that her reporting of it, as a woman religious in a position of inferiority within a hyper-hierarchical institution (Schneiders 2013), did not lend any credibility to the case when it was first brought to the attention of Church authorities (Bonavoglia 2006, 102; McCue 2022; Rastello 2023c; Wexler 2016).

FEELING COMPASSION TOWARDS PERPETRATORS

There is no doubt that the sisters' experiences with, and reactions to, the abuses elicit complex emotions and responses. Their consideration of the well-being of all who have been affected by, and implicated in, instances of clerical abuse is indicative of their compassionate approach toward the many forms of "woundedness." For example, Sister Jeanette, like so many others, articulated the feeling of helplessness and genuine concern that she felt for both victims and perpetrators: "It really saddens me ... I pray for those people that were abused and for their abuser. And then I have to realize and say to myself, maybe these people needed help, and nobody recognized it."

As one who considered clerical abuse so "appalling" that it was one of the issues that led her to feel "ashamed to be Catholic," and as one who personally "knows some abusers," Naomi's consideration was threefold. She felt concern for the victims, compassion for the perpetrators, and critical of the official response:

> I blame ... the institutional Church in a double way; first of all, for ... failing to deal honestly and lovingly with the victims of abuse and being candid about what has happened, but also in perpetuating this system in which ... priests ... can live very unhealthy lives ... I see very clearly that they are victims of a terrible system ... called the Church which in my experience has fostered loneliness and a way of life that is really unhealthy.

Others held similar stances regarding the controlling context underlying their compassionate outlooks. While she certainly did not condone their behaviour, Carol recalled feeling "very sad for some of [the offending priests] who have been charged with abuse" and that she believed that "they are victims of a Church that ... is ... just sexually deprived in its teaching ... it's sick, sick!" Similarly, while Sister Ella felt "sorry for many [of the perpetrators] because they're caught in a cult," Sister Noreen elaborated on her consideration for those who were both directly and indirectly implicated:

> Now I feel sorry for the individual priests, when I think there was a bishop above them who should've looked out and helped them and I'm sure they went for help, they were probably told to pray about it. So that's the next level … the higher up you go in the cover-up that's when it gets even more [critical to intervene] …
>
> I feel sorry for the priests who are in it with the right heart because they get painted with the same brush. There is a whole climate of distrust that has been created now … so on one hand, I'm glad people are being caught and on the other hand, I feel sorry for those priests who have really embraced their vocation.

Comparatively, Sister Adele recalled the mixed reactions of both contempt and compassion that she felt when she accompanied another sister to her ministry in a prison where "a priest who had been convicted of abuse" had been granted permission to "say Mass for a very small group" of prisoners:

> I [sigh] … was appalled … I remember when I first heard about it, I could hardly believe it could be and I just … felt so badly … I knew it was terrible. I felt awful it could have ever happened. I felt sorry for victims … but I just remember the confusion, I mean, I had every feeling you could have being at that celebration. I felt for this priest. He seemed … nice; he was a person … and whatever he had done, he was in prison. I felt sorry for all the prisoners … I thought … whatever they did, they're people … So … I felt compassion for him. I really felt compassionate for whoever his victims were. I felt anger at him and … that any of it had ever happened. I felt everything! I guess I didn't feel joy. But somehow it was part of my learning to just be there and to be able to be with all of those feelings and not have to even sort them out, or figure them out, or banish them, they were just all there at once.[12]

Sister Agnes also had a mixed reaction to perpetrators who still say Mass. Despite her frustration with sexually abusive priests being reassigned out of parishes and into convents to say Mass for nuns, who are themselves capable of leading their own spiritual celebrations, Sister Agnes clarified the compassion she felt in their regard, given the isolation they face from parishioners:[13]

> Yet my heart goes out to some of these men … in the case I'm thinking of … I've grown to [understand], he is suffering so much … I don't know that anything ever came out in the courts … but the parishioners spoke up and said they don't want him in the parishes.

For some women religious, their direct knowledge of the implications also informed their compassionate approach. For example, Darlene had provided extensive counselling in one of the first publicly disclosed cases of sexual abuse perpetrated by Catholic priests in Canada. She recalled her involvement: "I worked with victims, and I worked with perpetrators, victimizers." For Darlene, like many others, the abuses hit close to home. She recounted feeling a lot of "sympathy for [one particular perpetrator]" because he was the brother of one of the sisters in her community at the time. On the other hand, as a skilled facilitator working with priests in a community where abuses were previously publicized, Darlene witnessed first-hand how those accused of abuse were angrily rejected by their fellow priests in group settings.

Still for others, such as Sister Sarah, their sense of compassion took the form of a relational and reconciliatory approach – one that is no doubt complex, but that is nevertheless sorely lacking in the Church (Kinew 2017; Rastello 2023a, 2023b, 2023c):

> One thing that I think that the Church … really needs to understand is that there's more than a juridical justice that needs to happen, and that in the Church, justice is about relationships and I do also need to say that as much as I totally do not agree with … what perpetrators do whoever they are, that if we really believe in reconciliation, we have to understand what that means and … if we really believe in the dignity of human persons, it's ALL people, and that means a whole area, I think, around … understanding how to be in relationship with perpetrators and what that means. That, we really need to understand. Like I REALLY do not think we know how to be reconciled in the

> Church and ... I'm not talking about victims being reconciled or victims forgiving their perpetrator ... I'm not talking about ... priests who abuse being able to be priests, to be able to continue in that capacity ... but yeah ... we really need to look at ... the whole process of reconciliation.

It is to such complex aspects of accountability that we turn to next as we present how women have also directly experienced clerical abuse.

WOMEN TOO ... #NUNSTOO[14]

The clerical sexual abuse of children has justifiably scandalized the Church in recent decades, but men's sexual violence against women in the Church has not received the same scrutiny (Bouclin 2006; Chibnall, Wolf, and Duckro 1998; Heyder 2022; Marcel 2013; McPhillips and McEwan 2022; Voices of Faith 2018). As some critics contend, priests' sexual violence against women "far exceeds their involvement with minors" (Bonavoglia 2006, 85). This tendency to erase violence against women is consistent with broader cultural acceptance of the inevitability of violence against women, particularly when it is intimate partner violence happening in the relative privacy of women's homes. The nuns' experience with sexual abuse by clergy is complicated by the fact that their abusers live where they might also work, making the workplace and the home potentially overlapping sites of sexual violence for women religious survivors (Bouclin 2006).[15] This sexual exploitation of women religious and the corresponding denial and derision of those who speak out against it remain an urgent underreported, underplayed, and under-researched crisis across the globe (BBC News 2019; Chibnall, Wolf, and Duckro 1998; Fernandes 2022; Hidalgo 2007; Kavi 2022; Marcel 2013; McPhillips and McEwan 2022; Schneiders 2013; Thomas 2022; Wagner 2018).[16]

Sexual violence against sisters by priests can be seen as an extension of the institutionalized misogyny well-known to the Church, and arguably rooted in its Catholic culture and doctrine (Demasure 2021; Fisher 2012; Heyder 2022; Manning 1999; Meyer 2021). Unsurprisingly, like the accounts of other women abused by clerics, the sisters' testimonies have been met with denial, blame, manipulation, deprivation of independent legal advocacy, and elaborate cover-ups by the Church (Bonavoglia 2006; Bouclin 2006; Demasure 2021; Figueroa and Tombs 2022; Heyder 2022; Marcel 2013; McPhillips and McEwan 2022;

NPR *Europe* 2019; Schneiders 2013; Voices of Faith 2018; Wagner 2018). As Sister Loretta corroborated, Canadian nuns were certainly not spared this widespread abuse: "Oh my! When we worked in formation, you know, like in [a retreat centre], we had various congregations come there; so many of the women had been abused. It was just unreal ... Yeah."[17] Although women's rights advocates have denounced such cover-ups and have called for accountability for and prevention of "sexual violence against nuns and other women by Catholic priests worldwide," especially in mission countries,[18] very few gains have been made (McPhillips and McEwan 2022; NPR Europe 2019; Saldanha 2022).

As feminist theorists of rape culture explain, rape is about power and entitlement (Filipovic 2013; Friedman and Valenti 2008). It is not difficult to understand, then, that the Church's explicit designation of gender roles to subordinate women cultivates an environment where men's sexual violence against women is condoned (Bouclin 2006; Demasure 2021; Filipovic 2008; Fisher 2012; Manning 1999; McPhillips and McEwan 2022). Men's violent expression of misogyny through rape is not unique to the Church, of course, but the way the Roman Catholic Church has denied and hidden men's abuse of women is telling of their intense hypocrisy (Meyer 2021; Schneiders 2013). Sister Agnes expanded on the inextricably linked forms of exploitation:

> The priests who have sexually abused ... It's got to do with the putting down of women again ... In some of our motherhouses, the person celebrating Mass cannot be in a regular parish [because of sexual abuse] so he's with older women ... so if you can't go to a parish within a diocese, go to the nuns, you know.[19]

For Sister Agnes, women's exclusion from the altar, their experiences with rape by priests, and their not-so-subtle responsibility to contain abusive priests is part of women's relegation to the margins of power (Demasure 2021; Gervais 2018; Gervais and Watson 2018). Others have raised similar concerns when looking back on incidents both abroad and at home. Sister Kelly recalled observing a circumstance in earlier decades in a European country which she recognized unequivocally as "totally unacceptable domination" by a member of the Church's patriarchal hierarchy in the form of sexual exploitation of a woman (Schneiders 2013, 530):

> When I was in [a European city], one of the … professors was working with … a young woman who was having an affair with a cardinal from Rome. And this was going on for several years and she thought she was … so much in love with him and he was so much in love with her and he used to drive up … and at this stage she told him she was pregnant and she never saw him again … Now that's abuse!

Similarly, Carol pointed to incidents from her earlier days at her convent in Canada that were never reconciled as, at the time our interview, the perpetrator had never been held accountable and had remained a priest, while the victim continued to suffer in the aftermath of the abuse:

> Some of my classmates … were told, "Look it, I will have sex with you and that will help you" by priests that were coming in to run retreats! … I mean the gurus! … I know of gals that have left because of it and the convent denied them! The nuns themselves, when the sister went and said, "Father raped me," said, "It didn't happen. You must have led it on." [Name of former sister] is a bad, bad, bad alcoholic … But she was abused by one of the priests … from the time she was about twelve, thirteen, fourteen years of age; she worked at the rectory and she was abused by [a priest] … sad, sad, sad situation … I know of [another] one … abused by one of the great Spanish priests who'd come from Spain to teach us … BUT she got no support from the convent. No. None.[20]

While Carol was particularly frustrated that this former sister-peer was neither believed nor assisted by her religious community, as has been evident among women religious elsewhere (Heyder 2022; Meyer 2021; NPR Europe 2019; Voices of Faith 2018; Wagner 2018), Sister Joelle was comparatively relieved that sisters in her congregation who were similarly harmed as children and youth did receive mental health care: "a number of our women were victims of abuse by priests … And so they carry the scars and need support, treatment, and so … I'm aware of a number of times that that was provided for them." Nevertheless, the existence or extent of support for these women within their own congregations is not necessarily the main point of contention. Instead, what is more troubling is that rather than assuming their responsibility for the sexual exploitation of nuns and for sometimes forcing the nuns whom the priests impregnated to have abortions (Allen and Schaeffer 2001; Colwell and Johnson 2020; McPhillips 2019), the Vatican downplayed the matter by referring to it as a minor problem (Manning 2002), and the Church clergy deflected attention away from the entire sexual abuse scandal by condemning nuns for their feminist interventions (Bonavoglia 2006; Gervais and Watson 2018; Schneiders 2013; Wexler 2016).

Given such deflections of responsibility, the abuses perpetrated and denied by Church actors are ongoing, and victims are still suffering (Fernandes 2022; Heyder 2022; Kavi 2022; McPhillips and McEwan 2022; NPR Europe 2019; Schneiders 2013; Thomas 2022; Wagner 2018; Voices of Faith 2018). As with the harms exacted on children, some sisters have speculated on the underlying conditions of the abuses against women too. For Sister Clara, the overarching context was unequivocal: "patriarchy is an abuse of all the women." Yet, within an intimidating institution still deeply entrenched in patriarchy and misogyny (Daly 1973; Ó'Murchú 2011; Wexler 2016), there are few avenues for women religious to challenge long-held institutional beliefs that are still indoctrinating them into subservience (Figueroa and Tombs 2022; Filipovic 2008; Manning 1999, 2002; McPhillips and McEwan 2022; Meyer 2021; NPR Europe 2019; Wagner 2018; Voices of Faith 2018; Wexler 2016).[21] Carol remembered how their gendered conditioning to cater to priests visiting their convent went unquestioned: "nobody challenged, you know really challenged ... As sisters, as congregations, they did not challenge misogyny. They did not challenge ... exclusive language ... they treated the priests like little gods." Carol recalled how the expectation was that the nuns served them "in the breakfast room ... with the tablecloths ... and the linen" and she felt that "we [the sisters] were inferior ... there was no doubt about it."

To counter such ingrained patriarchal attitudes, Sister Ella proposed that instead of placing the onus solely on women and their capacity to challenge the institution, we must "target the source ... It's the men who need to be targeted." To do so, and to foster allyship for women religious, Ella was already engaged in these efforts: "Every chance I have to talk with men ... I encourage them to work with men. Men need to work with men. I'm convinced." Ella's recommendation relates to a fundamental flaw in the wider societal tendency to responsibilize potential victims, who are predominantly women, by expecting them to take the educational and tactical steps required to prevent their own victimization. Instead, Ella points to how imperative it is that men bear equal responsibility in all efforts aimed at ending the perpetration of violence against women (Connell 2003). And who better than to lead the way than the man who heads the Roman Catholic Church? Although Pope Francis did pledge to "fight against" sexual abuse and other "abuses of power" against women religious, including gendered conditions of servitude (Fisher 2012; McElwee 2019a), the structural transformation required by the institutional Church, especially of its prevailing patriarchal and clerical system, has not yet begun (McPhillips and McEwan 2022; NPR Europe 2019; Romey 2022; Schüssler Fiorenza 2016).

CONCLUSION

Navigating their complex feelings towards both victims and perpetrators forced the sisters to reckon with their membership in the institution that hid these offences. While some critics and survivors may understandably never distinguish nuns from the Roman Catholic Church and its problematic role in facilitating and perpetuating clerical abuse, some distinctions are warranted. First, the women religious represented herein neither accepted nor condoned the ways in which the Church's patriarchal hierarchy failed to adequately address allegations and actual accounts of abuses committed by priests; as such, their critiques constitute expressions of resistance, including loyal disobedience, against the Church's prevailing hush culture and its attempted silencing of sisters (Holtmann 2008; Murphy 2022; Ó'Murchú 1997). Second, while some sisters readily acknowledged that there were abuse scandals in which women religious were complicit, and, in some cases, active participants (Manning 2002; Meyer 2021; Watts 2024),[22] the sisters we interviewed did not report firsthand experience with priests abusing children. Third, while concerning in and of itself, nuns' perceived complacency must be understood within the broader context of the Church's explicit sexism. Certainly, some nuns' inaction or dereliction of duty[23] can be interpreted as an example of sisters having "packed up their privilege and slipped out the back" (Payne 2021; Rastello 2023a). But many sisters attempted to disclose instances of abuse and support survivors in life-giving ways with counselling and other forms of care (Faulkner and MacDonald 2009). Sisters have deeply regretted instances where they feel they could have done more to protect children and women against sexual violence by priests. Their own subordination within the Church helps to nuance their range of responses. As subordinates tasked explicitly with obedience, sisters often feared serious consequences from the Church and congregational hierarchies if they brought these matters to the attention of authorities on behalf of victims (Bonavoglia 2006, 102; McCue 2022; Rastello 2023c). Relatedly, in instances pertaining to their own victimization, such fears were further complicated by their status "as consecrated members of the Catholic Church … [through which] they may view themselves as a part of the Church leadership, leading to a conflict between needing to protect the reputation of the Church or disclose the harm they [and others] experience" (McPhillips and McEwan 2022, 5).

Mindful of theirs and the clergy's (in)actions, the sisters proposed ways forward which involve removing a range of barriers (Faulkner and MacDonald 2009; Ó'Murchú 1997). For Sister Penelope, the process entails moving beyond the inertia and the lack of genuine understanding of what is required for healing: "I don't really think the Catholic Church knows what peace is because they have made no efforts to try bring about peace and reconciliation with this whole issue with sexual abuse." For Sister Joelle, the Church ought to be stripped of its separate protective system that enabled the cover-up by allowing its decision-making related to abuse cases and financial settlements to remain hidden: "You know this parallel structure of the Church … as with … annulments and divorce … it's duplication [of civil and criminal justice systems]."

Despite Pope Francis acknowledging the sexual violation of women and of nuns in particular, by Roman Catholic priests (NPR Europe 2019), efforts to heal in community will continue without full accountability by perpetrators or authentic amends toward victims.[24] The context of reconciliation is additionally complicated in settler Canada as Indigenous scholars and activists criticize the tendency of settlers and colonial states to shift our gaze toward therapeutics and away from structurally produced struggles for sovereignty or healing for those continually harmed (Johnson 2019; Million 2013; Simpson 2014).[25]

In the spirit of radically reimagining an inclusive future (Manning 2002; Ó'Murchú 1997), some sisters expressed a desire for transformation. Darlene came to this sense of institutional falling-apart as she recalled a moment when she heard a prisoner call out to her as she walked past a local prison: "The prisoners were cleaning up and

I heard, 'Hello Darlene,' and I looked around and this is one of the priests whom I knew, in jail. He was there cleaning up and spoke to me. It was just ... Talk about the Church crumbling, you know?" Sisters Noreen and Maureen, as well as Mildred, conveyed the same point, but with rather wishful tones:

> You know, ever since the scandal of the abused children broke out, somehow I think all of this is gonna fall into place. I grieve for it, I grieve it. But I don't lose sleep over it ...
>
> The institution is crumbling and that's part of the crumbling, okay. This touches people so much when little kids are being abused ... that the institution's weakness is so blatant now ... and I say God has his ways ... of prevailing, right. And the monsignors are the first ones to go down! (Sister Noreen)

> I think ... it's a way of letting it die and I think it has to die before the new can come out of the ashes and it is killing itself. And like everything new that's born, the old has to go, and this is the way it's going. (Mildred)

> My hope is that the Church will realize that this is a way of cleansing and perhaps a new church coming from that ... It'll be a while before they [men clerics] see it. But ... a lot of things can happen and could be happening amongst the people themselves. (Sister Maureen)

The sisters may not have foreseen it at the time of their interviews over a decade ago,[26] but a "crumbling" of sorts has recently begun, not only through declining church attendance (Winkel and Heinz 2022),[27] but also in the selling of Church properties as part of one archdiocese's legal obligation to compensate clerical abuse victims, namely those who suffered extensive harm at the Mount Cashel Orphanage in Newfoundland (Gillis 2022).[28] Church officials were not forthcoming with reparations out of concern for the victims' well-being. Instead, they fought vigorously to avoid accountability in decades-long court battles that eventually culminated in an appeal court imposing vicarious liability on the Archdiocese of St John's secular arm – a once strategically separate corporate entity (Butler 2022). As disorienting as these sales have been for some parishioners who are losing their places of worship and spaces of community, they represent a long-awaited moment of accountability by the perpetrators and their aiders and abettors, one that will hopefully support survivors (Butler 2022).

Potential for change can also be found among the lay people themselves (Wexler 2016), of which nuns are technically a part. Sisters' "what if / if only"–type reflections show how they hypothesized different outcomes related to the abuse had women been in leadership positions within the Church:

> I know that the abuse question, well, one, would not have been as severe probably, and it would have been handled very differently. (Sister Joelle)

> There is still a hush hush around a lot of it, and ... I think if it was religious women [in leadership positions], it probably would have come to the forefront much quicker than it has. (Sister Penelope)

While such comments are of course speculative and it is impossible to glean how things may have been different under women-led governance, the sisters clearly thought about how their already-demonstrated leadership capacity could bring the Church into a new era of accountability, reconciliation, and peace, away from the harms and failures caused by a deeply entrenched culture of patriarchal domination (Chittister 2022a; Murphy 2022; Ó'Murchú 1997). Relatedly, with a sense of outrage and urgency over the ongoing abuse scandals, others, including University of Notre Dame scholar Kathleen Sprows Cummings (2018), have insisted that fundamental change in the Church will only occur when women are not merely given a "place at the table," but are fully integrated into a radical restructuring that involves a complete "reset [of] the table." If the current structure of the Roman Catholic Church does crumble, and the table is reset as a result of abuse survivors and their allies, perhaps then "something new can emerge" (Broz and Flynn 2006, 193), and lead to spaces of worship that are "safer for children" (Sprows Cummings 2018),[29] for women, and for all.[30]

6

Supporting Women's Reproductive Justice

Christine Gervais and Amanda Watson

> What I do is not so much anti as really advocating for the dignity of all people.
>
> Sister Sarah

INTRODUCTION

Reproductive rights represent yet another contentious issue upon which women religious' feminist orientations and faith-based traditions both conflict and coalesce (Gervais 2018; Holtmann 2011a; Wexler 2016). Perhaps surprisingly given the controversy surrounding reproductive injustice in the Catholic Church, some of the most trenchant examples of sisters' opposition to specific Church teachings pertained to contraception and abortion. As we illustrate the sisters' and former sisters' complex views on such matters, informed by their negotiation of feminism and Catholicism (Gervais 2012; Holtmann 2011a), we demonstrate how their advocacy for women's reproductive rights has been remarkably compassionate in the context of stifling Church doctrine. The sisters' accounts touched primarily on issues of women's autonomy, and their reports indicated a range of resistance, from feelings of ambiguity to activism for abortion access.

Given that they are perceived as representatives of the Roman Catholic Church, women religious have been understandably stereotyped as supporters of the anti-abortion movement in Canada and globally. The Church has been known for its opposition to contraception and abortion through its enforcement of Canons 2270 through

2274 and the 1968 encyclical *Humanae Vitae*,[1] even in some of the most grievous cases (Congregation for the Doctrine of the Faith 2009).[2] Many Catholic nuns, Catholic Women's League members, and Knights of Columbus have been recognizably opponents of abortion,[3] but the Catholic sisters interviewed in this study have found ways to consider and defend women's reproductive justice and health care needs as they reckon with Catholic mores (Catholics for Choice 2011; Wexler 2016). In doing so, they have resisted the Church's official anti-abortion and anti-contraception stance through their community work (Ruether 2003). Their stories echo and bring nuance to Catholic sisters' controversial positions on issues of sexuality and reproductive justice more broadly, as they have long contested the Church's widespread and excessive control over women's bodies in matters of sexuality (Bonavoglia 2006; Fisher 2012; Wexler 2016); dress, particularly via nuns' habits (Murphy 2014; Sullivan 2005); contraception (Bouclin 2006; Manning 2002); and such dehumanizing rituals as the "purification of women after childbirth" (Lee 1996, 43).

Considering how the sisters' views on gender equality were influenced by feminist movements in the late 1960s and '70s (Sullivan 2005; Bonavoglia 2006; Wexler 2016), so must their comments on abortion and contraception be situated within the specific context of abortion debates in Canada, which intensified in the 1980s and 1990s, a significant period during which the Supreme Court of Canada decriminalized abortion on the basis that legally restricting abortion infringes upon a woman's right to "life, liberty and security of the person."[4] While anti-abortion movements in Canada were not nearly the amalgam of religious and political leadership that they were in the US context (Bonavoglia 2006; Wexler 2016), anti-abortion rhetoric in Canada became a unifying avenue for Protestant and Catholic religious people who opposed the social rights framework being advanced in Canadian society (Saurette and Gordon 2016). Since that time, anti-abortion movements, founded and organized by Catholics but diverse in strategy and membership, have attempted to re-criminalize abortion by advocating for foetal rights (Cuneo 1989; Saurette and Gordon 2016). Despite legal rulings, concerns related to provision and access are still ongoing, as some of the sisters' stories make clear.

The sisters' ethical positions were not neatly tied to one side of this debate or the other, often reflecting ambiguity as they prioritized women's rights in unexpected ways. Whereas the encyclical *Humanae Vitae* forbade all forms of contraception, and the Vatican continues to constrain women's agency regarding sexuality and reproduction (Beattie 2014; Bonavoglia 2006; Bouclin 2006, 45; Manning 1999; Ruether 2008; Associated Press 2018, 2017), the women religious herein and elsewhere (see Reed 2004 and Schneiders 2013), along with other Catholics (see Catholics for Choice 2011), were in favour of contraception and were sympathetic about abortion. In the following sections, we examine how the sisters engaged in collective action against Church interference, and how they have lived with the ensuing backlash.

DISAGREEING WITH CHURCH DOCTRINE

While the majority of the sisters and former sisters' opinions were directly in opposition to Church doctrine, Mildred's stance conveyed even greater autonomy as it involved deeper ethical consideration beyond Church teachings: "When I have these … reflections, I don't usually associate them with the Church's views on things. But it's more, what is it that my conscience calls me to hear, when I make a decision, can I live with it?"

Those who disagreed with the Church's position were particularly concerned about patriarchal control, the obsession over abortion, and respecting women's autonomy. When asked to comment on the Church's official line on contraception, family planning, and abortion, Sister Kelly was unequivocal: "Yeah, I have big problems with that … I don't agree. Yeah, I don't agree with the Church's stance at ALL!" Sister Kelly shared a troubling anecdote to explain:

> An explicit example of male clerical control over women's autonomy regarding her reproductive rights is that of a woman who was refused absolution and humiliated by her confessor because she was under doctor's orders to take the "pill" since her health could not sustain another pregnancy … those stories are real, you know.

Here Sister Kelly articulated the feminist argument that an anti-abortion stance is not in fact "pro-life" as the Church's position is not about love, or about caring for women's lives. Rather, the Church deploys shame tactics to uphold its authoritarian control over women's bodies (Fisher 2012; Manning 1999). Referring to the Church's stance, Sister Benita echoed the controlling aspect of the institutional Church: "I have a real difficulty there, getting that balance … I have that balance, but I don't think they have that balance ... they're very, very strict." Whereas Church doctrine is unflinching on the issue of abortion, Sister Benita seemed to advocate a middle road between respect for foetal rights and respect for women's reproductive needs.

Some women religious, whether they wholly disagree with Church doctrine, seemed frustrated with how the accentuation of abortion as a moral transgression has led to vulnerable women's needs being overlooked:

> The fact that they put so much emphasis on abortion as if it's the ... only sin, the only way in which life is not respected. (Sister Edith)
>
> I see ... just the lack of vision on the whole ... [there is a need for] a larger vision because I'm anti-abortion but ... it's such a narrow ... they're fanatics almost; the Church is; it's all they ever get on is abortion! ... and I tell you ... the stuff I've seen over the years [regarding girls and women having abortions], and the Church wasn't there for them, and their families weren't even there for them, you know! So there's all human dimensions in everything. (Sister Clara)

Still others framed their disagreements with the Church's position on contraception around lay people's agency "in the whole area of sexuality" (Sister Joelle). Whereas Sister Joelle recognized the freedom of choice among "couples" generally,[5] others such as Sister Penelope referred to women's agency: "the whole thing on abortion too ... I think the Church is still taking a stand that goes against the responsibility of the woman herself." When Sister Penelope reflected on whether or not she felt that her rights as a woman had been denied by the Church, she turned her attention towards other women, especially women who considered abortion: "Not mine particularly but I think yes, women's rights in general ... like ... women who can't really, with their own doctor make a decision of whether or not an abortion is a good thing for their life, or a decision with their family ... Yeah, I feel that women have been denied." Sister Penelope readily situates abortion in the context of health and family life. Some sisters, such as in the example of Darlene below, conveyed the gravity of circumstances when women's reproductive autonomy is denied.

CALLING OUT HYPOCRISY FROM CHURCH HIERARCHY

While Darlene was still a nun, she was deeply troubled by the hypocrisy of the Roman Catholic Church with respect to abuse and abortion. She remembered multiple controversies involving not only the denial of women's reproductive rights, but also the systematic and widespread abuses against them:

> I also dealt with a man who had to choose to let his wife die and the baby to live and he had six children at home because of the pastoral advice … So I was very convoluted about this and while I will never say that I am pro-abortion, but some part of me is pro-choice and to respect the ambiguity of it, you know.
>
> I got more activist in that too when the Vatican … used their status at the UN to get the morning-after pill taken out of the rape kits during the Bosnian War. I felt really, really upset about that.
>
> And then I heard about the sisters in Africa who were being raped and who were having Vatican-approved abortions when they were pregnant. It was a policy, an under-the-carpet policy of the Vatican that in Catholic hospitals in Africa, they could have abortions.

The latter instance refers to the case of priests raping and impregnating schoolgirls, lay women, and nuns, and forcing them to have abortions or sending them to other countries (to hide them) to give birth to the children resulting from the sexually exploitative relationships (Allen and Schaeffer 2001; BBC News 2019; Bonavoglia 2006, 34; Bouclin 2006, 33; Demasure 2021; Manning 2002; McPhillips and McEwan 2022). Other women religious recalled Ontario-based incidents of allegedly forced and hidden abortions associated with priest-perpetrated sexual abuse:

> It absolutely just boggles my mind how anyone in [good] conscience, you know like Father [name removed], just went back in the paper, eh … And he had this girl get an abortion. While he gets up and preaches against abortion. You know it just gets my hair [up]; I get so angry, I could kill him.[6] (Sister Mabel)

Darlene's and Sister Mabel's examples substantiate the persistent insensitivity and hypocrisy on the part of Catholic Church officials (Gervais and Watson 2018). The Church's stance on abortion is doubly hypocritical in the context of its nuanced doctrine around killing life when it "is in the hands of men" – which permits killing by the state in self-defence as a sanction (Chittister in Bonavoglia 2006, 134), or arguably, as seen above, by male Church officials when the pregnancies for which they themselves are responsible inconvenience them (Allen and Schaeffer 2001). By contrast, when it comes to abortion, "When life is in the hands of a woman, it can never, ever, under any circumstances, for any reason whatsoever, be contravened" (Chittister in Bonavoglia 2006, 134). In this light, it becomes apparent how misogyny operates through preventing women from accessing bodily autonomy while condoning acts of violence by men.

While these cases enraged both Darlene and Sister Mabel, they also led Darlene to grieve as she struggled with ambiguity:

> I used to go to Call to Action, which was an American church reform group … so I went there and they were to discuss … pro-life, pro-choice kinds of things. And we were of both positions and … we were in groups with mixed positions and we simply told our stories and I cried my eyes out telling mine because here I am, a Roman Catholic nun, and … this is a very confusing and painful issue and I was keeping a secret [about my stance on abortion] which was not healthy spiritually or psychologically.

Darlene's account points to the extent to which disagreement with doctrine generated distressing repercussions for some women religious, especially in earlier decades as their opinions on women's agency were shaped by evolving societal attitudes about gender equality. Nevertheless, despite the evident emotional toll, Darlene and other nuns continued to resist complicity in causing harm by remaining critical: identifying and reconsidering the inconsistencies both blatant and subtle across Church statements and practices (Holtmann 2008; Ó'Murchú 1997).

The sisters underscored another dimension of hypocrisy, tinged with a troubling layer of irony, that pertained to what they perceived as a complex contradiction within the Church's stance against both contraception and abortion. Sister Theresa's opinion pointed to how the Church's strict policies prohibiting preventative options have *increased* the reliance on the reactive responses that it has fought so obstinately against: "I'm sorry that the Church is so … against contraception because I think they're responsible for more abortions because of their refusal of any kind of contraception." While Sister Theresa was compassionate towards women who contemplate or have abortions, it was apparent that she did not condone the practice. Nevertheless, her disapproving tone indicated her frustration over the restraints faced by Roman Catholic women.

Nowhere was the sisters' frustration with the patriarchal control of women's bodies more striking than in their condemnation of the Church following a particularly disgraceful announcement by the Vatican. At the time of the primary author's spring 2009 interviews, nearly half of the sisters raised their opposition to the Vatican's excommunication of a Brazilian mother and her doctors for authorizing and carrying out an abortion for her nine-year-old daughter, who became pregnant with twins while being sexually abused by her stepfather. Sister Kelly's outrage speaks to the incoherence of the Church's doctrine when it comes to whose body is criminalized:

> But that's … a good example of power and control and the boys' club … the stepfather is scot-free and … he's a criminal in the eyes of the law.

Sister Marian also expressed her outrage at the Church's position:

> Well, I'm fed up with the Catholic Church. Do you know that? Absolutely fed up with it! … They are so far away from reality … just the other day I read of a nine-year-old child who was carrying twins. Raped by her stepfather so the doctor said, I'm paraphrasing now, "this child … her body is not fit to … carry one child let alone two." So they aborted the foetuses. Now … the Church, Rome is on that now. Now I live with a sister in this house who was a labour supervisor, an OB supervisor for years. She said, [whispered softly] "they [the Vatican officials] are crazier than we are, you know. That child couldn't carry those … her body is not ready for that! Nine years old!" … Where is the compassion and the warmth and the inclusion and the understanding? … Now I never thought I would ever, I'm not for abortion. I really am not but that young kid seized my whole attention … for a nine-year-old child to be

carrying twins [softly]. I think those had to be aborted; I really do … Oh yeah. The Church is so hard.

Later in the interview, Sister Marian underscored her frustration on the same issue and her willingness to speak out:

I never heard any reaching out [reprimand] by the Church to him [the abusive stepfather] … that's what makes me mad … I get those vibes up … but that little kid, I can't get her out of my mind …. And all her life she's gonna be tagged.

While she was aware of the repercussions that both she and her religious community could face if she publicly criticized the Church about this case, she felt strongly about the plight of the little girl, and she expressed a willingness to take the risk:

But like that child, that nine-year-old with those twins, I would have to speak out against the Church about that, you know, I really would. Like who knows when life begins? The Church has arbitrarily set it at so many months or something … at conception … well who knows that?

As she too commented on the same story, Sister Josephine emphasized the need for empathy that was entirely absent from the Church's criminalization of abortion. As she questioned the Church's position, Sister Josephine invoked a merciful God in her unequivocal support for the nine-year-old girl:

I was frustrated with that … I did not think that was right … I thought that the stepfather … should have been hung by his whatever … there was no compassion there … and ah the child was … going to die and so were the babies. So you know … I wasn't too worried about [excommunication]. Again, I don't think God gets too upset about things like that.[7]

After considerable public pressure, including from women's rights advocates, and after realizing that it was "not sensible" (Sister Ella), the Church retracted its original statement on the excommunication of the mother and doctor, which demonstrates how feminist resistance had served women in small ways. However, such gains were short-lived, given that several months later, in its official newspaper *L'Osservatore Romano*, the Vatican reiterated its automatic canonical penalty of excommunication for all cases of abortion.[8] Like the above-mentioned incidents of priest-perpetrated sexual abuse and impregnation, this story, and the Vatican's ultimate overriding of the retraction, tells not only of the staunchness of the Church's hypocritical anti-abortion stance, but of the hierarchy's sustained support of men over girls and women even in cases of obvious abuse.

RESISTING CHURCH INTERFERENCE

Sisters described various ways of countering the Church's fixation on condemning abortion, from refusing to judge women's reproductive decisions, to supporting and showing compassion to women with unwanted pregnancies. For the sisters, regardless of their personal feelings about abortion, the Church's stance reflected a distinct lack of love and respect for women's reproductive needs, as well as a tendency to objectify and dismiss women in ways that erased the context of their reproductive health. Sister Benita was one who could not ignore how Church officials left women, made vulnerable by structural inequality, not only morally condemned but also unsupported in their pregnancies, despite insisting that they carry them to term. Frustrated that "all the church people were saying ... 'don't have abortions' ... but they weren't doing anything for the teens," Sister Benita founded a centre to provide residential, educational, psychological, and child-care support for adolescent mothers and their babies in Ontario. However, after the centre opened, she encountered interference by Church officials who expected her to identify the centre as a "pro-life" institution. She vividly recalled her refusal to adhere to the men clerics' expectation of anti-abortion advocacy:[9]

> [Priest's name] was the head of pro-life and he was the Episcopal vicar of [the] diocese ... So he phoned me one night and he said, "As the principal vicar of [the] diocese, I insist that you give up [the centre] or else put in all these things about pro-life that I'm going to tell you to put in." ... Well, if [the centre] isn't going to say absolutely that we are against abortion – I don't know how I could say it any other way ... When I said no, I said, "I'm sorry, Father, I can't do that." So I did stand up to him ... but he took a letter to the priests' meeting, and the letter was ...

> [full of] crazy things. That's what he wanted me to sign and say that I accepted it.
>
> But anyway, [another priest attending the meeting] ... said when he [the vicar] read the letter to all the priests, they just rolled their eyes and looked at one another, but nobody backed me ... they just sort of let it go.

Sister Benita's comments are reflective of her constrained circumstances in doing the major work of opening a centre, including the pressure she was under to conform to and in fact advertise the Church's anti-abortion position, as well as the complex power dynamics at play between priests and sisters. She courageously expressed opinions distinct from official Church policies, and such clear resistance was met with both hostility and support, even if the latter seemed unspoken.

In her 2009 interview, Judith echoed Sister Benita's courage in her reference to the well-known story of Sister Mansour:

> Sister of Mercy, Agnes Mary Mansour; she died lately; she took the job as head of social services for the state of Michigan ... All hell broke loose with the Catholic Church because of choice and because they [Michigan's department of social services] fund abortions for poor women and she refused to... step down. And they leaned on her community like everything! She was VERY brave! ... and Bishop Gumbleton stood behind her. And there were meetings and we went to them and we signed letters and everything. Anyway, she ended up having to leave the community ... But just to see a woman have to struggle like that. Who better would you want to head up social services in a state than a forward-thinking nun?

Judith was among several current and former nuns who mentioned Sister Mansour as they expressed solidarity with their counterparts in the United States who had signed, in 1984, "The *New York Times* ad" – otherwise entitled "A Diversity of Opinions regarding Abortion Exists among Committed Catholics."[10] Those who signed the statement were reprimanded vehemently by Church officials; nuns were threatened with excommunication if they did not recant their signatures and positions (Kaylin 2000, 227), while theologians' careers, including those of Rosemary Radford Ruether and Elisabeth Schüssler Fiorenza, were ultimately hindered.

A COMPASSIONATE APPROACH

Sister Sarah's reflection on her efforts to address her abortion-related inner turmoil revealed how her compassion ultimately prevailed:

> [It] is difficult … see what I do is not so much anti [chuckles] as really advocating for the dignity of all people … I grew up in a very pro-life family and so the whole abortion issue has always been a part of my life and it's always been something I've struggled with … it always created a lot of conflict in me and … my response to conflict is … to be able to listen and dialogue and … see what we can learn from each other.

In contrast to the Church's rigidity, Sister Sarah's openness to respectful exchanges of ideas has led to the empathetic approaches that many women religious bring to bear on women's personal and family struggles. Sisters Jeanette and Loretta represented the consideration shown by many of their counterparts:

> Well, the only issue I have is that … in the whole area of … abortion … some persons are not compassionate to a woman who may have been raped against her will and then she … aborted. I think … we have … [to] reach out and be compassionate too … I don't know her. I can't judge … I don't ah condone it, but I don't know the reasons behind what happened. I can't say they're right or wrong because I don't know. (Sister Jeanette)

> I worked with people who've had abortions and glory be to God! What they suffered … But you don't judge them, I mean. Oh! [sigh]. (Sister Loretta)

Neither Sister Jeanette nor Sister Loretta advocated for women's access to abortion in their comments, but they both resisted aligning themselves with Church doctrine since they did not feel entitled to pass judgment on women's reproductive decisions. Sister Loretta affirmed that the Church "gets caught up" in the issue of abortion, straying from Church teachings of compassion and love. Similarly, when providing examples of how the Catholic Church stifles people's rights, Sister Sophie referred immediately to "pregnancies" and "abortions" and felt "absolutely" that there was a greater need for compassion in that regard. Despite how the perspectives of the sisters might diverge on issues of reproductive justice, they articulated their rejection of the Church's authoritarian approach, and relied on values of empathy, compassion, and respect when interpreting women's reproductive needs. Carol encapsulated this stance thus:

> It's to say "just a second here" ... Let's not just say we're against abortion here; let's really try to understand it and let's put ourselves ... in the shoes of this woman who's poor and pregnant and raped ... But ... you can't do that with a lot of 'em. It's ... "I don't want to think," you know? And that's the tragedy of the Church is that many people that are there don't want to be shaken. They don't want to be called to wholeness ... some of my good friends that are the ex-nuns [say,] "just ... don't challenge me." I'm frustrated with black and white. You know, like, that's not life. Of course I don't want ... people to ... have abortions but ... what are the alternatives for some people? And I just can't stand the judgmental ... kind of self-righteous approach. And it's very often run by men, and the monies are coming from these right-wing Evangelicals. I think it's really wrong ... But then it sounds like I'm pro-abortion ... when you speak that way. It's kind of like if you don't, if I'm not for the war, I'm against our troops ... I mean Louise Summerhill ... the one who started Birthright,[11] she went to hold the hand of a young woman who was having an abortion. After she tried everything she could possibly do ... the girl still decided to have the abortion and went through it. And she went with her and held her hand through the operation. Like to me that speaks VOLUMES about compassion. It's not laying your stuff on them.

LIVING WITH BACKLASH

Abortion is undeniably one of the most contested issues around which sisters' intersecting feminist and Catholic identities and practices have been complicated by their conflicting personal, public, political, and religious priorities (Holtmann 2011a). As we explore in subsequent sections, both their historically and institutionally entrenched positions and their evolving stances have led to circumstances in which their resistance has been either fraught with ambiguity and distress on the one hand or embraced on the other.

While some of their opinions reflect the language of pro-choice groups (as shown in the remainder of this chapter), the complexity of sisters' positions was made evident in the late twentieth century when one congregation of sisters officially maintained their anti-abortion stance in the health care facilities that they then owned and managed. Defending that position led to distressing tensions between the sisters and local feminists in an Ontario city where one of only two local hospitals was being closed. The sister-owned not-for-profit hospital in which abortions were prohibited remained open while the public hospital in which abortions were performed was closed. The sisters, who viewed themselves as women's rights advocates, particularly in the areas of education, employment, housing, and domestic violence, were harshly criticized by local feminist groups. The backlash they encountered was particularly painful because it tested their own feminist priorities as they attempted to uphold their Catholic values. Sister Marian shed light on the emotional impacts as she elaborated on the context:

> [At the ... hospital] they don't do abortions; they never will and everybody knows that ... it was a big deal and I was ... coordinator of our health institutions in those days; it was terrible, you know. And I could understand. The cottage hospital was a good hospital ... it had rejuvenated and renovated and ... for somebody to snatch it away, I could understand ... but I was amazed at the depth of the ... anger against us and ... I'll never get over that. It was downright hate ... Oh, it was terrible. It was terrible. Even though ... the cottage hospital didn't do all that many abortions ... But it was the right, you know, for those who had wanted it. I'm not promoting it but ah.
>
> Oh yeah ... I was on council at the time and ... but one of these leaders that nearly creamed us ... when the split came ... she told us around the board table at the admin centre, she likened us to the apartheid regime in South Africa. Do you know I found that the biggest insult of my life because we wouldn't allow abortions. I'll never forget it. Then I go to volunteer with women in crisis and who's the chair of the board but this lady! Anyway, we got along alright!

Sister Marian explained the complexity of her position as coordinator of the not-for-profit hospital owned by her congregation, the only accessible health centre remaining in the small town, as restricting access to abortion threatened women's health. As the focus of her community service was, in fact, women's health and especially women in crisis, she found herself needing to defend the anti-abortion position of Catholics while facing scrutiny from other women aiming to protect women's access to health as critical services were cut. This speaks to the power of Church doctrine to frame abortion as a moral issue instead of a critical health need, as Sister Marian could not reconcile her Catholic values with advocacy for the full scope of women's health. Even though abortion is framed in polarizing terms within the rigid patriarchal control of the Church, the two women on opposite sides of the debate over providing abortion services at the remaining hospital still "got along alright" in their work with women in crisis.

EITHER SIDE OF ANTI-ABORTION PROTESTS

Darlene had experiences related to anti-abortion protests that further entrenched her feminist stance, yet they also left her feeling marginalized as a Catholic nun. In the first instance, she chose not to attend an anti-abortion demonstration; instead, she stood in support of the women affected by violence. Her account reveals the significant implications of her feminist choice:

> The Montreal Massacre ... was another big shift for me because ... when the Massacre happened, I was part of the leadership team in my community. So there were five of us on the team and ... two of us were really, really shook up, and we went to the memorial that we had in [city] ... the day after it happened ... and with this one other sister, we became activists in the feminist community ... and the women's centre and status of women. We became activists very publicly after that. The other three that very same night went over to the Morgentaler clinic, to be [anti-abortion] activists ... But that, in my head is very, very symbolic of how I was on the edge, because my community would have affirmed them [those who went to the anti-abortion protest] and would have dismissed us and so that was kind of a ... realization.

Darlene also experienced ostracizing attacks by anti-abortion protestors as she sought to be present and compassionate with a student who opted for an abortion. She remembered the troubling encounter:

> The whole right-to-life thing ... that's a very difficult and painful issue. But I had once gone to visit a student of mine, who had had an abortion... and the abortions were done in a wing, and so you could exit ... the hospital from that wing and I came out and here were all these local right-to-lifers ... I was still in the habit in those days ... so they recognized me: "Sister, what are you doing in there?" and they started to push and shove me ... and I said, "Well, you're not respecting my life right now, just get out of my way" ... They really were ... holding the rosary beads at me and ... they literally pushed me ...
>
> They were really very condemnatory to me. They were all Catholic; some of them I recognized from the [name] parish ... a couple of them were Catholic Women's League people and I had given them retreats ... they were just not nice to me and I said ... "You don't know what you're talking about; there's pain on both sides of this" ... But that's all I said because they just shouted me down ... So that wasn't a very good experience.

While acting counter to the Catholic Church's moral code as she stood by the young woman who had the abortion, Darlene recognized that her presence was essential as a form of non-judgmental ministering: "Besides, I knew some stories of very sad cases ... and this case was one of them ... She was suicidal that day too... and the fact that I was there ... and her story was just the worst kind of horror story you could imagine ... [and] in a sense I represent[ed] a church to them too, another side of church."

Stereotypes of religious institutions and their members may lead one to assume that when abortion-related demonstrations occur, all Catholic nuns would be found on the side of anti-abortion pickets and chants. While many current and former sisters did acknowledge that several of their conservative counterparts within their own religious communities have organized and/or attended anti-abortion protests, they themselves disagreed with a strict anti-abortion stance. Some nuns, such as Sister Joelle, conveyed fewer of the expected narrow religious biases and more of the surprisingly feminist stances: "Well, I don't toe the party line. I find the pro-life movement one issue and quite anti-Christian in its approach. Oh, no, I just get really turned off."

Such critical considerations form the backdrop of many sisters' unexpected abortion-related activism. While it would be rare to find a Canadian sister standing on the so-called pro-choice side of a street-level demonstration, some have refused to stand publicly on the anti-abortion side of the street:

> Well, I guess ... you say pro-life and that would be the word. I want to be pro all of life ... I don't believe abortion is a good thing and I want to be compassionate with anybody who's had one ... and I guess I feel really sad that for the most part, pro-life is used in a very narrow sense ... So I find I can't stand with a group that would call themselves pro-life because of the way they stand and maybe because of some of the other things they stand for that are not pro all of life ... So for me the pro-life stance means that we include everyone. It means we protect the life of the unborn. It means we don't go to war or we don't promote war ... It means we care for all as well as we can through all of life and now it even means caring for all of Creation; it's not just about humanity. It's about caring for this beautiful planet with all of the life on it. So I mean pro-life is so huge and I can say I'm pro-life if that's ... the description. (Sister Adele)

In reflecting on what solidarity meant to her, Sister Adele explained how she felt about a complicated scenario involving anti-abortion Church officials in relation to the World March for Women held around the turn of the millennium. We quote her comments in full because they indicate both a sense of solidarity with men from the Church and a related sense of hope:

> Solidarity is trying to really understand ... what people are suffering, and then trying to see how that can be addressed and collaborating with anybody and everybody who's willing to address it. So I think that's that inclusivity; it's like I want to be able to work with anybody. I might disagree with them on some other issue. I remember the March for Women, the CWL [Catholic Women's League] withdrew[12] because there were some groups that supported abortion who were part of the March for Women ... but again, there was good leadership at our

> diocese and on the part of some of the bishops because in spite of that, we had a big gathering and a Mass and then we came out from the Mass at the Cathedral to join the groups who'd come from [city] and join the rest for the whole thing. And we timed it so we could do that. And it was two women religious who really ... helped [chuckles] the archbishop to be able to make that decision! And there were just very few people outside who didn't agree with the fact that we had this but ... the cathedral was filled with women and some men ... it was the March for Women ... it was connected with International Women's Day in one of those years ... And I admired [the] archbishop ... because he went ahead and ... he and six others [bishops] came ... they were there! With all of us ... we celebrated liturgy together and we went out to join the march from there. So we went out with the Church's blessing to be part of that. Even though there would be some people there with whom we would disagree on some things and ah. But what this was about, we could all agree on. So for me it's important to be able to make those distinctions ... [and] there were women in the sanctuary, lots of us. I was there in the sanctuary too. I mean given the Church that we are, I was really grateful to the men who were there. Talking about solidarity! They were there in solidarity with us ... so given the structure of the Church and given that they were probably criticized for being there by some elements in the Church ... they were risking more than we were that day. And so, I mean I always want to give credit where credit is due. [chuckles] ... you know, and they showed up. And he more than showed up. He had it organized in the diocese ... invited the others and some of them came ... So you know, there's always some signs of hope if you look for them too.

Sister Maureen took a position similar to that of Sister Adele as she critiqued a Church-based boycott against a Catholic aid organization:

> There's been some leak about Development and Peace money going towards abortion. The money [from collections in parishes] is not going there now, you know; [people are being told to] put it towards wherever you'd like you know and that is bothersome. And I just think what's going to happen with Development and Peace and the excellent work that's been done you know?

Here, Sister Maureen made reference to how in 2009 Church officials recommended that parishioners redirect their donations that were usually allocated to Development and Peace during Lent because it was alleged that the Catholic-based international development organization was supporting contraception and abortion in economically developing nations.[13] As her account revealed, she was less concerned about the abortion aspect; rather, she recognized and valued the broader vision and benefit of the organization and thus perceived the Church's and parishioners' boycott tactics to be narrow-minded and limiting (Gervais 2018).

Taken together, the reflections of Sisters Adele and Maureen are illustrative of profound, yet somewhat unexpected, positions among women religious. That Catholic nuns partook in a pro-women demonstration and supported an international development organization that allegedly upheld women's reproductive rights, while some Catholic lay people, including women, avoided them to underscore their anti-abortion stance, points to the all-embracing understandings through which sisters have engaged in feminist and social justice activism (Holtmann 2008, 2011a, 2011b; Gervais 2018).

COLLECTIVE ACTION

While in the late twentieth century, the sisters tended not to publicly address women's reproductive rights, after the turn of the second millennium, some sisters and their congregations came to a pivotal point at which they felt compelled to speak out. As the subsequent sections illustrate, such collective engagement is reflective of the sisters' efforts to advance women's reproductive rights in the early twenty-first century. One congregation's astute argument, directed to Canadian bishops in its Canadian Religious Conference survey responses pertaining to reproductive justice, addressed a range of compelling concerns.[14] The rationale presented therein echoed Sister Adele's emphasis (previously mentioned) on "all of Creation" as they considered "life" as part of a much broader canvas:

> REALIZATIONS
> We recognize that though deeply concerned about individual morality as evidenced by its positions on sexuality … [and] birth control … the Church is less concerned about social injustices of global proportions, and at times its regulations may be contributing to these injustices.

> CRITIQUES
> We deplore the Church's condemnation of the use of condoms, resulting in misery, sickness and death for millions of people, especially children, infected with AIDS and other sexually-transmitted diseases in Africa and elsewhere.
>
> ASPIRATIONS
> We long to hear the challenge to speak up for care of all of Creation, to hear our church state unequivocally that there is no such thing as a just war.

Such astute assertions are illustrative of sisters' collective capacities to advance incisive feminist-based arguments (Faulkner and MacDonald 2009; Holtmann 2008, 2011b; Ó'Murchú 1997). Inevitably, and as previously noted, there were consequences to this uncommon resistance against the Church hierarchy. Although the sisters were frustrated with the clerics' predictable criticism of their steadfast stance, they were even more disappointed with the Church hierarchy's lack of official consideration of their report, in which they had invested much time and effort. Although such silence was not surprising, it is indicative of the Church's ongoing refusal to engage constructively on issues pertaining to women's autonomy (Manning 1999, 2002; Wexler 2016).

CONCLUSION

Issues pertaining to women's reproductive health are not as clear as they may seem from the official stance of the Catholic Church. As the sisters' comments in this chapter elucidate, attempts to constrain and support women's reproductive autonomy were uneven across communities and the sisters themselves. Many sisters reported contending with constraints posed by individual members of their own congregations who held traditional and canonical views. Sister Loretta expressed her frustration with a fellow sister's fixation on abortion:

> I guess if there's any issue that gets to me it's the pro-life people. I mean I don't believe in abortion … But they are so self-righteous. Oh my! I just find them very judgmental and very self-righteous … we have them in the community and they're very, very hard to deal with … because they seem to be people who have one issue … [Sarcastically:] Ah … you know, Bush is a wonderful man

> because … he has started that war in Iraq and thousands and thousands and thousands have died. But … he was a pro-lifer and so he was … a good man, you know that kind of attitude … it's the one issue that clouds everything else. And [they think] that everybody should be working in that area and it's the only area that ever existed [for them]. And … if … I say, "I don't believe in abortion" [and] somebody says to me … "Well, why aren't you out picketing?" [I respond], "Well I just don't feel like going out picketing right now." … Nobody in our congregation … would support abortion. I know that! But … it's not a one issue. There [are] many, many issues out there … Anyway … it's a whole vicious circle.

In reference to the same anti-abortion nun, Sister Ella relayed how their congregation coped with her position by directly calling her to account:

> You just don't carry around divisions, you know … we had an experience not very long ago in our own community where somebody was REALLY holding us hostage at a meeting because she wanted to get her points across. And finally one of the leadership team just said, "Hold it! We've heard this. We're tired of it. I for one don't want to hear it again." And a whole crowd of us said, "And we don't want to hear it again either!" [chuckles] We all joined in. Well, this woman got the message. She's a one-issue person. So like we're at it all the time trying to … I don't think she felt hurt, in fact … the first person who said, "I don't want to hear this again. I know your point of view. Please don't hold us hostage like this" … when we broke up [ended the meeting], she went right to her and I heard her say, "I love you! I don't want you to … feel you're rejected. I just … can't take it anymore! Every meeting we come to, you stand with this issue. We know it. We don't need your point of view so leave it please." [chuckles] … She thinks that we're not ah strong enough anti-abortionists.[15]

Sisters Loretta and Ella have managed to see a greater purpose in staying connected to the Church, despite their frustrations with members of their community who feel the need to agitate against reproductive (in)justice. Some sisters, however, have aligned themselves with many other former Catholics who have parted company with the Catholic Church on this issue (Catholics for Choice 2011; Kalven 2003; Wexler 2016). As alluded to above, the reasons were many, including frustration with, and resistance against, the blatant hypocrisy (Holtmann 2008, 2011a; Manning 1999, 2002). Darlene's comments illustrated how her sense of identity and alienation within her community hinged on abortion politics:

> I didn't feel safe to say [my secret stance on abortion] to anyone in my community. This one sister who was with me at the memorial [for the Montreal Massacre] actually died and I was the only one left in the whole community ... My sisters were wonderful; they came to my courses ... about feminist theology and ... they were very empowered by ... women in the scripture ... but at a certain point ... there was a part of me that wasn't there anymore, and it was a secret part of me and ... a struggle with the Church and a struggle with my community on that point and it wasn't voiced because I wasn't being honest ... I felt if I declared my ambiguity about abortion, for example, that ... my community wouldn't understand and that I'd be less effective in the other work that I was doing.

Darlene's struggle to feel safe in her community because of her ambiguity around abortion speaks volumes about the single-issue politics of abortion that continue to hinder women's health; but this context may be shifting in Canada. When documents leaked in May 2022 predicted the overturning of the 1973 *Roe v. Wade* decision, which provided constitutional protection for legal abortion in the United States, Canadian minister of families, children, and social development Karina Gould affirmed that her government was committed to expanding access to women's sexual and reproductive healthcare and that women travelling from the US could access abortion services in Canada (Zimonjic 2022). A month later, when the *Dobbs v. Jackson Women's Health Organization* decision granted states the power to restrict abortion and many states criminalized abortion, the majority of Canadians supported a woman's access to abortion whenever she[16] wants one (Sethi 2022). The sisters who voiced their opposition to the Church's stance on abortion remind us that even those presumed to fall on the anti-abortion side of women's health access because of their organization's explicit role in turning back the clock on women's rights are not persuaded by moral arguments against abortion (Holtmann 2008, 2011a; Manning 1999, 2002). As is the case with many issues, their work in community advocating for women has made the anti-abortion stance seem particularly lacking in compassion and local knowledge.

7

(Re)Negotiating Celibacy and (Re)Considering Sexuality

Amanda Watson and Christine Gervais

We have become so hung up on … sexuality, on the separation of the body and the spirit, you know. It's … horrible … Holy shoot!

Angela

INTRODUCTION

For faithful women religious in a highly regulated patriarchal Church and in intensely institutional convent settings, taking a vow of *chastity* was one thing, but practising what was eventually recast as *celibacy* was another.[1] Historically, vowed women religious were expected to abide by various canons intended to control their sexuality (Corwin 2021; Fisher 2012; McPhillips et al. 2022).[2] In the case of women religious, as with all lay Catholic women, their "virginity" was emphasized as a metric of morality (Castelli 1986; Fisher 2012; Manning 1999; McPhillips and McEwan 2022; Ruether 2011), just one aspect of sexist subjugation in a deeply patriarchal and misogynist culture (Demasure 2021; Elliott 2004, 2012; Ganim 2013; Ó'Murchú 1997; Ruether 2011, 2014).[3]

The sisters recounted a range of perceptions and strategies as they made sense of canonical constraints on their relationships.[4] From identifying celibacy as foundational to religious identity to relishing romantic or sexual intimacies, sisters' memories and manoeuvres represent a continuum of acceptance and resistance. It is clear in their comments that regardless of how it was interpreted and felt, the expectation of sexual restraint served as a rationale for particularly intrusive and gendered forms of surveillance in their daily and nightly lives (Corwin 2021; Fisher 2012; Ganim 2013). Instances of either acquiescence or disobedience to the promise of sexual abstinence temper the image of the docile and virginal sister and at the same time call into question how those who devote themselves wholeheartedly to chastity and celibacy find freedom in their commitment (Hidalgo 2007; Mahmood 2012; McPhillips and McEwan 2022).

This chapter examines the ways in which the sisters talked about celibacy and sexuality. In doing so, it unfurls the patriarchal and oppressive logics of celibacy while also attending to expressions of sexuality that escape narrow and singular ideas about sexual expression being confined to romantic relationships (Ganim 2013). The dynamic nature of sexuality across the life course, from expressions of desire for children and grandchildren that burn and fade, to delight in the sexual energy inherent to creative expression, comes to light in this collection of passages (Fisher 2012).

REFLECTIONS ON WRITTEN AND "UNWRITTEN RULES" ON CHASTITY AND "PARTICULAR FRIENDSHIPS"

Many sisters reported that what we might expect to be "cut and dry" (Philomena) rules on the vow of chastity were in fact difficult to understand and even harder to follow. Bernadine vividly described a memory of her formation director opening a book of instruction on the topic of chastity only to immediately withdraw from discussion with the empty promise that the sisters would "find out later." Bernadine went on to describe the catechum on the vows as a "joke," remembering a sense that there was "no training" or preparation for a life of celibacy. Claire also confirmed that "sexuality was never discussed." This lack of emotional or intellectual mentorship on matters of chastity is unsurprising, given how the language required to define celibacy is itself taboo in the Catholic Church. Bernadine remembered, "We couldn't even read the word sex, you know. Isn't that awful?" As Julia reminded us, stigmatizing women's own bodies had consequences for their bodily awareness and health: "I came from a family where my mother was that generation where you didn't talk about gynaecology; it was 'troubles down there,' you know, that kind of thing." Forbidding the mention of body parts that might be sexualized is to secure the stigmatization and shaming of sexual desire, to say nothing of the experience or pursuit of sexual pleasure (Fisher 2012).

Of course, the sisters learned to grapple with constraints on their relationships even when it came to friendships with other sisters. Dominique recalled a memory of being left to interpret the logic of being "single for God," reflecting "there was no sense of ... integration of sexuality and very little education of sexuality for those committed to celibacy." But in her memory, even with the lack of preparation to uphold a life of celibacy – with simple instructions to be "single for the mission" without explanation of how their own sexuality might feature in their lives or pose a challenge at times – there was a "big, big emphasis on ... the problems with particular friendships." She grew to understand this restriction on particular friendships as "prohibition against homosexuality," a coded euphemism for immoral behaviour that ought to be prevented and avoided (Corwin 2021). Justine echoed the same sentiment, reflecting on the code of "particular friendships" as the "big taboo" particularly salient in her memory. Dominique came to understand this controlling code only after cloistered convents opened up, directly connecting their physical setting to mental discipline. She reflected how "it only made sense later on, you know, when all the structures went." Outside of the enhanced physical discipline of their cloistered enclosures and routines, the homophobic and misogynistic underpinnings of the surveillance of their sexuality and friendships with other sisters had room to breathe.

The institutionalized scrutiny of women's friendships ironically acknowledges the inherent power and fluidity of women's sexuality, as sisters recounted extensive efforts to keep women cloistered but segregated from each other (Corwin 2021; Fisher 2012). Philomena, who further articulated a sense of insufficient guidance on how to interpret and devote oneself to the vow of chastity, remembered that while the vows were

> very cut and dry ... What the formation people said ... was [that the] rule was to be obeyed ... Ah ... actually with chastity ... you weren't even allowed close friendships with anybody, like they were frowned upon ... if you were getting too chummy with one person ... you were told by the formation director or by the superior of the house ... "Well, how come

> you're always with that person?" ... yet you're bound to have friends ... that you speak more openly with ... and that you do get closer to for sharing experiences ... But that was very much frowned upon and that was seen as something against ... chastity ... But that no longer exists.

Barring the sisters from intimate friendships of course speaks to a paranoia on the part of the Church that women's solidarity was a threat to patriarchal control over their bodies and minds (Corwin 2021; Fisher 2012; Ganim 2013). Frustrated with how the vow of chastity was highly regulated within the convent through scrutinizing and prohibiting certain interactions, Claire cast the stigmatization of close relationships in similarly opaque language:

> Well, certainly, particular friendships, I mean in terms of sexuality ... Oh absolutely! You were not to be in twos ... You always made sure you had three. You never visited another sister's bedroom. You know, those were the rules, the unwritten rules ... BUT with no explanation really about why. It was just "this is the rule." ... It was very much top down ... it was never explained. It was NEVER EVER, the word of homosexuality, mentioned.

Obviously understanding the rule as implying that sexual intimacy is something that is likely to happen in groups of two and unlikely to happen when three are present, the sisters were left to laugh about the absurdity. Claire also called up the strange way chastity and celibacy were enforced while not directly discussed when she remembered encountering dated idioms as a teenage girl over a half-century ago:

> We were told custody of the eyes was a value ... you kept your eyes down ... I mean those were old terms that ... for us as young teenagers in the '60s meant nothing.

Claire became comfortable with noncompliance over the course of her training for religious life, which was not always the case for others. Despite her compliance with the rules, though, Lola was equally critical of the excessive monitoring of presumptive relations, and she underscored the ridiculousness of the surveillance and the lack of information about its purpose:

> Oh lord! When I entered, I thought they were all crazy! [laughs] … I guess I see it a little more now but you couldn't go for a walk down to the river with one person, you know. And I'm thinking, What is wrong with them anyway? … But I don't know what they were coming out of … Like … I don't even think I knew what lesbianism was when I entered. I mean, I had never heard it … but anyway, we did it.

Lola did, however, eventually benefit from a loosening of restrictions on convent life, something that previous generations of women religious did not experience. A crisis of declining Church membership resulted in greater relational freedom for the sisters: "We … were encouraged to have friends … A lot of our older, older sisters didn't; that was not encouraged so they live very, very lonely lives … But … we had the opportunity to do that more and thank God for that!"

As the convent setting opened, so too did some cultural attitudes evolve, evident in the modified language of the vows. Carmel offered a comparison between the wording of her originally professed vow (circa the 1950s/1960s) and that which emphasized a greater sense of agency decades later: "In my time it was chastity, [but] celibacy [is what] we say now … because everybody has to be chaste in a sense. Celibacy is more of a choice."[5] These sisters maintained their skepticism despite the best efforts on the part of patriarchal Church leaders to stigmatize the very language of sex among women religious (Fisher 2012; Ganim 2013). Resisting doctrinal rejection of their sexual and romantic identities, they formed lasting critiques of convent life and the glaring omission in their education when it came to the vow of chastity or the decision to live a life of celibacy. When it came to these vows, however, not all sisters felt like something was missing.

IDENTIFYING WITH CHASTITY

Hearing from sisters who did *not* feel challenged by the same vow dispels any impression that the sisters uniformly experienced or struggled with the surveillance of their relationships and the norms of the institutional Church (Fisher 2012). With respect to her vows, Thomasina stated, "I didn't have a problem with them. They were what I expected." Sylvia similarly denied having any "big struggles" and Nina described challenges with the vows, including chastity, as minimal: "They didn't keep me awake at night." Esther connected making peace with chastity to maturity as she eloquently conveyed how the vow was variously interpreted: "Chastity, well, relationships … it wasn't a big challenge … But … I found that in mission life … if you were not mature … well, you were like teenagers. But I was able to … have good friendships and good relationships." And while these sisters' accounts seem to take the vow in stride, not recalling the commitment as particularly disruptive or shocking, other sisters *valued* celibacy as foundational to their lives as women religious. Julia described celibacy as "really important" and a "central dimension" of her life:

> I see myself in relationship with Jesus … and the whole bride-groom image is important to me; for some it isn't … But, for me it is; it defines basically my commitment … I remember making a workshop some years ago … and it was probably the early '80s, and we were … exploring the meaning of religious life today … and I identified at that time, that … if there were only the one vow, let's say, it would be for me, celibacy. It's non-negotiable.

The strong language of her conviction contrasts with those who felt any challenge at all. Elaborating a similar appreciation for the vow of chastity, Joy described finding strength in all the vows, including that one:

> Ah, the vow of chastity is, for me, it's the freedom to be of service to God's people. And … it's … sacred. Like the vows are all sacred. It's a communication within myself with God and my community I live with. And just like in, well, today … marriage vows, there's a fidelity to that. Fidelity and there's certain times that sometimes you're weak in one but … you look and you try to strengthen that area that you need to strengthen in the vows.

These longer quotations convey how the sisters situated a commitment to forgo sexual and romantic relationships in the context of a religious life devoted to serving God and the Church. Joy's sense of "freedom to be in service" and Julia's implication that celibacy was the vow that particularly defined her identity as someone devoted to religious life suggests that sexual or romantic relationships – and, perhaps by extension, marriage, motherhood, and family – require a kind of devotion that might compete with their ability to work in service of the Church (Castelli 1986; Fisher 2012; Ganim 2013; McPhillips and McEwan 2022). Still, Julia's appreciation of the bride-groom image, implicitly wedding herself to Jesus, allows the scaffolding of heterosexual marriage, and thus heteronormativity, to remain a stable touchstone of Catholicism (Elliott 2012; Fisher 2012; Ruether 2011; Titley 2017), even in the inner lives of celibate sisters.

Nadine remembered writing her own vows, imbuing the vow of chastity with the idea of loving less discriminately than a partnership might allow, again cementing presumed heterosexual and monogamous sexual relationships as the cornerstone of intimate relationships, while also displacing these from the centre of a life of love. She recalled:

> Well, I mean … I wrote my vows; I wrote what I wanted them to be about; we did that by the time I came along. So … if I begin with chastity … I certainly understood that it was about loving, and loving unconditionally … and the love that goes to the neighbour without distinction, this is the big thing about our congregation … so that was the thrust of the thing really.

On the topic of the congregation improving their support of the sisters and the support to keep the vows, she turned to the importance of friendship: "I think I've always been blessed with very good friends, friends that I have to this day; God has been merciful … it's made a big difference … that means a lot." Here Nadine called up the notion of God as compassionate to describe her sense of gratitude for a life full of friends.

Not all sisters thought about celibacy within the binary of punitive or valuable. Perhaps implying a critique of or resistance against the expectations of Catholic women's roles in lay life, several sisters recalled having boyfriends prior to entering religious life and expressed appreciation for the freedom and independence that religious life afforded them relative to the expectations of marriage as Catholic women. The ways in which they variously referred to their former partners – even "good" ones! – when asked why they pursued religious life clearly shows a preference for what they felt was its relative freedom and independence. June included mention of the work of caregiving as she recalled,

> I had a really good boyfriend before I entered. He was very disappointed that I was entering [laughs]! … Ah, he married … another lady … and they had eight kids so I think I'm blessed … At any rate … I really didn't have any, "Oh I wish I had had children" type. No. I was an only child. I didn't even like babysitting. So I'm happy the way I am.

Thomasina was equally keen to give up married life for service to the Church:

> I was going steady with a fellow … And I got a bit of a shock when I realized that he wanted to marry me. And then I realized that I … preferred the freedom … in doing my own thing.

Philomena reflected similarly about committing to the vow of chastity and forgoing a family of her own. As she reflected on how the thought of family "entered her mind," she also explained how she "never suffered from it as such," chalking her ease with the decision up to her career as a teacher. She had the "freedom to be with children all day long and to enjoy … the presence of children in [her] life." In doing so, Philomena called up the feminist ideal that people thrive in multi-generational, life-giving, and collaborative communities (Faulkner and MacDonald 2009; Ó'Murchú 1997), referring to her "many nieces and nephews." Still, the vow of chastity extended beyond the desire to spend time with children. Philomena trailed off referring to "the whole sexuality issue," claiming that "you have to learn how to channel your emotions … I think that's where chastity most presents itself, you know, is learning how to channel your emotions and your relationships with others." Even though she did not belabour the point, the notion that emotions must be channelled to cope with stifling one's sexual identity reveals the painful undercurrent of patriarchy once more (Fisher 2012). Carmel's recollection seems to round out the three prior comments as she remembered sensing an absence in her romantic life before entering religious life:

> I had a wonderful boyfriend who thought we'd get engaged. And … there was something missing. I just wasn't fulfilled and … And, ah, my main, main, main interest was always about helping the poor.

Reflecting further on what celibacy meant to her, Carmel claimed that the vow of celibacy was her "favourite one," as she associated and even credited the vow with her spiritual path enriched by the arts: "My whole journey in spirituality is a journey in literature and music … and I learned so, so, so much from the kids [I taught] certainly and … from literature and music." After she recounted stories in literature about regrets and sacrifices, she clarified:

> So … that's what celibacy means to me. Like, you know, that … there's more joy in it than giving up. Obedience I found a little challenging …

Despite her optimistic outlook regarding celibacy, Carmel's pivot to reflect on challenges with obedience was echoed by several sisters, who explained their struggles with the requirement that they lead a life of submission to the authority of the Church (Armstrong 1981; Elliott 2012; Fisher 2012). Like Carmel, in her over fifty years of religious life (at the time of her interview), Celine found obedience more difficult than celibacy:

> Well … chastity and poverty, there was no real struggle, no real problem. But obedience at times, you know, when you were told to do something in such a way and you [laughs] yourself … would have preferred to do it otherwise …

Martha put this challenge more provocatively, as she reflected on the "fun things" – swimming, travelling, spending summers together – that she was able to do with male friends despite her vows:

> I never found the [vow of] chastity too hard because I always had friends [laughs] … and I always had male friends, and … nobody ever questioned that … and they were often priests, my male friends … we did all kinds of work and … fun things … So that wasn't too much of a[n issue] … but obedience, that I thought sometimes was just stupid.

Imagining the sisters promising to remain deferential to representatives of Church authority is in fact challenging given what they have shared about their own activism on the topics presented throughout this book. Madeline affirmed that chastity came more easily than obedience, as she recalled the childishness of a vow that required that they do what they were told:

> Well … like chastity … I never broke that vow … I know I didn't, you know. Um, obedience … well … some of the things … were so childish that I never really … considered them … And poverty, I may have transgressed that.

Throughout the lives of the sisters interviewed, the meaning and enforcement of the vows evolved. Norma explained that she never found the vows "onerous," and pivoted to recall optimistically the historical context and her young age at the time of the ritual:

> Like by the time we were professing vows, so that was like '67, there was like a broadening of interpretation ... But um, forty years ago ... with the age and stage that I was, none of the vows were crippling.

Still, not all sisters reconciled their commitment to the vows so easily. In what follows, we turn to bigger questions of what living with the uncertainty of not having a family of their own may have meant for women religious who devoted themselves to religious life at very young ages.

LIVING WITH UNCERTAINTY

Many of the sisters referred to the struggle to stay committed to religious life, but none so evocatively as Evelyn. She shared her vivid memory of what she was thinking about as she stepped up to the altar to make her final vows:

> I was VERY aware that I would never have a husband and children. And ... I remember coming up in ... th[e] end of that [final] retreat saying, "Ah! It's you and I. Are you enough for me? Will you be enough for me?"

She reflected on the realization at this time in her life that she was missing her ex-boyfriend and her family, and she doubted whether she should be giving up what she knew as the intimacies of her social life:

> I began to realize that I'd never have children and I'd never have an arm around me, you know, as you would with a husband. Um, those kinds of things were eating away at me ... and then I kinda felt, well maybe I made a mistake. I seem to have wanted to leave all and had to in order to find out. But maybe I made a mistake. And so I went through a hard ... couple of months where I was in this real depression I would say.

And yet, even though Evelyn felt tortured by this uncertainty as she mulled over these questions throughout her preparation for that life commitment, she reported that the struggle stopped there, referring to the vow of chastity as a "gift" and repeating her sense that a joyful celibate life remains to her a "mystery":

> The day that I received the habit ... in a ceremony – in the chapel, I was alone in the afternoon, passing through really; I was just making a pop call and ah, I heard God say to me very, very clearly without a doubt, "[Evelyn], you're mine and you're mine forever." It brings tears to my eyes, it's so beautiful! And I left the chapel and I soon found the novice director who knew my struggles up to that point, my doubts and I said to her ... [whispers] "It's going to be okay" ... It all settled. It's like shackles fell off from me. And I never had a doubt from that day to this which is most unusual, especially in the times that we've been through, many of us have had doubts and hung in there and some didn't, you know, or couldn't.

Leaving the doubt of her decision behind, Evelyn was able to happily find belonging in community and feel a sense of gratitude for what she found on the other side of the vows. She thought about her great fortune at being able to support young women who also came through doubt and struggle, and realized in hindsight how she settled quickly into a sense of home in religious life. Other sisters echoed similar stories of moving from doubt and uncertainty to relative ease with their communities in religious life. At the time of her interview, Ava said she hardly thought about the vow of chastity, but recalled how in her thirties, she thought, "Gee, it'd be really nice to be able to get married and have kids." She elaborated on how she felt through that time, also pivoting to the community that her celibacy afforded her:

> So I mean I thought about it then! ... And it was sorta like choosing it again, you know ... And so for me ... you know there was a time when living that vow cost ... and I didn't ignore that. That's a reality; I'm a woman [chuckles], you know ... but it never led me to want to leave for that ... because I really knew I belonged here ... I do know what celibacy, CHOSEN celibacy and

> community have enabled in me ... you have a certain freedom of mobility ... and being a member of community gives me that too.[6]

Even though there was a time when living with the vow caused some strife, she reflected that she did not ignore the feeling, and instead embraced the sense of loss as an expected part of her womanhood. In doing so, she was able to focus on the fact that she did not want to leave the Church because she knew that was where she belonged.

Rachel picked up where this story left off, extending her description of the struggle with giving up a family to one that became more about forgoing the possibility of grandchildren. Nostalgically recalling the struggle of her earlier life, she explained how the "careful attraction" to men in her case remained a part of one's identity: "because we entered religious life didn't mean that kind of thing is gone ... But ... I'm fine with the vows now. I really am. I can't see letting any of them go." Rachel continued evocatively, though, detailing the pang of emotion brought on by witnessing her sister's joy as a grandmother: "I think almost as we got older, I'm getting okay with it, but I still feel it when I see my sister with the grandchildren, and so on. But ... then I mean the married people have problems too." Not to paint an unrealistically glowing picture of family life, Rachel wrapped the emotional reflection with a healthy dose of realism about heterosexual marriage.

Speaking to the attraction element as well, Julia also echoed the lack of emotional mentorship as they entered the novitiate. "You learned as you lived," she recalled, since "there was no sex ed or anything like that," nor was there "preparation for some of the struggles with celibacy later on." Julia related that in this context, she had "infatuations ... that [she] worked through" on her own. And while her words reverberated with a sense of isolation on that path, she was not alone in the experience. Cora explained that breaking her vows "wasn't an option," but she did struggle:

> Oh! Yeah ... yeah, of course! Of course that comes up, you know ... your sexuality doesn't die ... because you entered a convent. I mean it's there and you learn ... to be with it you know and ... live through it.

These sisters' realistic comments on the stability of their sexuality despite a life of celibacy provide refreshing contrast to the image of the asexual sister in the habit of popular culture (Fisher 2012). Cora went on to remember taking stock of the foreseeable longings, evoking an image of a young woman making a big life decision and all the emotions that must have accompanied it:

> I smile to myself because when I entered, you know, I made a list of all the things I was going to miss. Ah! I was going to miss having a husband. I was going to miss children. I was going to miss all these other things.

But despite her list of unfulfilled life events to grieve, she, like Carmel above, thought about the centrality of music and the arts in her life next:

> You know, I didn't [miss having a family]. When I entered, you know what I missed? Music ... Music. 'Cause there was no music other than choir practice ... and ... I entered in the old farmhouse [first convent building] and I used to go down to the root house to sing. All by myself I'd go down and sing [laughs]. Yeah. So that I found ... very difficult.

Perhaps Cora's move to considering the role of music in a happy life could be read as a means of coping with some sense of loss, but it also seems evident that the sisters continually come back to what the vow of celibacy – particularly their remaining independent of family commitments – offered them in return. Without the level of independence afforded to them through religious life, there might have been fewer opportunities to go down to the root house to sing, or to follow one's passion for literature and art the way Carmel was so rewarded by doing. Articulating the agency involved in this life direction and giving a sense of pride (Brock 2010; Murphy 2022), Camila reinforced her independence while also pointing to the impact of mentorship in supporting her through her transition to religious life: "Having a spiritual advisor before I entered and having ... reviewed all this, I did not find the difficulty that some people would find. I chose it. I chose it." But despite her conviction, she wavered somewhat, as she readily recounted the difficulties outweighing the ease when it came to the vows:

> Oh yes! More challenge always than ease with the vows to keep them, yeah. But ... I felt I was better prepared than some ... About five years after, the challenge for marriage like, you know ... celibacy is being alone ... relationship and for marriage

> of it being one … Well … I had a steady boyfriend and … at that time you know it was [a difficult choice] … uh huh.

As we have explored elsewhere about how sisters have left the Church when finding these challenges insurmountable (Gervais 2018; Gervais and Watson 2018; Gervais and Turenne Sjolander 2015), Camila was quick to respond to the question of "why stay?"[7]

> Ah, there've been a lot of temptations along the way. I made vows. I made permanent vows and like marriage vows, I honoured the vows … as hard as they were at times.

And when asked if celibacy was the hardest one, she implicitly referred to the intensifying culture of consumerism as bringing about new challenges for the vow of poverty in particular:

> Gosh … they were all challenging at times … I'd say poverty is the one that may trick me [now] I find but, ah … it's … kind of as individual as your prayer life, you know, it's how you're living it. And it's difficult because the temptations are greater in this age than they were then.

Lola, who also struggled with giving up family and children to take the vow of chastity – "There's always been challenges there. Always! It's never easy, you know" – explained leaning on companionship to help her cope: "But having friends, like being able to have … close friends, I find that really has helped a lot you know." Her reliance on friendship with other women made the surveillance of particular friendships mentioned earlier in this chapter especially stark and ironically misguided on the part of Church authorities who sought to control women's sexuality (Bonavoglia 2006; Corwin 2021; Fisher 2012; Ganim 2013).

Though most sisters pulled the vows apart when asked to consider their challenges with the vows, Simone clarified a broad commitment to religious life that does echo through the sentiments of the others. She explained how she looks at the vows "as one," as a "vow to consecrated life in community":

> When I look at the vows, I don't see them [as] all that different from vows that let's say married people make to each other. So

> for me … the difference is that I make these vows in community and it's a different kind of context … It's the communal piece, and definitely, living in community is a challenge in all those aspects: poverty, chastity, and obedience.

Simone's conception of the vows as communal shifted our lay understanding away from forms of discipline, resistance, and respective losses to consider the commitment to religious life as a whole and what it might preclude and offer. And yet, we note how she exclaimed with some humour:

> Oh yeah, chastity! How could I miss that one? [chuckles] I would say that that has been the biggest struggle for me [and it] has been right now in my life as a middle-aged woman … and I think … I'm in the process of just discovering … how the vow of chastity is really a vow of relationship and loving and … not that I didn't reflect on it or experience it as a younger person. But … I just feel a lot of what I do now as being a lot more sexual than I did before … that it's really an expression of my sexuality. A lot of what I do in terms of being mothering … generating life and wanting life for others, ah, suffering a lot … I mean I do experience it like that.

It is difficult not to pay special attention to the stifling of women's sexuality in Simone's words, as we know her approach to religious life focused on the communality of their joint commitments to a set of practices and sacrifices. But when prompted, she thought of sexuality more broadly as an expression of her identity than as attached to a particular act or orientation. This more holistic understanding perhaps explains why women's sexuality is such a threat to the Church (Fisher 2012; Ganim 2013; McPhillips and McEwan 2022). Even though Church doctrine refers to sexuality in such binary and homophobic ways (Curb and Manahan 1985; Loughlin 2018), if women live in ways more connected to their sexual identities, their creativity and talents might not be readily stifled in obedient service of the Church. Simone elaborated:

> I think too there was a difference in my congregations again. One, the first congregation was very … very rigid; it was … a vow of celibacy or a vow of chastity that was very much about

> what I couldn't have or what the negative piece of it … and it was a very narrow view of sexuality. Like, I think that that's what's happening to me now; my understanding of sexuality has continued to grow and I think that the vow of chastity in this other congregation and in the Church in general is very narrow. And for me I really understand all of creativity to be part of that … and … to know myself as a woman who's growing in her sexuality, discovering her sexuality through a vow of chastity – it has been a challenge. It's been very … painful and wonderful. And I think that's part of religious life that I need and that I would encourage anyone who's in this way of life to … really explore their creative side because for me … that's where a lot of that energy goes whatever that is going to create whether that's a new ministry or … a song or a drawing or a poem or whatever … that it has to be about creativity of something.

She is not the only one who thought about the vow of chastity as in some ways central to religious life. Miriam, who relied on prayer to avoid putting herself "in a place where there'd be temptation," also affirmed the vows "because I think it's expected of all people … well I mean some people say why can't you be married and be a sister, but it doesn't fit you know?" Nadine echoed the sentiment exactly: "Well, I agree, certainly. I mean if you're religious, you're not going to marry. So certainly that makes sense, right? It's an either or." And, from a place of realism about family and community life, Philomena agreed:

> Yeah, I think there's still a place for the vows. But I think they have taken on a whole new role … Not the old version but … I still think there's a place for chastity too because if you, like family life is very consuming in itself … and so you can't really live family life and live community life … if you opt for a religious community, like community should be given your priority.

What comes through these comments is the notion of community service above and beyond one's responsibility to the work of raising children or committing to marriage. In this sense, the vow commits one to receptivity to the needs of others, even strangers. Referencing Diarmuid Ó'Murchú,[8] Evelyn claimed, "the vow of chastity is the vow of relatedness. And see that's … how I experience the vow of chastity too." Evelyn explained how she does not know "what God has in mind for the new way of religious life" but she imagines it will be "very different," and may include "temporary times for celibate living" with a different understanding of what that can mean over the life course (Fisher 2012). Dominique felt similarly about the potential of the vow to provide clarity of call, but in her explanation, she also gestured to the future:

> I understood that celibacy, if you were going to be a community working for justice and compassion, then celibacy … is a good thing if you feel called to it. But I don't think it's for everybody obviously and I think there are other kinds of communities today … It doesn't require celibate women living in community to do the social work of the Church anymore.

EXPLORING SEXUAL AND ROMANTIC RELATIONSHIPS

Like their counterparts elsewhere (Fisher 2012), three women raised their past romantic or sexual relationships in the context of challenges with celibacy, and others recalled observing peers' experiences. Nadine and Esther reflected on how the struggle with chastity was a struggle in the context of missionary work in particular. Nadine remembered how she saw sisters "making other choices" or "struggling trying to find their way again," while Esther recounted the same observation of the mission context, where "there [were] lots of them" (priests and sisters) engaging in romantic relationships. Referring yet again to their lack of mentorship and preparation, particularly as they were thrust into missionary work in foreign locations, Esther reminded us that her peers

> never had any exposure. No exposure. And that's why it went on with the ones in the missions. They were thrown into something. There were no boundaries and they were not ready for that. So they were acting out a lot of stuff that ah, they never had a chance to grow up. So ah, some of them pulled through alright but others didn't. They ended up getting married and maybe that's the way it should be … It was … like, you know, whatever decision they made, we were supportive of them and helped them.

The three women who disclosed their own experiences of romantic and intimate relationships as vowed women religious recounted feelings of joy, pain, fear, and a deep sense of meaning, but certainly not regret. As Bernadine divulged not only having had "some struggles" with chastity, but that "there's still some struggles! [laughs]," a complicated story of heartbreak followed. After "never [having] had any relationship with men," Bernadine became enamoured with a priest in the co-ed setting of an educational retreat in the early 1970s:

> The mingling of ... the two sexes certainly just brought out some ... forgotten ... emotion ... I'm human ... and by that time, after twenty-five years, you're really, I guess we're looking around too, I don't know ... I fell in love. I should say that. I really fell in love; it wasn't just a slight thing.

Yet, it became "quite a year" as Bernadine was devastated when they "broke up" after "the priest left the altar" to marry "another ... nun" to whom he had been a chaplain: "They both decided to leave and they [got] married [chuckles] ... and with that, ah, my heart was broken ... that was my first real agony to experience, to let go." As we have problematized in the chapter on clerical abuse, one can certainly not overlook the priest's patriarchal privilege in this love triangle, particularly given his authoritative role as chaplain (Bouclin 2006). Nevertheless, Bernadine's account sheds light on how vowed nuns have also experienced complicated romantic encounters, not unlike those of their non-vowed counterparts (Fisher 2012).

While during her first "three years" as a nun, Angela "was so damn busy" that she "didn't even think of it [the vow of chastity]," it was also in a co-ed setting later in life that her "unchaste" moments originated. Angela excitedly recalled how stimulating she found the shared retreat and residence space at the progressive spirituality institute in a foreign country, and her initial sexual discoveries:

> [That university] was so rich! God! God is in your sexuality. Wow! ... and just studying ... with men and almost living with men in a sense, ah, was just so, so freeing, you know, just so wonderful!
>
> I made a mixed massage weekend and I remember journalling after ... and saying that if anybody had told me that massaging a priest's butt would deepen my spirituality, I'd say they were crazy. But that's what happened!

Unlike Bernadine's experience of heartache, Angela found consolation in the distant memory of her parents' reasonable approach as she put into perspective the "failures in my life ... in the area of chastity" as a middle-aged woman, even after disclosing them to "a confessor ... on occasion":

> I think that the common sense of my father and kind of a balance that when I was unchaste, it wasn't the end of the world, you know ... and especially after [my experience at a progressive university]. But I was already ... fifty... and for me ... I don't think I feared God as much as maybe some religious and ... it's funny. My own home, you know in some ways, whatever the priest said, whatever the nun said, you didn't question. But on the other hand, there weren't beatings when you did wrong things. So ... I think my parents kind of modelled loving authority.

Claire was similarly able to put the sexual encounters of her convent life into perspective. She did so, as she discussed "breaking" the vow of chastity, by recognizing the importance of human bonding and the implications of gender-segregated learning and living arrangements (Fisher 2012):

> Yeah, yeah. Without knowing it. However ... I would not even confess that in the confessional ... when I was a sister ... and I surely wouldn't now! [laughs]. But then ... my rationale, I mean ... I am a warm loving person. I need affection and I need to give affection and this is friendship. I went to an all-girls' high school and then into an all-girls' convent, you know, at seventeen, eighteen. So I mean, my experience of dating was VERY limited.

Yet despite such self-compassion, Claire's recollection of having had "a number of" sexual encounters in the convent also brought to mind the ensuing emotions and confusion over the realization that they had been "lesbian experiences" which were set against virtuous expectations and homophobic suspicions. Claire's pursuit of relationships exemplifies the resistance presented in this book, as she reclaims her body and sexuality despite punishing Church doctrine forbidding women's sexual pleasure outside of marriage, in religious life, *and* between women:

> My first sexual experience … was in the convent. Blew my mind and terrified me! … But I mean … I had never heard the word lesbian. So … it was total denial for me … It was filled with guilt. Not me recognizing my humanity and being comfortable. No! TOTALLY feeling guilty. Suppressing the guilt. Ah, carrying it for YEARS! Until I recognized, "I can't live this. This is inauthentic." But … I was still a really good nun! And popular out there … but if anybody really knew who I was, they would not like me. That kind of guilt, you know. Subtle … destructive … self-loathing … imposed by a lack of understanding of what was happening and no place to really discuss it.

Such long-term isolation was rooted in prior instances of castigation by both her convent superiors and her local pastor, all of which were especially confusing given her own lack of awareness of same-sex relationships at the time:

> As a postulant, I … went to teachers' college with some of the ones that were older than I. And I can remember … we were having a dance down in the college … gym. And … we were dancing around … and I got called into the novice mistresses' … office because one of the professed sisters had complained that I danced three dances in a row … with another professed sister … I was so pissed off … I didn't know anything about lesbianism.
>
> But I can remember going to … our parish priest and I said, "Can you believe I was called on the carpet for god sakes for dancing three dances with somebody?" And he said, "Well there isn't any hanky panky going on, is there?" That was his response to me! … This was before I had any sexual encounter. That was two years later … I mean it didn't even cross my mind … So no. I was truly naïve and innocent. So when I started having a different experience, then I was kinda like, "Oh my god, what's happening here?" But still, nobody really to talk to other than the person, you know.

Whereas Claire readily admitted to having been confused in some regards, she appeared more certain about other aspects of those relationships. After having disclosed that her "first" sexual experience "in the convent" was with "the principal at [her] school when [she] was a young teacher," she was quick to dismiss any concerns related to abuse despite the ten-year age gap between them and her partner's position of authority over her:

> No. Not at all ... They ... were just love relationships ... I think there was just a natural attraction and we became REALLY good friends. I loved her dearly and she loved me dearly and we had FUN together.

Many readers may feel skeptical about the power dynamics of such a relationship, and one should certainly not overlook countless nuns' experiences of abuse at the hands of both superiors and priests in convent settings (Chibnall, Wolf, and Duckro 1998; Fisher 2012; Poggioli 2019; Wagner 2018), abuse that continues to be hidden and denied (Araujo-Hawkins 2021a, 2021b; Fernandes 2022; Meyer 2021; Voices of Faith 2018). Nevertheless, that Claire did not consider that she was preyed upon, and that she disclosed "a number of" intimate encounters, points to the nuanced contexts of relationships in institutional settings; and for some, as we explore next, such encounters may even serve as an opportunity to reconsider the vows of chastity with greater openness towards both heterosexual and queer relations that are genuinely consensual and loving.

CALLS TO REIMAGINE THE VOWS

Even among those who still saw value in the vows for religious life, there was a sense that change is needed: less rigidity, and more compassion for the social, spiritual, and physical needs of religious and lay people (Fisher 2012). Simone explained how the Church seemed to be moving in this direction, as she witnessed "more opportunity [for support] ... for people." She went on to share that it is the open communication, community solidarity, and openness to share and support each other through struggles that give her hope and joy in religious life:

> And what's most nourishing for me is being able to share my life with others to be able to talk openly about struggles about joys and struggles and not feel confined. But I wouldn't say that ... it's always absolutely perfect either you know ... because ... in religious community, even in the new model, there are still some

> things that may or may not be able to be spoken about you know. Like I think that there are still parameters that are there … left over from an older model.

The old way of thinking about the disciplinary power of the vows stifled what support there could be for sisters with respect to their commitments to religious life (McPhillips and McEwan 2022). While some of the sisters' stories above recognized the value that their devotion to the vows had brought to their lives, particularly with respect to the freedom to enjoy what they might not otherwise have prioritized in family life outside of their lives of service, the sisters did not make light of the pain, sacrifice, and isolation many of them experienced – particularly in their younger years, but still, for some of them, through to their senior years (Corwin 2021; Fisher 2012; McPhillips et al. 2022; Schneiders 2001). The issue is hardly simple for the sisters, even though the vows themselves are meant to be all-encompassing. But as Claire reflected, perhaps the practice of requiring everyone to commit to the vow of chastity or celibacy could become a thing of the past. She admitted that

> it's part of the expectation that you take some of the crap, you know. So … you're not just there as an individual … the whole notion of community is that you work for the common good. So I do understand that and … if you're going to be celibate, then be celibate. But understand it. Should they be? That's a whole other thing. Honest to God, I have said, "Enough already!"

Martha was equally impatient with what she sees as purely a mechanism of control. On whether the vows should pertain to sisters today, she says,

> [I] don't think so at all … Sometimes I think they could be a control rather than a spiritual thing … More damaging and more authoritative. It's a good way to control people, from the top of the Church down.

Cora also thought about the vows as outdated, at least in the literal way they were interpreted in mid-century religious life in Canada:

> I don't agree with them in the sense that we um understood them … sixty years ago. In fact our cluster has just worked

> with ... a book ... it's the vows in the environmental sense ... what those vows mean today. And when I – we didn't ... learn that.

While she did not elaborate on the "environmental sense" of what the vows might mean, Cora's expression seemed consistent with many sisters' stated desires to consider women religious as full people with dynamic and varied sexual identities and lives (Fisher 2012; Ganim 2013). In a similar vein, Bernadine offered the notion of "optional celibacy," since she questioned how the vow shapes the work of priests and nuns today: "the deacons who know about life and who know about working with their families and everything, have much more power with the people ... Oh much more relationship." And on this topic, she knows: "we have to change the Catholic Church." While such conviction toward the need for the Church to evolve was unmistakable in the individual opinions above, as we show next, it was also manifest in collective resistance efforts.

COLLECTIVE ADVOCACY

Given that many of the sisters recalled having to process their sexuality and come to terms with their vows alone, or at least without sufficient confidantes and institutional guidance in earlier decades, there is a certain satisfaction in uncovering an example of communal openness to discussing these aspects of religious life. Specifically, the sisters' resistance to "the Church's sexual straitjacket" (Bonavoglia 2006, 99) was made explicit in one of the congregations' calls to action presented alongside those of a number of other Canadian women's religious orders to the Canadian bishops in the mid-2000s. As a testament to their organizational capacity for conscientization and collective advocacy toward greater emancipation regarding sexuality (Faulkner and MacDonald 2009), we include a short selection of their shared "statement[s] of disagreement and protest" (Ó'Murchú 1997, 114):[9]

> REALIZATIONS
> We recognize that for more than a millennium celibacy was not a requirement for clergy.
>
> CRITIQUES
> We deplore the amount of energy that goes into any issue dealing with human sexuality.

> We deplore the rigidity of leaders regarding issues such as married clergy, celibacy, and inclusion of women.
>
> We deplore the demand for conformity [and] lack of opportunity for debate, especially on issues related to sexuality.
>
> ASPIRATIONS
>
> We hope that when bishops feel they must write about human sexuality, they will consult trusted married couples.

Not only is the sisters' resistance to the Church's stifling stance evident herein (Elliott 2004; Holtmann 2008; Ó'Murchú 1997), but so too is their openness to evolving and encompassing outlooks on celibacy, ones that thoughtfully include a life-giving reimagining far beyond the patriarchal renunciations and negations of their own and others' sexuality (Faulkner and MacDonald 2009; Fisher 2012; Ganim 2013).[10]

CONCLUSION

Whether the sisters were inclined to keep their sexual identities, feelings, and relations under the radar or express them confidently with clear intentions of disrupting canonical constraints and, in so doing, rendering all facets of their "*humanness*" more constructively transparent, their collective stances reflected diverse strategies toward the same supportive ends. The sisters' personal articulations about and, in many cases, against the regulation of their sexuality were deliberate, contextual, and transformative, and were thus indicative of their autonomy and their resistance to both religious and societal constraints against women (Avishai 2008; Brock 2010; Burke 2012; Faulkner and MacDonald 2009; Holtmann 2008; Ó'Murchú 1997). Taken together, the sisters' wide-ranging expressions and experiences of sexuality gave a sense of the complexity of understanding and stifling of one's sexuality in a community of varied support and suppression (Fisher 2012; Ganim 2013; McPhillips and McEwan 2022). As the next chapter elaborates, the Church is always considering and reinforcing its controlling moral stance on sexuality. The sisters' reflections show that these moral codes are constantly being met with opposition as communities are empowered to fight for the inclusion and autonomy of their members.

8

Resisting Compulsory Heterosexuality

Christine Gervais and Amanda Watson

The condemnation of homosexuality [is one of] the two issues around which I feel truly ashamed to be Catholic.[1]

Naomi

INTRODUCTION

Despite the *Canadian Charter of Rights and Freedoms* (1982) protecting against discrimination based on sexual orientation, the culture of the Catholic Church is fundamentally homophobic (Loughlin 2018; Callaghan 2018). For many Catholic and secular members of the 2SLGBTQI+[2] community globally, Pope Francis's comments on inclusion, safety, and non-judgment of all members of the Church regardless of sexual identity have represented enormous progress for members of this community, particularly compared to the vitriolic homophobic and transphobic comments of his predecessors (Allen 2013; AP in Vatican City 2023; Kirchgaessner 2018; McElwee 2016a; Pullella 2023; Schenk 2022; Thomson Reuters 2013).[3] But the Roman Catholic Church's condemnatory teachings and exclusionary practices, to which Naomi refers, remain entrenched.[4] With respect to sexuality, the catechism of the Catholic Church, under Canon 2357, explicitly states that "homosexual acts are intrinsically disordered ... are contrary to the natural law ... [and] under no circumstances can they be approved" (Traina 2018). Moreover, although Canon 2358 states that "they [referring derogatorily to gay and lesbian people] must be accepted with respect, compassion, and sensitivity,"[5] Pope Francis has assured Catholics in numerous public statements that while people come to diverse sexual orientations through no fault of their own and should therefore be received without judgment, any sexual activities outside of heterosexual marriage are still officially considered sinful and condemnable. Gay marriage remains banned as "morally problematic" (Mayer 2014), calling up controversy akin to that around abortion (Bonavoglia 2006). The painful experiences of those affected by such ongoing stigmatization cannot be overlooked (Hunt 2024; Schenk 2022).

Compulsory heterosexuality, as explained by Adrienne Rich in 1980, refers to heterosexuality as a political institution rather than simply a sexual arrangement. Rich argues that the institutions which have traditionally been controlled by men presume sex and gender roles where women's labour is exploited and relationships between women are rendered suspect.[6] In the context of the Church's entrenched position on heterosexuality as natural and morally superior, the sisters' attitudes and approaches towards diverse sexual relationships and expressions warrant our attention as they reflect inspiring instances of resistance agency (Murphy 2022), strategic resistance aimed at inclusion and collectivity (Holtmann 2008), and compassion (Faulkner and MacDonald 2009). We begin this chapter with Claire's and Justine's testimonies of marginalization by Church officials. After exploring the former and current sisters' disagreements with Church doctrine and their concerns for those who have been ostracized by compulsory heterosexuality in the Church, we highlight how they individually and collectively model inclusivity (Corcoran 2017),[7] and incisively demand institutional change within the Church.

FORMER SISTERS' EXPERIENCES OF EXCLUSION

Beneath the confidence and pride with which former sisters Claire and Justine identified as lesbian during their interviews, there remained an undeniable layer of painful memories associated with their experiences of marginalization within the Roman Catholic Church due to their sexual orientation. Their accounts illustrate how the institutional Church's homophobic and misogynistic moral stances on sexuality manifest in devastating ways in both the personal and public lives of women religious who identify as gay or lesbian.

Like sisters elsewhere whose retrospective reflections revealed how they "unconsciously" chose to join women's religious congregations because of their sexual orientation (Fisher 2012; Kaylin 2000, 175),

Justine came to the realization that she probably did so but with neither the vocabulary nor a full grasp of the choice. The extent to which she was able to parse her rationale at the time was likely shaped by the societal and religious repression prevalent during the mid-twentieth-century context in which she became a nun:

> So I began to feel … in these latter years since I've been out of the community in the last twenty years or so that … [my identity as a lesbian] … probably that was one of the reasons I entered the convent. You know when you think back. I would have NEVER thought that when I was seventeen! But now to live among women and good women.

Yet what may have partially led her to enter a religious community of women also contributed to her eventual departure from the Church. Although Justine remained a practising Catholic after she withdrew from religious life in the early 1970s, she left the institutional Roman Catholic Church in the early 1990s because of "the way they treat gays; the way they treat women." Despite the disconnect she felt, she did occasionally attend Mass afterward in solidarity with a group of women she had been supporting for decades in a Latin American country, but her decision to attend occasionally came with risk. She reflected on hateful comments from a priest during a Mass in 2008 and ostracizing comments from a parishioner at another celebration:

> I walked out last summer, last Mass I was in [village] … I said "I'm not staying and listening to this." He [the priest] was talking about … gays getting married … he was screaming his head off about it and I said to [a sister from my former religious community], "I'm not staying." And so I left. I visited all kinds of people in the town, up and down [the main street]. [I] bought a blouse and it was a good morning! I met them [sisters from my former religious community] after and also I said I wouldn't go back either in … the one [church] they go to in [another city] … because … I was there one day, and at the end of the Mass, somebody got up and said … "There's going to be a retreat in marriage encounter or something like this and we invite anybody to come" … and he used some derogatory word … for gays and ah I was crying after too … you know.

After Justine recounted this painful experience, we discussed how part of her struggle with the Church was in relation to her sexual orientation. As she confirmed that tension, she broke down in tears and concluded: "Yeah. So I won't go back there ... Yeah! Big signs up. Everybody welcome, blah, blah! I was not welcome."

Claire's experience of marginalization echoed Justine's. While referring to canonical terminology as she reflected on how her human rights as a woman had been violated,[8] Claire's critique of the institutional Church's official stance focused on the Church as narrow-minded, exclusionary, and hypocritical:

> Well, my whole sexuality is denied ... I'm intrinsically evil ... You know, made in the image and likeness of God. But ooh, just a minute! Not if you're gay! You know, [as if we were] taught, like duped ... Under the umbrella of this Church, this hierarchical Church that says I am intrinsically disordered! Well, I'm saying, "and so are you" [laughs – referring to Church officials] and we all are then. You know, like, I'm not willing to continue to fund an organization that labels me intrinsically disordered.

Her clarity of mind on the subject was reinforced in a personal experience in a rural parish in Ontario where Claire and her same-sex partner led the choir:

> I left. Well, let me put it this way ... At first, I'm standing there facing the congregation for the final hymn. As Father [name] says, "Now we've got to write our letters to protect marriage!" You know, "We can't be having these same sex marriages!" [My partner's] behind me running the overhead projector and everybody in the parish knows that we're a couple ... and I can feel myself going chickachickachicka [representing her temperature rising and face flushing due to her growing anger upon hearing the priest's words]. So I go in afterwards and I said ... "How dare you with the lack of sensitivity?" [He says,] "Well, we have to protect marriage!" You know, "Well, if gays get married and heterosexuals start falling apart, what does that tell you about heterosexual marriages?" [I said,] "It's not going to affect most of them, father!" Anyways so that was number one. Then the next time he spoke, I still kept going [to church] for a while ... he spoke about the lepers in society ... and he

> named the drunks, the abused, then he could not name the homosexuals you know, and I went in to see him afterwards, I said, "You know what? The drunks, the abused, you can't even say the word homosexual." [He said,] "Yes but it's the sexual thing." And I said, "You know you're so genital, it's just pathetic! ... It's all about genitals. You don't understand sexuality beyond the genital. So, of course you know 'til death do us part' means, you know, physical, biological death. It couldn't mean the death of the love to you guys, you know! You don't understand those concepts. You gotta keep the people in a death-wielding relationship."

Despite both her feelings of marginalization and her steady critique, Claire and her partner continued to lead the choir because they believed in sharing creative and uplifting music with the parishioners of their rural community. Yet, their willingness to persevere came at a cost:

> Then, then it was walking into the church, you know, there'd be a petition about poverty at the back of the church and he'd say, "Look, Development and Peace, they have a petition at the back of the church. They want you to sign it. It's about poverty."[9] You know, it's [placed] on the back table. The same-sex thing, that one, he had the table out on the sidewalk. You had to literally fall over the table on the sidewalk to get people to ... sign it ... So that was the straw that broke the camel's back. I said, "I won't be back," and then I said, and it was in about June, so I said, "I won't be back," and in the summer we didn't play anyway. And [name of fellow choir member] stopped playing too then ... in solidarity, and then I said, "[Name,] look, you've got teenage kids. You need to be taking them to church. You know, don't worry about me." [He said,] "I'm not going. We're not going ... If they don't accept people like you guys, I don't want to be a part of it either."
>
> There was a parish mission going on and they put out this letter to people who were disenfranchised from the Church, [and it stated that the parish priest] will come and do a pastoral visit, you know. So I ... sent him an email and I said, "Yeah, you can come and see me." [During the visit] I had said, "Maybe we, [fellow choir member] and I would come back during Advent

> at the beginning of December." And he said, "Well, I don't know." So I said, "Well, we should have a visit." So [my partner] wouldn't stay for that visit. She didn't come home that night and he and I went at it, and there were kind of like conditions put on my coming back. And the conditions were, now that it was public, I said, "Bullshit, it was public before I ever left! It was public when you were saying, 'We've got to protect marriage.' You know we never tried to hide who we are." So it was ... I could come back and play if I stopped going to communion because now it was a scandal. If I would, ah, profess that there was no sex going on or something, and I said, "You know what Father, even if there wasn't, I'd never do that because you know what, I believe in same sex because that's who God made us to be, so you know. But again Father, you're stuck with the genitals. You don't see relationship or love at all, you just see genitals. And you can put rules around genitals, you know."

Claire's direct confrontation with the priest shows enormous courage of conviction given the inevitable risk that she would be further disenfranchised from her small-town parish. Accusing the priest of being "stuck with the genitals" offers incisive critique of the culture of homophobia and the political institution of heterosexuality being about power and control – rules – over development, peace, or social equality (Fisher 2012; Manning 1999, 2002). Her example, like many in this chapter, underscores the cost of tolerating and building resilience within a deeply homophobic culture. It is one that also resembles other nuns' experiences with resistance against the Church's overemphasis on sex and same-sex relations, and its overuse of pamphlets and petitions in that regard (Murphy 2022).[10]

Despite the solidarity expressed by the choir member, Claire and her partner not only felt marginalized by the institutional Church due to the parish priest's restrictions, but they also felt unsupported by some of the parishioners:

> The other side of it [is] this silent majority. You know? Yeah! Sure, I played and they loved it for how many years? But did any of them say to Father, you know? Did any of them ever say to me? "Geez I'm so sorry. Is there anything we can do?" "Can we write a letter?" "Can we stand up for you?" Nothing! Nothing! ... That's when I said, "You know what? This is a sick

> organization! These people don't think. They're taught not to think. And if they think, they have to keep it quiet because we are a SILENT group of people. We are forced into a culture of silence. Conform or leave. We don't need you." ... So I left!

Justine's and Claire's experiences of confusion and exclusion were echoed by women religious in other countries who have also been devastated by the Church's prohibitive stance and for whom such deep hurt has led to either their sporadic attendance at Mass or their full departure from the Church (Kaylin 2000, 183–4; Wexler 2016). As we show next, such painful personal manifestations of exclusion did not go unnoticed by sister-peers who have also disagreed with Church dogma and have held compassionate outlooks.

COUNTERING THE CHURCH'S STANCE

The current and former sisters' inclusive outlooks were apparent in their disagreements with the Church's official position that had resulted in the distressing and sometimes agonizing marginalization of those who identified as gay or lesbian or who sought same-sex marriage:

> I don't like their black and white stance on homosexuality. (Sister Theresa)

> The ostracization of ... gay people really bothers me. (Sister Clara)

> I feel strongly about it ... I think it's terrible for a church to be contrary to love, you know. (Sister Sophie)

> I don't like the stance of ... condemnation. (Sister Corinne)

> I disagree with the Church. I disagree with the priests in the Church ... who will not give communion to people. (Sister Carmen)

In a similar vein, Sister Rita drew on social justice language as she expressed her concern over the marginalizing impact that the Church's position has on gay and lesbian people: "there's ... still ... a lot of [stigma] ... attached to that so where are the human rights there [on the part of the Church,] you know?"

Echoing Sister Sophie, when asked how she felt about the Church's position on same-sex marriage and relationships, Sister Adele remarked: "Well, I feel really sad because they're people and they're real … and I still think our Church is very exclusive … certainly exclusive of gays and lesbians." Based on a similar concern and nuancing the concept and practice of love as the "real" Catholic and Christian stance, Sister Noreen reinforced the importance of acceptance by distinguishing the official Church's exclusionary position and the oft-cited and inclusive Catholic conception of the Church as the people of God: "I mean, homosexuality again, you know, if you understood, it has to do with … people have no choice … it's the institutional Church's thing … but the Church in general, there's love, there's acceptance." The sisters' disagreement with the Church's homophobic stance was also evident in the ways in which they quietly rebelled against the Church's absolute prohibitions. For example, Claire recalled how she and her sister-peers resisted the marginalizing regulations of convent life, especially those pertaining to close relationships:

> The thing about particular friendship, you've probably heard that from some of the nuns. … well, BIG, well, big thing! I mean … the rules were so foolish that we made fun of them, to survive.

Officially, as noted earlier in the chapter on celibacy, particular friendships were prohibited because such one-on-one relationships were thought to undermine one's commitment to communal religious life and to one's faith in Jesus (Fisher 2012); however, sisters came to understand that the term was "a veiled reference to lesbianism" (Kaylin 2000, 174).

Echoing Claire's sentiments, many sisters were unequivocal in expressing their frustration with the Church's stance on sexuality:

> Same-sex marriage is another big issue. (Sister Edith)

> Well, I find … it's not cut and dry … I think ah the Church speaks and it gives the message and some think we have to listen to the message. But I think what is needed is the dialogue with the people and that's ah the pastoral dimension. The message is one thing. But it's the pastoral dimension. (Sister Carmen)

> [I feel] disappointed because I don't feel that they support it enough … as a way of being, a way of living. (Sister Penelope)

> Oh absolutely yes, I think that's just terrible the way some of the churches won't even allow them [gays and lesbians] to go to communion, you know, oh ya! (Sister Sophie)

When asked her opinion of the Church's position on same-sex relationships, Sister Kelly's response was the same as when she reflected on the Church's view on contraception and abortion: "Yeah, I have big problems with that." When asked if she thought the Church's stance on these issues was exclusionary, her response was emphatic: "Oh yes, yes, yes! And again, I've worked with beautiful, beautiful people who are lesbian or gay … [sigh], deeply spiritual people you know."

When asked how she felt about the exclusionary approach that the Church has taken on sexuality, Sister Agnes recalled her frustration with sermons and the way in which sexuality has been stigmatized alongside murder and abortion:

> It really bothers me that homosexuals don't feel more welcomed in the Church … a … cousin of mine once removed … had to take what he calls a sabbatical from church. He didn't want to. 'Cause he needs to be nourished; he likes to be nourished at church. But the pastor was throwing in too much. Murder, abortion, homosexuality, you know they don't go together. They don't go together! That type of thing.

Naomi was also deeply troubled by the Church's control over sexuality because such "power plays" have severe consequences for those excluded. Later in our interview conversation, Naomi further underscored her frustration and embarrassment with the way the Church has dealt with sexuality: "Well, I mean, the abuse is appalling. I think it's that and the issue of the condemnation of homosexuality are the two issues around which I feel truly ashamed to be Catholic and wish that there were another name for those who want to be in the tradition but not carry the name." That Naomi expressed distress as she explained the tension between her Catholic identity and her outlook on equality is indicative of how sisters approach complex human relations with considerable care because they are concerned about the injustices affecting those relationships (Faulkner and MacDonald 2009; Holtmann 2008; Murphy 2022; Ó'Murchú 1997).

While some sisters may have shared Naomi's embarrassment with respect to the institutional Catholic Church's homophobic position, none were more incisive with their critique than Claire, who lived in constant fear until she retired over the possibility of losing her employment and pension within a Catholic school board in Ontario:

> Everybody knows [about my relationship with my partner], but it's not spoken about. And that's what REALLY bothers me about the Catholic Church. You know that culture of silence. "There are no gays in the Catholic Church." That … kind of stuff which is total bullshit. You know, the notion of not dealing with sexuality, PERIOD, I think is the greatest sin of the Catholic Church.

Curiously, however, Claire revealed that she was not too focused on "the homosexual question." Nevertheless, when discussing sexual exclusion, Claire was unequivocal in her compassion and in her critical view of the Church's missteps:

> But it's one area where people don't want to look … and even the convent doesn't. And they NEED to! You know they NEED to because … this is what I keep referring to as the culture of silence is so evident. It's kind of like, "if we don't talk about it, it doesn't exist." You know, and that's the Catholic way.

Juxtaposed against the stereotypical image of Catholic sisters acquiescing to Church teachings, many current and former sisters have clearly grappled with the Catholic Church's overt promotion of compulsory heterosexuality. Yet in a comment countering the hush culture, Sister Carmen demonstrated an unfailing faith and optimism characteristic of sisters who hope for a more progressive and inclusive approach:

> Well, I'm hoping that homosexuality and lesbianism will be greatly accepted … and I certainly … disagree with the Church; I disagree with the priests in the Church … who will not give communion to people.

Not all current or former women religious shared Sister Carmen's optimism regarding a shift in the institutional attitude toward same-sex relationships. In her 2009 interview, which occurred prior to Pope Francis's advocacy for a non-judgmental approach, Justine noted how discouraged she felt and how she did not feel hopeful that the Church would become more welcoming in its approach: "I don't have any faith in the Catholic Church doing anything for gays." While some women such as Justine were frustrated with the Church's less-than-progressive attitude, the sisters themselves were far more inclusive, and as we show later, their inclusivity constitutes an expression of alternative communities and life-giving strategies of resistance (Faulkner and MacDonald 2009; Ó'Murchú 1997).

COMMITMENT TO CONTINUED LEARNING

While most sisters' supportive stances towards sexual inclusion were unambiguous, for many, their opinions were the result of reflection and ongoing learning, indicating their commitment to self-improvement via their own conscientization (Ó'Murchú 1997), as well as their desire for institutional change. While at the time of her interview, Sister Clara expressed concern about the marginalization of gay and lesbian folks, she explained how her acceptance and eventual solidarity developed over time and with some struggle. By way of example, she referred to one of her former students' same-sex wedding that she chose to attend secretly – a choice that she did not make lightly at the time.

> Now I have struggled with it. Um, the first time I encountered it ... I found it the strangest thing ... like it was altogether new to us, you know ... and I struggled with someone I know, who I ... love dearly ... but I came through my own struggle with this profound belief. When I made my decision on the wedding, I have no right to judge ... I wasn't judging them; I was trying to understand it.

Others, such as Sister Ella, also shared comments indicating they had contemplated the issue carefully and without ego: "Some of those issues I don't think we know. As I said about homosexuality, like we have to learn! What would God want? It's not what I would want that's important anyway." In a similar vein, Sister Corinne remarked that the first essential step toward inclusivity had to involve an openness toward compassion-filled awareness and understanding:

> There's so much we don't know about sexuality … So that the Church also has to learn. There's a lot to be learnt. And a lot to be done … I don't like when they condemn … I don't like the stance of … condemnation … I used to go along with that attitude that they were terrible people, but now I just changed my attitude and I just find that they are humans and they deserve our respect and they deserve our understanding … And we're supposed to … have compassion as sisters of [name of religious community].

While the sisters herein criticized the institutional Church's regulation of sexuality for its intrusive control over lay people's behaviour, they seemed similarly concerned for its implications for women and men religious. While acknowledging the institutional constraints as she reconsidered the vow of chastity, Sister Sarah focused her reflection more constructively and compassionately on the importance of working towards an acceptance of sexuality in religious life:

> I think that there are still parameters … and I think sometimes some of those parameters are left over from an older model … one of the questions that I personally have is, in encouraging people, say in the model that we have today … to look at our vows especially, say the vow of … chastity and really encouraging people to look at their sexuality and be comfortable with who they are. I really do still wonder whether a woman in religious life, if she is a lesbian, if she would actually be comfortable … and feel safe. Now I do know in our congregations in another province, I know for sure of a couple people that are lesbian and who have been able to be open about it. But I'm really convinced that there are others … that live fulfilled lives but I'm not sure and maybe … that's not something that everybody feels they have to be open about but for me, I still feel that … there is a bit of a constraint.

Openness to the nuances of sexuality also played a significant role in the ways in which some of the women attempted to counteract the Church's exclusionary measures. In recalling conversations with a trusted friend, Sister Sarah conveyed the importance of inclusivity and the need for people with potentially marginalized identities to feel safe being themselves in their own religious communities:

> [G]oing through what middle-aged women do, um, in terms of … sexuality, it can be a … time when women are very aware of themselves sexually. And so there can be a lot of conversation around … sexuality and I know there's this one person that I often share with and in our conversations, like I know sometimes other people are within earshot and one time I said to her, like, "I wonder how exclusive our conversations [are]? Like do they exclude people?" Like when people are free enough … to speak about their own sexuality … how do we do that in an inclusive way? … I think, we don't know how to do that … and I don't know if we can ever really work that out just because of the levels of trust you have in community … It's not like everybody knows everyone's sexual orientation. That's sometimes not really necessary to know.

Sister Sarah's reflection on potentially exclusionary impacts on one's audience and inadvertent bystanders is a testament to nuns' overall awareness and critical consideration of the impact of discrimination on community. As we show next, similar to women religious elsewhere (Murphy 2022; Wexler 2016), many sisters sought to transform their thoughtfulness into action as they not only called on the Church to address its own internal injustices and open its doors to all, but also sought to model such inclusive practices.

TOWARD INCLUSION

> Women religious have "stepped over [institutional Catholic Church] taboos to walk the way with the divorced and homosexual and unchurched."
>
> Chittister (1995, 29)

In their quest toward inclusion of "*everybody*" (Sister Benita), many women religious have been advocating for sexual diversity to be welcomed by the Roman Catholic Church. Both their individual efforts and collective advocacy serve as evidence of their activism in the face of the institutional Church's entrenched exclusionary mindset, including past convent rules prohibiting "particular friendships." During their 2009–11 interviews, many sisters and former sisters were not only accepting of sexual diversity, but they were also compassionate in their understanding of the frustrations and feelings of exclusion felt by gay and lesbian people.

Darlene, for example, noted that her stance on this issue was on the opposite end of the political spectrum from that of the institutional Church: "Well I'm on the … left side of all of that, you know." In discussing their views on sexuality and in deeming the Church's official position as contradictory, other sisters made their sense of inclusivity known:

> Yes, of course. It's crazy! It's just so dysfunctional. I don't know what else to say. (Sister Ella)

> I don't agree with it at all … Christ is not a Christ of exclusion. I believe in inclusion, like gays, lesbians, women, all … right across the board, there's so many that you can't even name them. (Sister Mabel)

> I don't think God gets too upset about things. You know … [sigh] … if God made people the way they are … maybe I'm wrong, but why would He do that if He didn't accept it? (Sister Josephine)

Echoing Sisters Josephine and Ella, Sister Joelle focused on the notion of a God that desired self-actualization for all:

> Well, I don't agree … What is it the pope calls it? A [pause], a deviation? I believe that … everything God created is God and with the medical and scientific knowledge we have now, we understand that orientation is not a choice and therefore, I think God created all of us to be fulfilled in all ways, and within a loving, you know, permanent commitment. Why would we deprive lesbians and gay people from fulfilling their lives?

In contrast to the Church's official stance, and much like Sister Rita's position below, Sister Jeanette sought to be unbiased, and thus, in her view, Gospel-inspired and faith-based, in her inclusive approach (Holtmann 2008; Murphy 2022; Ó'Murchú 1997):

> You can't judge the person because we don't know the reasons behind it … I don't have anything against people who are homosexuals or lesbians … To me … that's the way they feel called to live! So they're not doing anything to me! Or they never say to me, "I don't agree with you being a religious." You know, so like you have to go about being compassionate and that's the Gospel, being compassionate.

For many women religious, their supportive consideration of lesbian and gay members of their communities did not derive solely from abstract debates with sister-peers within the confines of convent walls. Rather, some of them recounted experiences and relationships with parishioners enduring exclusion from the Church and thus being painfully deprived of opportunities for worship:

> We haven't walked in the shoes of the lesbian, and we haven't walked in the shoes of the homosexual … you know what I mean … I think it's just to be open and understanding because, I'm thinking of one homosexual man who's gone through hell with not being accepted, you know, and I think, geez … he's such a fine man, you know. (Sister Rita)

Still, when others conveyed their people-centred and non-judgmental approaches, they drew on instances of inclusivity exemplified by the spiritual communities of which they were proudly members. Whereas for Sister Adele, it was a uniquely progressive Catholic parish in Ontario, for Darlene, it was an internationally dispersed peace and justice–oriented ecumenical group:

> I don't pretend to understand a whole lot around … gays and lesbians … at all … I'm no expert. I don't have experience. [But] I have a little experience listening to people. I just know they're people! … People are people. And you know, Jesus … would welcome all … Our parish says, "Everyone is welcome," and so we don't ask at the door, "Who are you? What gender are you? What's your sexual preference?" … We say, "Welcome!" …

> I just can't believe that we're called to exclude anybody. (Sister Adele)
>
> On the sexuality stuff, in terms of coming full circle about … homosexuality and all of that. The … community, just last year, made the most wonderful statement about sexuality. Honestly, I was so proud. It was something to the effect … "Staff and members and associates can be transgendered. In the mystery of sexuality, who are we?" And absolutely no discrimination … it's the best statement … It was just totally wide open; I just was delighted with it. (Darlene)

That Darlene and Sister Adele have opted to avoid exclusionary traditional Catholic parishes in favour of inclusive spiritual spaces is a testament to their intentional participation in life-giving "alternative communities" which resist against the Church's oppressive practices by fostering relationality, diversity, and creativity (Faulkner and MacDonald 2009; Ó'Murchú 1997, 115).

MODELLING INCLUSIVITY

> I think people have a right to live!
>
> Sister Loretta

Another way in which women religious demonstrated their advocacy in support of the rights of gay and lesbian members of their communities is by modelling inclusivity to others who tended to be exclusionary. Contrary to what people might expect from a Catholic nun who is most often viewed as a compliant member of a conservative institution whose official stance is homophobic, many sisters have encouraged others, often members of their very own families, to develop more open and compassionate attitudes. Three women recalled conversations in which they dialogued with relatives whom they referred to as "anti-gay" to encourage them to reconsider their positions and to become more understanding. Sister Maureen seemed to encounter the most opposition from a conservative brother, who allegedly disagrees with her on most social matters, and was unwilling to change his mind on the issue because "he has a hard time with same-sex marriage; he has a thing … about that."

Sister Loretta, whose stance regarding what she referred to as "the whole gay and lesbian thing" was unequivocally supportive, had many encounters with her own sister:

> My sister ... like, ah, gay people ... I mean that really ... used to throw her for a loop ... She had four boys and a girl, and she said, "If anyone ever said they were gay ... I wouldn't be able to handle that!" But you know as we talked, and talked, and talked about it and she did meet a few people who were that way, she changed, you know. She really changed.

Like Sister Loretta, Sister Ella recalled concerns that her own sister-sibling had regarding her nephew at various life stages, especially earlier ones during which his mother was concerned that he might be gay because he liked to play with toys stereotypically associated with girls. Ultimately, however, Sister Ella was successful in guiding her sibling towards welcoming the young man more fully and non-judgmentally into the family:

> When he was a little guy, my sister was concerned. You know, he'd play with Barbie dolls; he didn't play with airplanes; they were pushing trucks at him or hockey sticks, and she would say, "What is he going to become?" And when he finally, as a young man, went home to tell her that he was gay ... and it was coming out ... [in] print, and he was afraid that she would see it before he got [to] telling [her], and she called me in tears.
>
> I said, "Look it, do you remember years ago, you expressed your concern, 'What's he going to become?'" Honest to God, you know, she learned to accept him just as he is! If this is his given, it's an innate quality, who are we to [judge]? ... Oh, he's the greatest young man! He's holding his family together ... now since my sister has died ... He comes here [to the spirituality centre]. He loves to spend time here, and we talk about it openly ... and he has a partner now which ... for him, that's very important ... Anybody who talks to me about the Church's stand, I say we don't know enough! I wish we would just all shut up! For another twenty-five years ... We don't know! Why don't we let people just be and honour wherever people love each other ... and if they're forming community in a healthy way, let's just honour that.

Similarly, as a writer on issues of social justice, Sister Clara used her platform strategically to disseminate messages of understanding, compassion, and inclusivity worldwide:

> The global family of God means so much to me, and ... not just religious but we should all be ... It's a growing awareness that we're all members of the family of God and nobody, no race or religion is better than. I try to get that through ... in my last paper. People look down because they're homosexuals or lesser human beings. That's not what the global family of God's all about! And if you really believe you were a neighbour in the global family of God, and you'd really believe the Gospel calls you to love your neighbours as yourself, and ... you can do something consciously ... you can!

Whether they were personal or public, the sisters' consciousness-raising efforts conveyed their firm belief in the dignity of all people (Ó'Murchú 1997); and as we show next, such an enlightening conviction also informed their collaborative endeavours.

CONGREGATIONAL SUPPORT AND COLLECTIVE ADVOCACY

In recent years, women religious congregations' supportive stance appears to have taken various forms, including respecting sisters' autonomy in relationships. For example, both Claire and Justine reported instances of what they perceived to be a sense of openness on the part of their former congregations:

> People have asked me, "Have you ever seen a lot of lesbianism in the convent?" And I have to tell you, I didn't ... And do I now? Yes! Whether they're ... sexually involved or not is a whole other story. But I can tell you four or five couples in ... [my former congregation] that have always been moved together, you know, 'cause they would say, "I'm not going without them," you know. Now is that condoning? ... Like forget the sexual part ... just the emotional ... dependency ... I don't know. (Claire)

> Even [my former congregation], I noticed ... their, ah, acceptance of deep friendships within the community. I can see that, which

is lovely! It shows such a growth ... within the ... community in the younger and in the older. (Justine)

Moreover, similar to how they sought to address other aforementioned societal and religious issues, midway through the first decade of the twenty-first century, one of the religious communities represented herein took additional steps to collectively counter the institutional Roman Catholic Church's official anti-gay stance. In their responses to the previously mentioned Canadian Religious Conference's survey,[11] the congregation noted the following aspects, including ones that revealed their awareness of the systematic and structural contexts:

REALIZATIONS

We recognize the importance of meaningful rituals and liturgies to celebrate God's love in widely differing cultures and in a way that is inclusive of people regardless of marital status or sexual orientation.

We recognize that, though deeply concerned about individual morality as evidenced by its positions on sexuality, homosexuality, same-sex relationships, birth control, etc, the Church is less concerned about social injustices of global proportions, and at times its regulations may be contributing to these injustices.

CRITIQUES

We deplore the fact that many feel unwelcome at the celebration of the Eucharist because of their marital status or sexual orientation.

We deplore the Church's reluctance/refusal to promote compassionate and Gospel-centred ministry to gay and lesbian members of God's people.

We deplore the lack of welcome in our faith communities for our brothers and sisters from the gay community.

We deplore the demand for conformity [and] lack of opportunity for debate, especially on issues related to sexuality.

ASPIRATIONS

We hope ... for the day when whoever comes to be with us on Sunday will be welcome to the Table.

We hope for a faith-filled, vibrant Church community, living a wholistic spirituality, walking in love with our God, our sisters and our brothers in a new era of openness, trust and inclusiveness.

That women's religious orders felt compelled to formally address such exclusionary tactics is once again indicative of the organized and determined ways in which sisters have been challenging the status quo, explicitly calling attention to inconsistencies with Catholic teachings, and defending their stances towards greater understanding, compassion, and respect for the dignity of all members of their communities (Faulkner and MacDonald 2009; Holtmann 2008; Murphy 2022; Ó'Murchú 1997). While the Canadian women religious represented here may not have been picketing as publicly or criticizing the Church as openly as renowned advocates such as Sister Jeannine Gramick have been in the United States and elsewhere,[12] such direct critiques against the Church hierarchy and its institutional policies represent unusual, courageous, and thus significant forms of advocacy and resistance on the part of sisters in Canada (Brock 2010; Faulkner and MacDonald 2009; Holtmann 2008; Ó'Murchú 1997). While such contestation was said to have aggravated men in the Church hierarchy, the backlash in Canada was not as severe as it was in the United States, where sisters, and particularly the Leadership Conference of Women Religious (LCWR), were accused of "corporate dissent" under the Vatican's doctrinal assessment initiated in 2008 (Bonavoglia 2006; Wexler 2016). In the context of that investigation, the sisters' ministry to gay and lesbian people and vocal protests against the Church's position on same-sex relationships were deemed unacceptable since they were "not in agreement with the Church's teaching on human sexuality" (Congregation for the Doctrine of the Faith 2012). But the direct acts of opposition, advocacy, and solidarity by sisters in Canada can be seen as strategic, and successfully so, as they introduced family and community members to a more inclusive and less harmful way of understanding sexual diversity and, for some sisters, reintroduced church as a place of love and acceptance. As such, what the sisters sought to achieve through their resistance in solidarity with gay and lesbian members of their communities was an obvious reflection of the Gospel messages of love, acceptance, and reconciliation (Holtmann 2008; Murphy 2022; Ó'Murchú 1997).

CONCLUSION

As the sisters' remarks in this chapter have made evident, the Church's entrenched attempts to secure compulsory heterosexuality, and women religious' efforts to counter such exclusion and exploitation, have remained contentious. Until very recently, the Church continued to actively reprimand sisters for their pro-equality initiatives (Fraga 2021; Schenk 2022; Yeagle 2022), and, given recent moves across the US, and now across Canada, to restrict access to trans-affirming health care and education around sexual health, diversity, racism, and reproductive autonomy, we do not underestimate the need for renewed commitment to resistance and struggle. Cultural attitudes around 2SLGBTQI+ people and families may have shifted towards acceptance in some respects in recent years, but this progress is not inevitable and is constantly being challenged. Despite papal gestures towards non-judgmental inclusivity and the decriminalization of gay people and relationships by states – including Pope Francis's 2021 recognition of Sister Jeannine Gramick's New Ways Ministry and his 2023 consideration of blessing people in same-sex unions – the Roman Catholic Church, including some of its most conservative cardinals, continues to stigmatize gay and lesbian people in the strongest of terms through canonical constraints, mixed messages, and hypocritical practices (Fraga 2021; Gibson 2016; Hunt 2024; Mayer 2014; McElwee 2016a; San Martín 2018; Schenk 2022; The Associated Press 2023; Thomson Reuters 2024; Traina 2018; Wexler 2016; Yeagle 2022).[13] By contrast, along with their oppositional outlooks, the women religious featured herein have intentionally sought to move far past the convent rules that once prohibited "particular friendships" by initiating and modelling life-giving inclusivity (Murphy 2022; Faulkner and MacDonald 2009) – a testament to how far many sisters and their religious communities have progressed in their acceptance and, in the words of Sister Ella, in their honouring of sexual diversity.

Epilogue

Christine Gervais and Amanda Watson

What women are prepared to do so courageously (and in the eyes of many, so outrageously) is precisely the decisiveness which we all need if we are to bring about a better world for humanity and for our planet.

Ó'Murchú (1997, 111)

Since this book's opening account of a six-year-old girl's defiance against the Church's patriarchal power, we have illustrated wide-ranging instances of resistance on the part of women religious. The sisters' counternarrative throughout this book was itself a form of resistance as their insightful perspectives not only challenged stereotypical assumptions of nuns, but also called attention to the harm caused by many Church tenets and societal attitudes, as well as to the discrepancies between the Church's teachings and its practices (Heyder 2022). In doing so, they have tried to usher the Church into a new age of reckoning.

While the sisters endured multiple forms of gendered, economic, and political oppression within and beyond the Church, their counternarratives show how they persistently engaged in individual and collective resistance against dominant normative religious and societal practices (Chittister 2004; Holtmann 2008; Johnson 2002a; Murphy 2022; Romey 2023). Whether they were as spirited and outspoken as the six-year-old who eventually became a nun, or strategically soft-spoken, subtle, and stealthy with their subversive strategies, they navigated personal, institutional, and societal experiences of both subjugation and resistance in inspiring ways. As such, these chapters may serve as a handbook for those who are navigating and countering oppressive institutions and individuals that threaten the autonomy and well-being of those most marginalized in our communities today.

Imperative and timely issues emerged in trustworthy interview conversations with the women – issues that rarely, if ever, surface publicly among sisters in Canada. Of particular importance were their incisive critiques against the patriarchal and hierarchical underpinnings of the Roman Catholic Church, which were often disclosed passionately. Although Canadian women religious have addressed widespread social issues in public forums, making visible their resistance (Holtmann 2008), their challenges against Church policies have not been openly broadcast; partly out of fear of repercussions (Brock 2010), the sisters have tended not to confront them as publicly or as vociferously as their counterparts elsewhere (Bonavoglia 2006; Chittister 1995; Reed 2004; Wexler 2016). This more discreet style of resistance may in part be related to feelings of ambivalence when it comes to how to live a life of Catholic service while meeting the needs of community that require breaking one's loyalty to the Church (Holtmann 2008; Ó'Murchú 1997). Yet, such tempered conduct should not be misperceived as inactivity on their part. As we have shown, many sisters advanced sharp criticisms, often directly against priests and bishops, while others sought to shape institutional change by calling for legal, language, and policy reforms within and beyond the Church – all of which clearly reflects women's resistance (Faulkner and MacDonald 2009, 12). In fact, it is in such behind-the-scenes spaces where they have had to bear the brunt of the blowback from the Church hierarchy; as some nuns confirmed, priests and bishops sought to "put us in our place" (Sister Kelly) and are still "trying to keep their thumb on us" (Sister Sophie).

Like members of the women's movement decades earlier in both secular and religious settings (Faulkner and MacDonald 2009; Osiek 1986), the sisters' twenty-first-century recounting of their own resistance against patriarchal domination can be seen as part of ongoing conscientization efforts (Brock 2010; Heyder 2022; Ó'Murchú 1997). The fact that feminist and social justice efforts are as urgent three decades into the twenty-first century is indisputably concerning (Hunt 2024; Schneiders 2013; Romey 2022). Yet, women religious persist against "the vehemence with which the Vatican seeks to silence [their feminist] questions" (Ruether 2003, 11) and the clergy's ongoing efforts to delegitimize their women-centred initiatives (Chittister 2014; Schneiders 2021). Given the extent of such misogynist manoeuvres, we think that the sisters' persistence shows their remarkable hope for a more just future (Johnson 2014).

Indeed, for the injustice raised by the sisters herein to be addressed and ultimately prevented, substantial transformations are required on various fronts where discrimination and exclusion endure, including in the areas of canon law, religious rituals, clerical attitudes, institutional policies, societal stances, and research and media (under) representations (McPhillips and McEwan 2022; Murphy 2022). As multi-generational authors, our reflections on the possibilities and limitations of transforming institutions from within will continue beyond the publication of this book. We are indebted to many courageous feminist scholars, authors, and activists before us[1] and hope that this willingness to resist in the face of deepening threats continues to move feminist projects along. In this spirit, we echo the sisters' and others' calls for ongoing feminist and social justice research and action in which women's voices are validated, their experiences legitimized, and their rights prioritized over oppressive patriarchal systems.[2]

As Broz and Flynn (2006), as well as Chittister (2004), Holtmann (2008), and Manning (2002), have urged, as women, we must pay attention, speak the truth, challenge the status quo, and advance difficult conversations. We recognize simultaneously that by telling the stories of a particular group of feminist and social justice–leaning women religious, and arguably a relatively privileged one (Romey 2023), there are stories that remain untold in this book – stories that continue to be suppressed by the very institution we examine.[3] We are particularly mindful of those who have been tormented by the actions or inactions of women religious, and of others who continue to be harmed and haunted by the colonial, patriarchal, and hierarchical structures of the Roman Catholic Church and other Christian churches.[4] Neither women religious nor men clerics can simply "[pack] up their privilege and [slip] out the back" (Rastello 2023a; Payne 2021). Rather, they must confront the patriarchal and colonial expansion in which they have been complicit in pursuit of accountability and de-colonial practices (Kinew 2017; Michaelson 2021) – beginning with listening openly to learn, understand, and commit to long-term action (Heyder 2022; Wilson-Raybould 2022; Voices of Faith 2018).[5]

Signs of progress are evident in papal gestures towards inclusivity in the areas of reconciliation (Winfield 2023), pastorality of doctrine (Gaillardetz 2023), sexual inclusion (The Associated Press 2023), and the most recent synod (Giangravé 2023), but there is still cause for concern on multiple fronts because, both canonically and institutionally, little has changed (Chittister 2023; Hertzler-McCain 2024; Romey 2023; White 2024a). While shifts in papal tone may deserve recognition, without changes in Church teachings, they are ultimately inconsequential, and will likely remain so given the extent to which sexism is entrenched in the Church's structure (Murphy 2022; Ó'Murchú 1997), including its "flow chart" (Bruni 2015). In fact, some patriarchal constraints have been re-entrenched canonically, and thus major obstacles towards inclusion and genuine healing remain in the areas of women's full participation and ordination, reproductive justice, and sexual inclusion, as well as reparation for and prevention of clerical abuse (Hunt 2024).[6]

Other related barriers that many sisters mentioned include how younger generations of priests with ultra-patriarchal and traditional leanings have led to disappointing setbacks in parishes, whereby parishioners of varying ages, genders, identities, and roles have been disparaged and ostracized, often to the point of withdrawal from their parish and the Church. Mildred contextualized what Sisters Agnes, Joelle, Penelope, and Rita, among others, had also concernedly mentioned:

> I feel more frustration in the way these young men, so-called leaders, hold back the growth of people and they act as tyrants in some ways. They're an obstacle to the growth and the sad part is that unconsciously, they think they are doing a good job because the training is so bad. And so, if you can backtrack on that, there's where the problem is.

This trend among younger priests is alarming, though exceptions continue to inspire. An observation of one such exception by the primary author around the time of writing offers hope for greater respect of women's contributions in the Church. In the spring of 2023, Christine Gervais was invited to give a talk to a group of Catholic women at their final meeting prior to the summer break at which special awards for years of service were being granted. As is typical of many such meetings, a priest was present. In this case, the priest was relatively young, and comparatively, the women's respective decades of *volunteer* service to the Roman Catholic Church far outnumbered his years of *paid* service.

By all accounts, many young priests within his cohort have reputations for archaic patriarchal practices, but the young priest in attendance that evening had distinguished himself from the others by his jovial personality and inclusive approach, both of which were evident at the meeting. Two promising gestures stood out that night.

In contrast to the masculine entitlement of priests that sisters have described at women's celebrations, and that Sister Carmen had disapproved of decades ago at Catholic Women's League (CWL) meetings, this priest seemed to actively avoid being the centre of attention. In the first instance, the local group's leader had written a prayer for grace which she had offered for him to say or even replace. He respectfully declined by noting that it was hers to share since she had written it. After she said grace, she invited him to add a comment to which he simply and cheerfully replied "Amen!" Laughter ensued. Shortly thereafter, he was invited to be first in the buffet line, which he also declined by heartily clarifying that his own mother had never granted him any special treatment since he became a priest, so these women should not do so neither. Instead, he ended up being one of the last to fill his plate.

While this man's respect for women's leadership in their own meeting space may be unique to his personality, it was nevertheless refreshing as a pastoral approach, one that models an inclusive way for clergy to engage. Of course, overcoming patriarchal domination in the Church cannot depend on a few thoughtful priests, not to mention the *unlearning* of an engrained deference to patriarchy by some women in the Church. But we are heartened by these glimmers, as individual people make up the institutions that we seek to transform.

There is no doubt that *institution-building* – an oft-repeated recommendation for the advancement of women's rights (Kerr 1993) – is a warranted strategy given the pervasive exclusion of women in the Church, but it is daunting in this setting. As an institution, the Church has repelled such *building*, and thus has been painfully slow to change (Chittister 2023; Coco 2013). Thus, echoing Broz and Flynn (2006), for some current and former sisters (Darlene, Naomi, Noreen, Maureen, and Mildred), institution-*crumbling* in the case of the Roman Catholic Church offers a more desirable path, in the hopes that "more room for women" could be made (Darlene) and that "the new can come out of the ashes" (Mildred). Such a radical and arguably abolitionist outlook is indicative of how women religious can and do "resist dominant practices … in favour of more fluid, resistant and life-giving strategies to enable change in their own lives" (Faulkner and MacDonald 2009, 11), and in the lives of other women and marginalized groups.[7]

Such life-giving strategies – pursuing leadership roles for women, supporting women's reproductive health, embracing loving relationships across sex and gender, organizing in grassroots ways for social justice with marginalized communities, and protecting women and children from violence at the hands of priests – as forms of resistance make way for women's self-determination:

> I believe that's how the changes are going to come in the Church ... We find ways to work around it. (Sister Loretta)

> If we want to have a ... service ourselves, we will ... we don't need a priest to be present for it ... and you just don't inform the ... hierarchy that those kinds of things are happening ... we have the freedom to do so. (Sister Penelope)

> We're called to be ... midwives of new ways ... I feel called to ... new things and moving forward. (Sister Adele)

In the decade since they spoke about these alternatives, activists, survivors, and journalists have pushed Church abuses even more into the broader public consciousness. We wonder if the sisters might be even more emphatic today given the ongoing scandals of the Catholic Church, as well as the powerful cultural reckonings brought on by the #MeToo, Idle No More, Black Lives Matter, climate justice, and just economy movements that have occurred since the original interviews.

In planning for the future, most women's congregations are focusing inward on their own demise and on the logistics required to care for aging sisters, maintain or liquidate properties, downsize or close ministries, and entrust or discontinue social programs (Romey 2022; Schneiders 2021). Amid such major changes, though, many still prioritize broader societal issues, particularly ones related to sexism, racism, climate change, and socio-economic inequities via awareness, advocacy, financial assistance, and infrastructural support (Chittister 2022b).

As impressive as such priorities are among mainly Third Age women,[8] their resolve to address these priorities all while managing their institutional demise is particularly remarkable. Having intentionally carved out their own identities and initiatives beyond the Church, sisters' enterprises and spaces serve as models of their self-determination, and as such, constitute forms of resistance against patriarchal power (Faulkner and MacDonald 2009, 14; Holtmann 2008; Murphy 2022; Ó'Murchú 1997). Sister Joelle's congregation, for example, provides a unique infrastructure, a context of responsibility, and arguably a place of financial privilege (Romey 2023),[9] upon which their feminist and social justice advocacy is made possible:

> I do think the call ... now for religious is to be prophetic ... We have a network, we have supports where often lay people don't ... and so ... they can't afford to do as much ... So I think it behooves us to assume that role more and more, and I find myself willing to do so ... To speak more and more freely.

Sister Adele held a similar view of her community's competence, which she situated within the context of inevitably evolving circumstances. Echoing Sister Sandra Schneiders's (2021) contention that religious life's "corporate ministry has probably run its course" and former sister Carole Ganim's (2013) belief that "its structure ... ha[s] outlived [its] usefulness" (204), Sister Adele felt that its demise was predictable and desirable given the problematic aspects of institutionalized religious life. At the time of her interview, she focused on the potential of their cooperative capacity in the meantime:

> I don't know about our particular spirit living on. I mean I think it's the spirit of God that lives on in the whole. And so, if people forget about us, I don't know if that matters [chuckles], you know. But I think it's not about us. Right now, we're here. We're alive. I think we have lots to offer and we're doing our best to offer it ... and we're doing it in collaboration, and that's what matters. I mean, whether people remember who [we are]; it's if they feel the effects in the world, that's what matters.

Sister Adele's orientation to the spirit of what matters is inspiring. It is not only *what* the sisters prioritize, but also *how* they do so – countering patriarchal power while upholding the most meaningful tenets of their faith to serve others (Holtmann 2008; Murphy 2022). Clearly, the sisters have taken responsibility to ensure that their collective organizations, and the "alternative communities" they created within them, genuinely reflect their values (Holtmann 2011b; Ó'Murchú 1997, 115). Imagine how leadership might change under this influence. Reflecting on their relative resistance and compliance and the extent to which they have failed and succeeded in their efforts, their wisdom is a gift of knowledge to future generations on remaining steadfast and strategic in the struggle against patriarchal domination. While it is incumbent upon women religious to "lead the way" (Romey 2022), observers and activists can look to the sisters for guidance on deinstitutionalizing the Roman Catholic Church and other patriarchal institutions (Chittister 2022a, 2022b).

We recognize that for some observers, drawing on nuns for inspiration may be fraught given their religious affiliation and complicity in abuse. Like many of us who struggle with our institutional affiliations, and who are familiar with the feelings of ambivalence, alienation, or frustration that arise as a result, the sisters are uniquely situated either within or, as Sister Ella proudly noted, "on the edge" of the Church, and are well-informed about what an inclusive church can and should be (Murphy 2022). These sisters are also grappling with what it means to be leaving behind not only the Church after a lifetime of working toward inclusivity and institutional reform, but also their religious communities where such ideas were fostered and nurtured among peers. As Sister Marian reflected over ten years ago now, "We are diminishing. We're going off the scene. So our role now is, What is our legacy?" We draw inspiration from Sister Linda Romey's (2022) renewed call on nuns to lead the urgent struggle against patriarchal power in the Roman Catholic Church as the ultimate legacy project:

> There is still time for women religious to lead the way. Freeing the world of patriarchy could be a phenomenal legacy for us to leave those who come after us …
>
> Patriarchy has too many incentives for those who live by it – including churchmen – for them to want to change it on their own. That means it falls to those of us who are on the perimeter to force change …
>
> It may be too late to save the current form of religious life, but for the sake of what may emerge in generations to come, for the sake of women everywhere, for human wholeness and the survival of our world, we must end patriarchy now.

Dismantling patriarchal structures in the Church would undoubtedly "be a phenomenal legacy for [sisters] to leave" (Romey 2022), modelling for all of us how to fight for what seems impossible and resist the temptation to "[pack] up [our] privilege and [slip] out the back" (Payne 2021; Romey 2023). Throughout their interviews, the sisters radiated power and resilience through their own self-determination and collaboration (Murphy 2022), and that power can "and … must" be harnessed to "change the unchangeable" (Chittister 2004, 160). The sisters' various examples offered a nuanced model through which both privilege and powerlessness can be interwoven strategically to serve subversive ends (Gervais 2018).

In such endeavours, we hope that the sisters heed the advice they gave to other women over ten years ago when the primary author asked them how women can and should articulate their own feminist positions:

If you believe in something, stand up for it. (Sister Josephine)

Speak out. Don't be intimidated. (Sister Mabel)

Such calls to question and act echo decades-old pleas by the renowned Sister Joan Chittister, who warned: "Don't be afraid to speak ... Be afraid what will happen to the whole truth if you don't" (Chittister 2012, 101).[10] Chittister and other outspoken sisters quoted throughout offer such mantras for our own and others' inevitable sense of ambivalence as we navigate complex patriarchal institutions and hierarchies in our lives.

We close this epilogue with a reminder to ourselves and readers that efforts to shape an inclusive Church are not solely the responsibility of women religious. We have relied on the feminized unpaid and devalued caring and organizing work to our own disempowerment for far too long. Clearly men of the Church who have lived on the purchase of gendered labour bear this responsibility.[11] It will be a long path of unlearning for the clergy who must let go of the institutional Church's "medieval mind[set]" and of the patriarchal and hierarchical structures that have benefited them but have stifled them too (Chittister 2023). When churchmen learn to step aside so that others, especially women, can work in solidarity as equals (Holtmann 2008), they might realize what is offered to everyone in "reset[ting] the table" together (Sprows Cummings 2018). We hope that those with privilege, especially men, will be inspired to do this work and seek the communion that comes from fully listening to, and actually "learning to learn" from, the people who resist their oppression – thus, not only from women religious and other lay women (Chittister 2004, 165),[12] but also from that tiny six-year-old girl who knew back in the 1940s, as well as from Indigenous leaders in Canada who continue to remind us into the 2020s, that love, not wrath nor fear nor exclusion, should centre our human activities.[13] It is from that awareness that are sown, and have always been sown, the seeds of respect, dignity, compassion, freedom, and equality for all.

Notes

PREFACE

1 The convoy emerged in reaction to COVID-19 pandemic-related restrictions.
2 Beyond CBC News and other news outlets, we also draw on other sources including the *National Catholic Reporter*, *Global Sisters Report*, FutureChurch, Benetvision, etc. We are aware of the specific orientations of these sources of information and opinion.

INTRODUCTION

1 The sister who shared this childhood account asked that her identity not be affiliated with this story; thus, to further protect her anonymity, we do not reveal her pseudonym either.
2 In this instance, a "missionary priest" refers to a Church cleric who would visit parishes on "Mission Sunday" and/or during a week-long "missions" period (often during Lent) in which he would give sermons intended to reinforce local pastors' messages and/or offer an external perspective on Church-related topics, all of which were designed to encourage a commitment to reflect on particular pre-selected theological or evangelical themes. Being a member of a foreign missions society was not a prerequisite for priests visiting parishes for this purpose. Thematic emphases during such "missions" in parishes varied over time and were shaped by pre- and post–Vatican II priorities.
3 The capitalized terms "Roman Catholic Church," "Catholic Church," and "Church" are used interchangeably as they represent the official institutional Church, and particularly its Romanized and thus formalized form. The term "church" in lower case refers to a church building, as well

as to wider conceptions and non-institutionalized forms of religious gatherings and practices (Chittister 2004; Johnson 2002b; Wittberg 1994; Winter 2002). Our use of the capitalized version of "Church" is intended only for the purpose of clarifying these distinctions; it does not imply that we think that the institutional Church warrants capitalization because it is more important; in fact, the capitalization is in some ways a rhetorical reflection of how the Church hierarchy itself attributes and expects that prominence. For more on how these distinctions are manifested in religious practices among women religious, see Gervais and Turenne Sjolander (2015) and Johnson (2002b).

4 Not only is the gendered dimension significant, but so too is the age difference. A female child challenging a male adult, be it publicly or privately, either within or outside a church, was certainly rare in the early 1940s.

5 "Women religious" is the term scholars use to refer to vowed women in the Catholic tradition who are commonly known as "sisters" or "nuns" (Smyth 2007, 8). While we recognize the distinctions among them, we use "woman religious" and "sister" and "nun" interchangeably.

6 That the two influences in this instance are both "father" figures is not to be overlooked given the patriarchal structures of both the Church and family systems that have been mutually reinforcing throughout history. Nevertheless, it is essential to acknowledge that not all priests are "hell, fire and brimstone" preachers, nor do all fathers within families exert their patriarchal power, as was made evident by this future sister's recollection of her father's educational and empowering approach.

7 We intentionally chose "equity" over "gender equality" to reflect how sisters have not only sought to promote and facilitate gender equality for girls and women, including themselves (Thompson 2021), but they have also worked tirelessly, particularly in more recent decades, to address structural and societal conditions that affect variously marginalized populations. Given that some of their efforts have focused not only on equal opportunities, but also, and more so, on fairness, the term "equity," compared to "equality," constitutes a more accurate representation of some of their social justice endeavours. Relevant examples are clarified throughout this book's chapters. Furthermore, one would assume that such dual devotions (Catholicism and equity) should be complementary and mutually reinforcing, given the fundamental premise of Jesus-informed Christian and Catholic teachings that sisters herein align with; however, institutionally they have not been, and in fact, they have been rather paradoxical, and downright damaging as a result (Chittister 2004;

Johnson 2002a; Schneiders 2013; Gervais 2018; see also, for example, Holtmann 2008, 217, on women's complex relationship with "a church that has taught us to recognize injustice, yet refuses to reform").

8 Or at the very least problematize and nuance the stereotypes – many of which have been depicted and perpetuated through mediatization – that ultimately influence the unique hold that sisters and their convents have had on the "cultural imagination" (Sullivan 2007, 103), including the mid-1960s American sitcom *The Flying Nun* and the early 2020s British detective series *Sister Boniface Mysteries*, whose storyline is set in the 1960s.

9 Such clarification is particularly important for multiple reasons. First, we have been reminded recently of how "resistance" is even more widely understood, given the currently popularized military and civilian "resistance" in Ukraine against the Russian invasion in 2022. Second, the notion of resistance is further muddled in the context of the so-called "Freedom Convoy" and its troubling and discriminatory implications across Canada in 2022. Third, it is essential to understand and recognize resistance in all its forms, given how both past and current acts on the part of nuns have been dismissed and demonized by patriarchal powers both within and beyond the Catholic Church (Chittister 2004); thus, our illustrations herein serve to acknowledge and appreciate sisters' acts of resistance as credible and constitutive, given how they are often aimed at generating structural transformations and improving the lived realities of marginalized populations.

10 Consider the roles that nuns played in subjugating Indigenous Peoples to maintain a colonial and white supremacist order in the Americas (Burns 1999; Williams 2022) and in the conditioning of gendered control across various institutions, including the Magdalene laundries (CBC Radio 2014, 2017; McPhillips and McEwan 2022; O'Malley 2016; Gott 2021, 2022; Titley 2006). For more on how nuns variously experience and exert power, and are thus considered both handmaids of and contributors to patriarchal control, see McPhillips and McEwan (2022), who draw parallels between nuns and the characters in Margaret Atwood's *The Handmaid's Tale*, first published in 1985.

11 For an expanded clarification of these resistance strategies, see Ó'Murchú (1997, 113–15).

12 According to Burke's (2012) interpretation of Avishai's (2008) distinctions, whereas resistance agency emphasizes women's efforts to oppose and transform elements of their religion, empowerment agency refers to women's reinterpretation of religious tenets and practices to enable their empowerment. In her critiques of the concepts of agency and in her

reconsideration of feminist projects, Burke (2012) shares Mahmood's (2009, 2012) view that resistance agency is limited insofar as it does not consider compliant women as agentic, and it problematically assumes that women inevitably oppose gender-traditional religious practices. She thus points to other forms of agency (including instrumental and compliant), and even non-agency, to demonstrate the ranges of women's complex engagement with religious practices (Avishai 2008). Nevertheless, given our focus on resistance, we draw selectively on Murphy's (2022) utilization of Avishai's (2008) and Burke's (2012) concept of resistance agency, given that it remains applicable to many of the sisters' views and actions featured herein. Still, we support Burke's (2012) proposal for future feminist sociological studies to consider the varied meanings of both agency and non-agency across a range of religious contexts, including gender-traditional ones. Moreover, where applicable, we remain open to Mahmood's (2006, 2009, 2012) analyses of agency because they consider the complex interplay between resistance and compliance, which is often reflective of nuns' experiences within the institutional Roman Catholic Church (Burke 2012; McPhillips and McEwan 2022).

13 While Munn and Bruckert's (2010) conceptions originally applied to prisoners' resistance, their clarifications and exemplifications are relevant to other contexts in which resistance occurs. Their proposed strategies and tactics of resistance are clarified both in footnotes and in the text at the outset of chapter 1.

14 For more on the study's methodological considerations, see Gervais (2018, 11–18).

15 In the years since the original interviews, some of the participants served again, and thus at very advanced ages, on their congregation's leadership teams.

16 Some of the sisters referred to "new age" movements and practices, reflecting a broad range of alternative spiritual beliefs (e.g., cosmology) and healing practices (e.g., yoga, Reiki, meditation) that have been popularized since the 1970s. Despite their controversial appeal and their unconventional status, new age practices are documented herein as they reflect women religious' evolving societal and spiritual encounters.

17 As cited in Bornat and Russell (2004).

18 When Pope Francis replaced Pope Benedict XVI in 2013, an ominous cloud of conservative control over the Church seemed to have been lifted.

19 2SLGBTQI+, the acronym used by the Government of Canada at the time of writing, stands for two-spirit, lesbian, gay, bisexual, transgender, queer, intersex, and diverse sexual communities using additional terminologies.

20 Such critics include Miriam Duignan, co-director of Women's Ordination Worldwide, as quoted in Giangravé (2023).

21 Such advocacy involved the sustained efforts of grassroots organizations including FutureChurch and the Women's Ordination Conference, as confirmed by those organizations' leaders Deborah-Rose Milavec and Kate McElwee respectively (Hertzler-McCain 2023).

22 Further details about the canonical re-codification in 2021 are found in this book's chapter on ordination.

23 Not unlike the manipulation wielded by other politically, economically, and socially powerful men with similar allegations and convictions against them who also attempt to cover up their abuse and deflect potential prosecution and evade accountability.

24 In May 2024, Pope Francis publicly apologized for his use of a homophobic slur in a private meeting at the Vatican (Thomson Reuters 2024). It is alleged that he used the same slur again a couple of weeks later in June (White 2024b). Critics questioned if the comments were errors in judgment at this late stage in his papacy or a reversion to outdated and unchanged Church doctrine that continues to deviantize homosexuality (Shine 2024).

25 The issues cited from Stefanovich's 2022 article are based on insights shared by Natan Obed, president of the Inuit Tapiriit Kanatami. It is also important to note that the Roman Catholic Church has not even remotely reached the degree of accountability required in relation to its role with residential schools, mainly because of its long history of denials, cover-ups, withholding information, manipulating its accounts to evade financial responsibility, and so on.

26 The issues cited from these articles are based on insights shared by former member of Parliament, Truth and Reconciliation Commission commissioner, Grand Chief of Treaty 6 Nation, and residential school survivor Dr Wilton Littlechild, and former Canadian senator and chair of the Truth and Reconciliation Commission Murray Sinclair. It is also important to clarify that in the first apology on Canadian soil on 25 July 2022, Pope Francis did not mention sexual abuse when he referred to the harms inflicted against Indigenous children in residential schools, nor did he recognize the institutional Church in its entirety as being responsible for the abuses, as was expected from the Truth and Reconciliation Commission of Canada; instead, he referred to some individual Church members (Bergen 2022). In later speeches or homilies (i.e., in Ste Anne de Beaupré, Quebec, and in Iqaluit, Nunavut), he referred to sexual abuse, and he used other wording ("by not just a few Catholics") to convey greater accountability

on the part of the Church, but he still stopped short of communicating full institutional responsibility (CBC News 2022; CPAC 2022).

27 The issues cited in these news articles are based on commentaries provided by Phil Fontaine and Natan Obed.

28 Considering that it constitutes the basis for the Church's colonial violence against Indigenous Peoples, we intentionally draw on an Indigenous source of knowledge and advocacy to explain the Doctrine of Discovery in extended detail: "The Doctrine of Discovery emanates from a series of Papal Bulls (formal statements from the Pope) and extensions, originating in the 1400s. Discovery was used as legal and moral justification for colonial dispossession of sovereign Indigenous Nations, including First Nations in what is now Canada. During the European 'Age of Discovery,' Christian explorers 'claimed' lands for their monarchs who felt they could exploit the land, regardless of the original inhabitants. This was invalidly based on the presumed racial superiority of European Christian peoples and was used to dehumanize, exploit, and subjugate Indigenous Peoples and dispossess us of our most basic rights. This was the very foundation of genocide. Such ideology led to practices that continue through modern-day laws and policies" (Assembly of First Nations 2018, 2; Edward 2014). For more on how the Doctrine of Discovery provided a justification for the domination of Indigenous children in residential schools, including threats and harms against them by nuns and priests, see Michaelson (2023).

29 As this manuscript was being written, the world witnessed Afghanistan being taken over (again) by the Taliban, which resulted in repression against all its citizens, and especially against girls and women, who lost countless gains, including access to public, educational, and employment spaces (The Associated Press 2022b). Concerns have also been expressed about the implications for South Korean girls and women of the anti-feminist stance of the new South Korean president (Rashid 2022). In addition to widespread devastation, the Russian invasion of Ukraine involved sexual violence against women, and it led to the differential treatment of racialized refugees fleeing into neighbouring countries (The Associated Press 2022a; United Nations 2022a, 2022b).

30 As seen in 2022 with the overturning of *Roe v. Wade* in the United States, and in some instances, even in the most literal (i.e., military) sense, as seen with the Russian invasion of Ukraine.

31 There are several instances of nuns' contemporary resistance on display around the world, and they must be acknowledged and contextualized; for example, see generally *Global Sisters Report* (http://www.

globalsistersreport.org), and specifically Sister Ann Rose Nu Tawng, Myanmar's famed kneeling nun (UCA News 2022).

CHAPTER ONE

1 In their original and colonial form, "foreign missions" typically consisted of women and men religious engaging in evangelizing endeavours in conjunction with charitable contributions in other countries. The Church's clergy typically directed nuns to set up foreign missions; given their vow of obedience, sisters rarely had any agency over such assignments.

2 For example, missions carried colonizing agendas of the missionaries' home nations, and sought to convert to Christianity those perceived as an uncivilized population. In particular, their evangelizing efforts were imbued with a perceived superiority of a white, Christian, and Eurocentric culture relative to that of the local or originating peoples. In Canada, the damage of domestic missionary work carried out under such pretences was most recently spotlighted in 2021 and 2022 by the confirmation of unmarked graves of Indigenous children, forced to attend residential schools and often subjected to abuse by both men and women Church staff (McCue 2022). Since a full critique of the undeniably problematic context of religious foreign missions is beyond the scope of this chapter, for more details in this regard, including the ways in which evangelization was orchestrated under charitable pretences, see Chin (2003), Rutherdale (2003), and Scott (2005).

3 See Val Marie Johnson (2019), "'I'm sorry now we were so very severe': 1930s Colonizing Care Relations between White Anglican Women Staff and Inuvialuit, Inuinnait, and Iñupiat People in an 'Eskimo Residential School.'"

4 Specific demographic and country-specific details are withheld to protect the women's identities. Of the thirty-two women interviewed, eleven volunteered officially and/or for extended periods of time, while nine others visited their communities' foreign missions either as leadership representatives or as peers supporting their colleagues' work.

5 Sister Maureen's involvement in Latin America was in support of development initiatives with her congregation's associates; Naomi's involvement in Africa occurred after she left religious life.

6 For more on how these missionary projects are variously understood both within and beyond the contested concept of educationalization, as well as within the context of sisters' encouragement of grassroots democratization, see MacDonald (2019).

7 While often the sisters articulated this shift as a conscious transition, one cannot ignore the impact of the pressing conditions in which they carried out their missionary work in drawing their attention to human rights issues. For instance, Sister Maureen, who worked in a Latin American country, discovered the disappearances of women through her work in preschool education, and subsequently drew Amnesty International's attention to the issue.

8 While Naomi's example may be critiqued as white saviourism, it indicates how the women's conceptualization of "protest" falls on a spectrum whereby some considered it to be frontline support (e.g., empowerment initiatives), while for others it implied social movement activism (e.g., marches).

9 Despite these positive contributions, we acknowledge the past abuses perpetrated by women religious in the context of education, such as their complicity in the harms against Indigenous children in Canada's residential school system and their lack of reparations in that regard (McCue 2022; Nakonechny 2021; Finkel 2006; Truth and Reconciliation Commission of Canada 2015a, 2015b, 2015c).

10 Munn and Bruckert (2010) outline three strategies of resistance, each with their own sets of tactics and helpful skills and competencies. "Subversive" strategies tend to be more covert or subtle means of sabotaging the activities of the powerful (145). "Contestation" is defined as "an overt challenge based on negotiation, ability to reason and discursive strategies" (143). Lastly, "counterforce" strategies tend to be more bold, direct, and, for lack of a better word, *forceful* than strategies of contestation and subversion (144).

11 Such solidarity efforts may also now be considered as a form of allyship in which sisters sought to amplify voices and to use their privilege to support marginalized groups' activities. We recognize how Ó'Murchú's (1997) reference to conscientization parallels that of Freire and Gutiérrez; as such, the sisters' late-twentieth- and early-twenty-first-century applications of this form of resistance may be seen as part of their ongoing engagement with liberation theology in the present day.

12 Liberation theology emerged from the work of Father Gustavo Gutiérrez in Peru in the late 1960s (see *A Theology of Liberation* by Gutiérrez, published in English in 1973 following the 1971 publication in Spanish which had developed over several years). His philosophy questions the hegemonic understandings of the Church's role in traditional charitable and evangelical work, and refocuses the "meaning of Christian living" to one committed to working in solidarity with the poor for the end of

the social and economic inequalities as the conditions of their suffering, rather than the short-termed mitigation of the signs and symptoms of poverty (Peña 1994, 37; Bruno-Jofré and Jofré 2015; Keeley 2016; O'Kane 2003). For a woman's account of a perceived papal silencing of liberation theology in action, see Gretchen Raydems-Schils's story in Wexler (2016, 141).

13 The Vatican II documents *Gaudium et Spes*, *Lumen Gentium*, and *Perfectae Caritatis* were particularly influential in sisters' mid-to-late-1960s reconsiderations as they responded "to the call by Pope John XXIII for a renewed mission in Latin America" (Bruno-Jofré 2007; Bruno-Jofré and Jofré 2015; Coburn 2015; Foisy 2012; Foley 2015; MacDonald 2019; Rogers 1998; Schneiders 2009; Thompson 2016b).

14 The Medellín documents emerged from the Conference of Latin American Catholic Bishops at Medellín, Colombia, in 1968, which propelled a shift within the Catholic Church in Latin America towards liberation theology and socio-economic justice. Bruno-Jofré, MacDonald, and Smyth (2017) contend that the Medellín documents served as an important inspiration for religious congregations working in that geographic region.

15 As mentioned, the contexts within which the sisters engaged in social justice practices were often fraught with complex, precarious, and interrelated social, economic, and political issues. These circumstances often produced moral grey zones that were difficult to navigate and in which it was hard to advocate for one particular perspective. For example, whereas many other citizens and even other sisters from Sister Penelope's community joined a boycott against the Coca Cola company for its problematic role in human rights and labour issues in the Latin American country where she served, she refused to participate in the boycott because of the company's sponsorship of certain events and development projects in the town in which she worked.

16 Formation involves the discernment process that one follows in preparation for their commitment to religious life, including the initial postulancy, and then novitiate training which culminates in the professing of final vows (*Global Sisters Report* n.d.).

17 Despite the movement within the Catholic Church as a result of Vatican II, both the employment of liberation theology and the social justice activism of women religious were not unanimously embraced nor, in some cases, even tolerated by the clergy or laity (Bruno-Jofré and Jofré 2015; Keeley 2016; Peña 1994).

18 In Judith's quotation, "chapter" refers to the governance-based meetings held by women religious communities every few years.

19 Capitalized words and expressions in the quotes signal that the women emphasized the terms through raised voices or stronger intonations.
20 See, for example, Ortiz (2002) and Keeley (2016).
21 Similar to other Canadian religious congregations, the sisters herein took their missionary training – both pre-travel and on-site – very seriously (MacDonald 2019).
22 We acknowledge the privileged position and relative safety from which Sister Shannon and her peers benefited as foreigners in this situation, including the moments of laughter.
23 As we show later, she seemingly introduced another tactic of contestation by enlisting the solidarity and support of the community.
24 Given how many of Sister Josephine's reported actions are indicative of multiple strategies, either concurrently or consecutively, and sometimes subversion and counterforce appeared to be operating simultaneously through her actions, Munn and Bruckert's (2010) resistance model may be imagined as more circular than linear, showing the multiplicity of resistance efforts.
25 Here, we are equating counterforce with activism. But subversion and contestation from Munn and Bruckert's (2010) model may also be considered forms of activism.
26 Judith is referring to the self-immolation of Jan Palach on 16 January 1969 during the uprisings against the Soviet Union's 1968 invasion of Czechoslovakia. Palach died from his injuries three days later on 19 January 1969 (not 1968 as Judith stated). For more information, see Blažek, Eichler, Ježek, Nachmilnerová, Šerých, and Šulc (n.d.).

In Spanish, the JEC refers to Juventud Estudiantil Catolica; in English it is known as the Youth Movement of Young Catholic Students; for more information on the JEC within the Catholic Action movement, see Peña (1994, 39).
27 Historically, a convent, especially one that housed both the main residence and the central administration offices, including those of the mother superior, was referred to as a "motherhouse."
28 Hence, as already noted, a circular version of Munn and Bruckert's (2010) model that illustrates the interconnection of resistance strategies rather than a pyramid model may be more analytically relevant.
29 For more on the psychological and emotional costs of nuns' resistance, including alienation, see Brock (2010).
30 We acknowledge that there are elements of othering and privilege in Sister Noreen's last comment in this quote; they should be understood within the context of both a complex political climate and personal health circumstances.

31 In noting this shift, we do not imply that the sisters' later work was not infused with white saviourism. Some of their early-twenty-first-century reflections fell short of acknowledging their own privileges and white-saviourist desires, and of engaging in Cole's (2012) expectation of "constellational thinking" on a range of global issues.

32 See further details about the survey in which such a statement was included in the "Advocacy" section in chapter 2.

33 See Titley's (2017, 4) critique against an overemphasis on "heroic personal sacrifices" in relation to nuns' "achievements."

CHAPTER TWO

1 We acknowledge that their initial social justice work may not be considered resistance. While in some cases its qualities of resistance are very apparent, in others, it remains more "humanitarian" and edges away from activism.

2 While, in this chapter, we emphasize women religious' accomplishments, we neither deny nor minimize Catholic sisters' complicity in oppressive operations in health care, social work, and education (Titley 2006, 2017). Previously and throughout this book, we acknowledge the roles that sisters played in gendered conditioning (Thompson 2021) and moral obedience in all sectors (Gervais 2018; Gervais and Watson 2014). While we fully recognize their problematic affiliation with a range of settler-colonial projects, including the abuse perpetrated by women (and men) religious in Canadian residential schools, our emphasis in this section is on the gendered implications (e.g., lack of recognition) of their roles as women vis-à-vis the Church's men-led hierarchy. To our knowledge, the women religious interviewed for this study were not directly involved in residential schools. Nevertheless, we recognize the importance of holding the entire Roman Catholic Church accountable for the undeniably systematic and institutionalized intergenerational harm it inflicted on Indigenous children, their families, and their communities in residential schools, at day schools, and during the Sixties Scoop (Manning 2002; McCue 2022; Truth and Reconciliation Commission of Canada 2015a, 2015b, 2015c). The sisters' concerns regarding abuse by representatives of the Roman Catholic Church are presented in the chapter on clerical abuse.

3 In keeping with their commitment to humble service, the women interviewed were not actually seeking "recognition" for their contributions. Thus, Sister Kelly's comment should not be perceived as either boasting or complaining. Rather, it was a well-founded critique against the patriarchal Church that has always promoted its own androcentric history without

respectfully acknowledging the contributions of others, and especially of women. As critics such as McGuinness (2013, 197) and Brock (2010) have pointed out, the men clerics could not have established such a broad institutional Church network without sisters' free labour and congregational infrastructure.

4 The visibility of women religious may be impacted by two main factors. First, while they may be present in public, they may not be recognized as nuns since most of them no longer wear habits and some may not wear the pins or pendants that represent their own religious communities. Second, given the advanced age of most sisters in Canada, many are no longer able to participate actively in public events.

5 Sisters were also among other firsts outside of Catholic traditions in Canada, including Sister Elaine MacInness, who was Canada's first Zen Buddhist roshi (master) who taught yoga and meditation in prison (Csillag 2005), as well as Sister Kay Morrell, who was reportedly Ontario's first accredited instructor of T'ai Chi Chih (Sisters of Providence of St Vincent de Paul 2005).

6 Sister Mabel reported that the centre was still in operation at the time of her interview in 2009.

7 See chapter 4 on women's ordination in this book for a brief discussion of the systematic religious discrimination and legal barriers that Catholic women religious still face regarding ordination as either priests or deacons.

8 For more on the Church's exploitation of nuns' "wageless labour," see Brock (2010) and Titley (2017).

9 Cesar Chavez was an American civil rights activist who championed farm labourers' rights. Naomi's reference to the lettuce boycott is related to the Salad Bowl strike organized by the United Farm Workers in the United States in the early 1970s in support of better wages and working conditions.

10 At least for those who are not already familiar with sisters' social justice activism.

11 For more information about the Nuns on the Bus, see http://www.nunsonthebus.org and Wexler (2016), particularly chapter 5, "Sister Simone Campbell."

12 Sister Ann Rose Nu Tawng, also known as Myanmar's famed kneeling nun, became a global icon of peace when she knelt on the street in front of police and soldiers in Myitkyina, Myanmar on 28 February 2021 (*UCA News* 2022).

13 Sisters' anti-war and anti-nuclear activism in the United States has involved them protesting against the School of the Americas (SOA;

renamed the Western Hemispheric Institute for Security Cooperation post-9/11) and other missile installations, which in some instances led to some nuns' relatively lengthy incarceration for civil disobedience, including into the twenty-first century (Reed 2004, 122; McGuinness 2013, 183).

14 The sisters' concerns and actions related to gender-based injustices are explored in Gervais (2018).

15 Not just in the economic sense, but also as it pertains to one's culture, ethnicity, class, ability, sexuality, gender, sex, and age.

16 "Action" refers primarily to the activities carried out to tangibly support marginalized people and to address their immediate needs; such social action most often takes on a charitable form (Holtmann 2011b). "Advocacy" encompasses creating awareness about issues and/or speaking with/on behalf of marginalized people (Holtmann 2011b). "Activism" involves concrete and potentially confrontational steps (e.g., protests, letter-writing, etc.) to draw attention to issues and to effect social change (Mangion 2008, 112); it bears greater similarity to the second dimension of social action that focuses on first identifying the structural sources of inequalities and then engaging in efforts to change those "unjust structures" across political, economic, and even religious terrains (Holtmann 2011b, 141). We diverged slightly from Holtmann's ordering of the concepts by featuring action before advocacy so that the latter was presented immediately before activism because we thought that the social justice– and solidarity-based elements of advocacy formed the building blocks of some of the more transformational aspects of activism.

17 The name of the drop-in centre is withheld not only to protect the identity of the sisters and their religious communities, but also to respect their wish to keep their charitable contributions anonymous.

18 The sisters have provided guidance to the staff regarding grant applications.

19 While "advocacy" and "activism" may be considered synonymous, for the sake of clarity, "advocacy" refers to awareness-oriented activities, whereas "activism" refers to political engagement, including open critique and public protest.

20 The survey response statements are included verbatim; however, the title and full reference of the document is intentionally withheld to protect the sisters' identities. These excerpts were found on pages 3–5.

21 While this critique pertains to several progressive publications, it is also directly related to a publication produced by Sister Clara to which Sister Rita refers; the concern is illustrated in the last section of this chapter on "Negotiating Pushback."

22 The statement in quotations is drawn from page 4 of the same booklet from which the realizations, critiques, and aspirations are drawn, but it remains anonymous to protect the sisters' identities.

23 While "Native spirituality" is commonly used in popular and religious discourses, and it was employed in the interviews with the women religious, to emphasize the importance of inclusivity and diversity, we employ "Indigenous spiritualities" or "Indigenous peoples' spiritual traditions," since they are more encompassing. Furthermore, while this section draws attention to positive aspects of nuns' engagement with Indigenous spiritualities, it is essential to acknowledge how some sisters in past centuries contributed to the destruction of Indigenous Peoples' spiritual traditions through residential schools and other Christian/Catholic evangelization and colonization tactics.

24 Relatedly, one of the congregations represented herein was also part of the aforementioned groups of Canadian women religious that called on Canadian bishops in the early 2000s to recognize that First Nations' experiences with the Church were "negative" and "that many in the church do not understand, nor attempt to understand and appreciate, the culture and spirituality of … Canadian First Nations." For details about the survey in which such a statement was included, see the "Advocacy" section in this chapter.

25 We acknowledge that while Sister Clara's comment is intended to reflect her critical and inclusive approach, it also conveys a sense of privilege given that those who experience racism would not find it "impossible to imagine."

26 This example was in specific reference to the Idle No More movement.

27 For more information on Percy Schmeiser's case, see Salvian (2018) and Democracy Now! (2010).

28 For more information on the International Union of Superiors General (UISG), see http://www.uisg.org/en/about/.

29 In this light, they seek to draw attention to the sacred nature of all life by focusing on the "story of the entire universe." They do so, in many instances, by promoting the Charter of Compassion and the Earth Charter.

30 The women religious herein referred to "clusters" as part of their circular forms of local governance, in which sisters formed small groups of peers of their choosing to share various responsibilities related to mutually supportive spiritual, health, and social care. For more on the origins of clusters among nuns in North America, see Ebaugh (1993); for more on how they became part of sisters' decentralized governance practices in Canada, see Gervais (2018).

31 Some women's religious communities in Ontario have even won awards for their green buildings. Their counterparts in the United States have advanced similar green building projects (McGuinness 2013, 189).

32 This wording is drawn from a sign in the kitchen of a spirituality centre that the primary author visited while conducting field work in Ontario. The full message read: "Thank you for helping us care for our lovely universe."

33 Sister Clara's anti-state stance extends to international levels of governance and applies to her advocacy for ecological and human justice since she is anti-IMF (International Monetary Fund), anti–World Bank, and anti-WTO (World Trade Organization), among other "state" governing bodies.

34 Sister Clara's subversion tactics have included pointing out absurdities in political, economic, religious, and gender-based contexts; her conscientization and contestation has entailed drawing attention to incongruities in similar contexts, as well as open engagement; and her counterforce tactics have consisted of various forms of political action, including active protests (Munn and Bruckert 2010; Ó'Murchú 1997).

35 Sister Clara's abovementioned concerns about culturally based discrimination and Sister Adele's overview of their group's approach bear some similarity to Sister Joan Chittister's post-9/11 anti-racist and pro-religious diversity call to action. Recalling the discrimination that women religious endured when wearing the "medieval habit," she encouraged sisters in her congregation and elsewhere in the United States to accompany Muslim women as they ran their daily errands in public as a gesture of support and as a measure of safety (McGuinness 2013, 196).

36 While "piques" may have been the intended term, the interview participant said "perks."

37 Analytical insight contributed by Sarah Gilliss.

38 Among many other examples, see Salgado (2022) on sisters' ongoing willingness to learn about and engage in justice-oriented and ecologically minded endeavours. See Ajiambo (2022) on how sisters contribute to the prevention of the sexual exploitation of women.

CHAPTER THREE

1 Rosalind Gill (2008) refers to "commodity feminism" to describe the extent to which the language of women's empowerment has been commodified by corporations as a marketing ploy.

2 As Romey (2022) has duly noted, as have various historians of women religious, many of the archives of women's religious congregations "contain instances of churchmen silencing ... sisters." For more on the

history of religious anti-feminism and anti-woman tactics by Roman Catholic churchmen, including the demonization of female spirituality, see Elliott (2004, 2012). For an historical overview of Christian feminism's response to patriarchy and of women's contributions to theology and Roman Catholicism, see Natalia Imperatori-Lee's *Women and the Church* (2024).

3 For a more recent theological analysis on both the tensions and synergies between feminism and Catholicism, see Julie Hanlon Rubio's *Can You Be a Catholic and a Feminist?* (2024).

4 We recognize Sarah Gilliss's contribution to this analytical observation. We also acknowledge that Sister Noreen's interpretation reflects the cautious ways in which individuals may assert agency and retain autonomy (Bruckert 2005; Murphy 2022).

5 The Leadership Conference of Women Religious (LCWR) is the association of the leaders of congregations of Catholic women religious in the United States. It is distinct from the more traditionalist Council of Major Superiors of Women Religious (CMSWR), which was not subject to the investigation carried out by the Vatican's Congregation for the Doctrine of the Faith (Clark 2012).

6 These excerpts were on pages 1–5 of the document submitted by one of the sisters' congregations represented herein. It remains anonymous to protect the sisters' identities.

7 Sister Loretta's colleague passed away before the study began so the primary author was not able to interview this sister.

CHAPTER FOUR

1 For example, girls and women have been included as acolytes, altar servers, sacristans, pastoral associates, communion ministers, readers, committee leaders, and council members, and, in some rare cases in certain forward-thinking churches, as homilists.

2 See Article 5 of Substantive Norms enforceable by the Vatican's overseer, the Congregation for the Doctrine of the Faith.

3 In the New Book VI of the Code of Canon Law, released on 1 June 2021, outlining "Penal Sanctions in the Church," under the section "Offences against the Sacraments," Can. 1379 § 3 re-iterates what was previously stated in earlier decrees and modifications to them by the Congregation for the Doctrine of the Faith in 2007, 2008, and 2010 under Pope Benedict XVI (Congregation for the Doctrine of the Faith 2012; Zagano 2021a); it specifically states that "[b]oth a person who attempts to confer

a sacred order on a woman, and the woman who attempts to receive the sacred order, incur a *latae sententiae* excommunication reserved to the Apostolic See; a cleric, moreover, may be punished by dismissal from the clerical state" (Holy See Press Office 2021). This further entrenchment of the ban against women's ordination under Pope Francis is not surprising, given how he has on a number of occasions over the years, including in 2018, reiterated Pope John Paul II's "closed door" policy on this issue (McElwee 2018; San Martín 2018).

4 Not only has such male supremacy been documented and defended since the beginning of Christianity, but its foundation can also be traced back to, and is a contemporary oppressive vestige of, religious laws of earlier millennia, including those under Judaism, all of which were, and arguably are still, intended to dismiss and dismantle Goddess religion and female deities, and to ultimately hold women – as daughters of Eve – forever haunted by, and accountable for, Eve's so-called original sin, which most people of Judeo-Christian and Islamic traditions have been conditioned to believe in from a very young and impressionable age, through the male-constructed myth of the Garden of Eden (Stone 1976, 228, 241).

5 For a historical account of the complex origin and evolution of the Catholic Church's anti-woman tactics and its criminalization of female spirituality in earlier millennia, see Elliott (2004, 2012).

6 For another example of the exclusion of women from the Church, see Lee (1996) and Roll (2003) on the churching or purification of mothers after childbirth.

7 Rather ironically, while the Ontario Human Rights Code (2019) protects against discrimination on the basis of sex and gender in the area of employment, individuals in religious offices are excluded from the protections of the Province of Ontario's *Employment Standards Act* (2000).

8 One of the reasons that religious institutions may be insulated from recent human rights gains is because their theological rules are not easily "justiciable" by the courts; for example, a case brought before the Supreme Court of Canada in 2018 involving the expulsion of an individual from a Jehovah's Witnesses congregation by the congregation's ruling committee was ruled by the Supreme Court to be "non-justiciable," on the basis that the court had no right to dispute disagreements over religious principles, including those pertaining to membership in religious organizations (Supreme Court of Canada 2018).

9 In fact, in July 2019 the Anglican Church of Canada elected its first female primate (the religious head of the Church in Canada), Archbishop Linda Nicholls (The Anglican Church of Canada 2022, par. 20).

10 The Orthodox Church in America includes the Archdiocese of Canada.

11 For an experiential account of how an elderly Canadian woman religious (Sister Mariette Milot) struggled with the prohibition of women's ordination, see the Pauline Voisard film *Je vous salue Mariette* (2010).

12 In her 1986 book *Beyond Anger: On Being Feminist in the Church*, Sister Carolyn Osiek relates the appropriateness and implications of women's anger to a range of gendered barriers in the Roman Catholic Church, one of which is women's leadership and ordination.

13 In some cases, most of the sisters had not been officially made aware of the priest's abusive past; in certain instances, while assumptions may have been made, many sisters came to know of the abuse only when charges were laid, and it was made public in the media.

14 Nuns have also struggled with hierarchically based constraints in their own institutionalized religious communities. But as we have explored elsewhere (Gervais 2018), many of the women's religious orders have established inclusive and non-hierarchical governance approaches in the late twentieth and early twenty-first centuries. For more on how other lay women have felt about women's "second-class status" within the institutional Catholic Church, particularly in relation to ordination, see Gretchen Raydems-Schils's and others' stories in Wexler (2016, 151).

15 The excerpts included here were found on pages 1–3 of the congregation's submission to the Canadian Religious Conference.

16 Among these attestations, the community of women religious also included concerns about improving the access of the laity in rural and remote areas to religious services and access to church leadership roles for married individuals and non-celibate men.

17 A doctrinal assessment is conducted by the Vatican's Congregation for the Doctrine of the Faith, which scrutinizes Church-affiliated religious groups to ensure their canonical conformity.

18 Although the Vatican defines it in positive terms, an Apostolic Visitation constitutes an intrusive investigation by delegates of the Holy See in order to investigate the policies and practices of a religious institution and compel its compliance to Catholic Church dogma. This particular visitation that began under Pope Benedict XVI's reign was followed by a monitoring period under Pope Francis's leadership which resulted in at least fifteen religious orders being summoned to Rome for further scrutiny (Araujo-Hawkins 2016; McElwee 2016b, 2016c; Stockman 2017).

19 The criminalization is canonically based within the Roman Catholic Church and is therefore not enforceable in criminal or civil justice proceedings. Nevertheless, the decree reflects how patriarchal and

hierarchal power has been constituted and reproduced through the enactment and enforcement of Canon Law. *Latae sententiae* refers to a sanction that is automatically incurred upon the commission of the offence. For other details on the sanctions, see Sub-Articles 1 and 3 of Article 5 of the Congregation for the Doctrine of the Faith's Substantive Norms. The "automatic" nature of the sentence is indicative of the extent to which the Vatican seeks to prohibit opposition. The lack of due process in these cases is undoubtedly designed strategically to silence women. It should also be noted that it is not only women who are affected by this decree. The Vatican is also punishing (e.g., excommunicating) priests and bishops who support women's ordination; see, for example, Roy Bourgeoys in the United States. Many people, including former Sister Judith, were upset about the repercussions for supportive priests: "the TERRIBLE punishments on priests who have supported that [women's ordination] are just ... inhuman."

20 See Elliott (2004) for a historical account of women's experiences "as quintessential laypersons barred from ordination and locked in an enduring position of deferential subordination" (48).

21 In addition to the long-held gendered restrictions set by Canon 1024, in the late twentieth century, both *Ordinatio Sacerdotalis*, written by Pope John Paul II in 1994, and *Responsum ad Dubium*, issued by the Congregation for the Doctrine of the Faith in 1995, not only excluded but also officially silenced women on the matter of ordination (Congregation for the Doctrine of the Faith 1995). While the 2010 decree involved the aforementioned list, it was actually in 2007 and again in 2008 that the Vatican's Congregation for the Doctrine of the Faith declared that women priests and the bishops who ordain them would be excommunicated *latae sententiae* (Congregation for the Doctrine of the Faith 2012).

22 As stated by renowned feminist author Sister Joan Chittister in a speech heard by Sister Kelly.

23 While her strong stance on resistance is quite evident in the passage to which Judith refers, the poem's ending is also suggestive of life-giving and spirituality-infused forms of resistance (Faulkner and MacDonald 2009; Holtmann 2008), and thus her reference to the poem overall was not likely coincidental: "For we have not come here to take prisoners / Or to confine our wondrous spirits, / But to experience ever and ever more deeply / Our divine courage, freedom and Light!" (Hāfiz and Ladinsky 1999, 28).

24 Judith is referring to the Vatican's controversial investigation of the Leadership Conference of Women Religious (LCWR) and the apostolic

visitation of religious orders in the United States (Chittister 2013; Kristof 2010, 2012; McElwee 2013; Schneiders 2011).

25 As the primary author has shown elsewhere (Gervais 2018), many sisters sought to move beyond this limitation by concentrating on what they perceive to be authentic Gospel lessons that emphasize Jesus's teachings.

26 The women's church group that Sister Carmen refers to in her example is the Catholic Women's League (CWL), which has traditionally consisted of a group of church-going Catholic women (in each parish) who support church and community events, often through domestic service, including the preparation of meals and cleaning for funerals, parish celebrations, and fundraisers. Such gendered labour, particularly by lay women, including women religious, is recognized by critics (Chittister 2023; Romey 2022; Schneiders 2021) as having been indispensable to the survival of the Roman Catholic Church. For more on the CWL, see http://www.cwl.ca.

27 Unfortunately, despite her personal interest in participating in such organized movements, Sister Joelle felt restrained by her institutional responsibility: "Now the women's ordination protest that happens every Thursday in a lot of places, was organized while I was in leadership, and so I didn't participate; just tactically, it wasn't the thing to do." When asked if she struggled with that choice, Sister Joelle replied, "Yah, definitely."

28 By moving forward with their own ordinations, the Roman Catholic Women Priests have intentionally and proudly "challenged and broken the Church's Canon Law 1024" because they have considered it to be "an unjust law that discriminates against women" (RCWP 2023).

29 Call to Action is a reform-based organization that originated in the United States; it calls for justice, transparency, and equality in the Roman Catholic Church; for more information on its origins and current emphases, see Call to Action (2023).

30 Women's presence at the Last Supper counters traditional and institutional Catholic teaching that maintains that only the male disciples surrounded Jesus during his final Passover meal.

31 Yet as many sisters pointed out during their interviews, they were certainly expected to serve meals to men clerics in rectories and convents. Similarly, women religious, and more recently lay women, in their service-based roles, have often been involved in the preparation of the Eucharistic gifts and the altar prior to the commencement of Mass; however, they are not allowed to be directly involved in the sacrament of the Eucharist or in the concelebration of the Mass.

32 This gender-based exclusion is also found in the Jewish tradition, where historically women prepared the Seder (Passover meal) but were never

allowed to partake in it; this deprivation led some women to adapt the Seder and create "women-centred" rituals (Broner 1999).

33 We acknowledge that a kyriarchical theological analysis may be relevant to the radical reconstruction that the sisters herein are contemplating (Holtmann 2008). Yet we do not engage in such an analytical framework. It is also important to note that none of the sisters made reference to kyriarchy in their interviews. For further clarification on kyriarchy, see Schüssler Fiorenza (2001, 2016), and Thompson (2016a). For further details related to feminist calls to move beyond the Church, see Hunt (2005), Schüssler Fiorenza (1993, 2005), and Ruether (1983, 2005), among others.

34 Sister Noreen manages the deprivation strategically – by prioritizing both her Catholic and feminist identities through her continued, albeit selective, participation in a Catholic parish. For example, in addition to detaching herself from the hierarchical institutional church, Sister Noreen is among the seven of this study's participants who have intentionally become, and have remained, parishioners in forward-thinking and inclusive parishes that enable both lay women and women religious to give homilies.

35 Advocacy organizations such as Women's Ordination Worldwide (WOW) and the Catholic Network for Women's Equality (CNWE) have broadened their mandates to reflect wider emphases and practices (Catholic Network for Women's Equality 2020; Ruether 2003). Feminist scholars have made similar points about the importance of moving beyond the priesthood; Schneiders (2004, xiv) noted that, "[f]rom a narrow focus on women's ordination from mid-1970s, the agenda has broadened and deepened ... Nothing short of the full recognition of the full humanity of all women, in family[,] society, and Church can respond to the feminist vision."

36 For more on how "creativity is unleashed when [clerical] rules are deliberately broken" or, in the sisters' case at least, when they are bent, see Elliott (2004, 7).

37 Sister Corinne's optimistic outlook in 2009 echoes that of renowned Sister Christine Schenk's 2021 reminder of women's historical role in reshaping the Roman Empire as an indicator of their potential in changing the Roman Catholic Church (Schenk 2021).

38 Sister Theresa's original prediction was correct insofar as women's ordination was not achieved during the late Pope Benedict XVI's papacy, nor in her lifetime; he resigned on 28 February 2013 and died on 31 December 2022. Sadly, Sister Theresa also passed away prior to this book's publication.

39 The announcement by Pope Francis that a commission would study the possibility of women deacons was prompted by questions and a proposal by representatives of the International Union of Superiors General at a meeting with the Pope on 12 May 2016 – a meeting at which Pope Francis had also reminded the audience of the harmful attitudes of both feminism and clericalism (Vatican Radio 2016).

40 See for example the advocacy efforts by organizations such as FutureChurch, Women's Ordination Conference, Catholic Women Preach, etc.

41 For more on women's persistence towards this progression via the "Ministry of Irritation," see Chittister (2024) and Women's Ordination Conference (2022a).

CHAPTER FIVE

1 This critique was part of the call-to-action statements that one congregation of women religious submitted as part of their responses to a mid-2000s Canadian Religious Conference survey. The statement is a testament to their awareness, anger, and alarm regarding abuse by Catholic clergy.

2 The first widely known case of extensive clerical abuse in Canada came under greater public scrutiny in 1989 upon allegations of a decades-long cover-up by state and Church officials at the Mount Cashel Orphanage in Newfoundland (Manning 2002; Catholic Church, Archdiocese of St John's 1990). Numerous other Catholic Church–related abuse scandals across North America, Europe, and Australia came to light around the same time and in the years that followed, including the *Boston Globe*'s now-infamous 2002 "Spotlight Investigation" that uncovered the extent of the abuse in the Catholic Church in the United States (*Globe* Spotlight Team 2002). Sadly, such cases continue to surface (BBC News 2021; Butler 2022; CBC Radio 2014, 2017; Cooke 2022; Gatehouse 2014; Gott 2021, 2022; Hatton 2022; Mustian 2022; O'Malley 2016; O'Riordan 2016; Queen 2019; Rukavina 2019; Whitfield 2019).

3 The media's efforts at "keeping up the pressure" have taken many forms, including ongoing news coverage of trials, civil suits, and most recently instances where Church properties are being sold to pay reparations to victims of clerical sexual abuse on the one hand (Butler 2022), while churches have been constructed when reparations to survivors of residential schools have been deceitfully avoided on the other hand (Warick 2021).

4 It is worthwhile to compare how Sister Jeanette pointed to full institutional accountability back in 2009 at the time of her interview, yet, in 2022, even after considerable pressure to do otherwise, Pope Francis's official apology ultimately fell short by not acknowledging that the Roman Catholic Church, in its entirety as an institution, was wholly responsible for the abuse suffered by Indigenous children in residential schools in Canada (Bergen 2022; Sinclair 2022).

5 We acknowledge nuns' roles in racially segregated residential, industrial, and reservation day schools designed for the "conversion and control" of Indigenous children across Canada (Gresko 2007; McCue 2022) – assimilation tactics orchestrated by the Department of Indian Affairs and across a wider Christian church system rationalized through "malevolent ideologies" including the Doctrine of Discovery (Assembly of First Nations 2018; Michaelson 2023, 82). Survivors' testimonies documented in the Truth and Reconciliation Commission of Canada's final reports on residential schools point to a range of encounters and experiences with Catholic sisters, including life-altering neglect and starvation, religious and cultural indoctrination, and emotional, physical, and sexual harms (Truth and Reconciliation Commission of Canada 2015a, 2015b, 2015c). For more on nuns' abusive roles in orphanages in Canada, see Watts (2024) and Manning (2002) in which they situate these concerns within the wider Church. For relatively recent revelations of nun-perpetrated sexual abuse against children in the United States, see Araujo-Hawkins (2021a, 2021b).

6 The extent of such backlash was also evident in allegations related to the 1969 murder of Sister Catherine Cesnik in Baltimore, Maryland, a case that became more widely known through the Netflix docuseries *The Keepers* (2017).

7 While it is by no means intended as an excuse, it is important to underscore that through the power of the vow of obedience, clergy often commanded congregations of nuns to manage residential schools. Thus, while nuns' involvement was undeniably problematic, it was also fraught with gendered coercion to which they too were subjected (Gresko 2007), and it is indicative of the patriarchal, hierarchical, and institutional power to which all involved were subjected. As a feminist historian, Gresko's emphasis in her 2007 chapter "Gender and Mission" was on the gendered subordination of sisters in the context of their involvement in residential schools in British Columbia. Di Mascio (2013) recognized that Gresko's (1975) earlier research shed light on the appalling conditions of residential schools and their life-long impacts on the former students.

8 For more on how girls' experiences of abuse by priests have been overlooked, including in media reports, see Marcel (2013).

9 Sister Penelope's frustration in 2009 with how parishioners' donations to churches have been subsidizing abusive priests' living expenses is comparable to the anger expressed by critics (both Catholics and non-Catholics) in 2022 over the Church's ongoing dependency on, and explicit expectation of, parishioners to contribute to the court-mandated compensation to residential school survivors that Church authorities themselves had evaded for far too long (Taylor 2022; Warick 2021). Her dissatisfaction is also relatable to the shock and frustration conveyed as recently as 2022 and 2024 by Catholics in Newfoundland and Labrador who have risked losing, and in some cases have lost, their parishes on account of court-ordered settlements that the Church cannot pay without selling some of its land and assets (Gillis 2022; Roberts 2024). In both instances, some parishioners are digging into their own pockets either to compensate survivors abused by priests or to buy back their parish buildings while Church leaders allow offending priests and implicated bishops to go about their lives. Nowhere in these scenarios is it apparent that abusive priests themselves are being held financially responsible, at least not on a personal level.

10 Sister Mabel could only offer counselling support to her nephew via long-distance phone calls because she was working abroad when he reached out to her for help.

11 The comparison is not intended to imply that one sister's approach is better than the other. It is simply meant to show how sisters variously negotiated their affiliation with the Church as they supported survivors and victims who were harmed by other Church officials. We are also not suggesting that Sister Sarah was seeking to avoid her affiliation with the Church. In fact, her willingness to face the survivors' frustration speaks to her attentiveness toward accountability, as a representative of the Church. It must also be understood within the context of her positive relations with Indigenous people, who reportedly trusted her with, and welcomed her into, their sacred ceremonies when she lived in a northern community.

12 Sister Adele's reflection aligns with Sister Helen Prejean's compassionate approach towards both prisoners and victims, and their relatives. For more on the complex circumstances and human consequences of criminalization, imprisonment, and the death penalty through the lens of a nun's spiritual journey, see Prejean (1994).

13 Sister Agnes's example points to one of the seemingly few cases where there are actually consequences for the abusive priests, and where parishioners' views on the matter were taken seriously by Church officials.

14 The hashtag #NunsToo in relation to the #MeToo movement has been variously applied; we draw from Wagner's (2018) use of it. We also acknowledge the importance of the wider #NunsToo movement and the role it played in drawing further attention to this issue (Colwell and Johnson 2020; McPhillips 2019; Meyer 2021; Poggioli 2019).

15 Future studies may consider how the clerical-based harms experienced by nuns are understood within the wider context of gender-based violence, and if/how there may also be commonalities with intimate partner violence.

16 As was seen in the relatively recent case involving an allegation of repeated sexual violence by a bishop against a nun in India (Kavi 2022), and in Pope Francis's 2019 admission that sexual abuse and sexual slavery of nuns by clergy was "still going on" in various parts of the world (BBC News 2019).

17 The sexual abuse to which Sister Loretta referred was perpetrated by both priests and the victims' relatives.

18 See the "A Call to Accountability" campaign (Feminist Majority Foundation Blog 2001).

19 Given how Sister Agnes's anecdote points to both sexism and ageism, it would be worthwhile for future studies to undertake an intersectional analysis of such simultaneous forms of discrimination to shed further light on their implications for women and women religious in the Roman Catholic Church.

20 Carol's reference to the woman's struggle with alcohol dependency was not intended as victim-shaming but rather to underscore the long-term and complex effects of abuse.

21 For more on women's experiences with the institutional church's misogyny, see womanist theologian Diana Hayes's critiques featured in Wexler (2016, 89).

22 For more on how Catholic sisters were involved in physical, sexual, and emotional harms against children in general, see Böhm et al. (2014); in Canada, see Manning (2002) and Watts (2024); in Ireland, see McDonald (2009) and Titley (2006); in Scotland, see Scottish Child Abuse Inquiry (SCAI) (2018); in New Zealand, see Te Rōpū Tautoko (2022a, 2022b). As McPhillips and McEwan (2022) contend, additional research on harm perpetrated by women religious is warranted.

23 In terms of the provision of care and guarantee of safety, especially in their roles as teachers and nurses.

24 We acknowledge the improvements under Pope Francis's leadership, not only in light of his apology to residential school survivors in Canada at the end of July 2022, but also given his mid-July 2022 "zero tolerance" instruction to male religious orders to "never tolerate the abuse of children" and to "end the practice of moving abusers to other countries" (Arocho Esteves 2022). Nevertheless, survivors and advocates, including the late Barbara Blaine (founder of Survivors Network of those Abused by Priests [SNAP]), have remained sceptical about reforms towards full accountability and support even under Pope Francis's leadership, and that is why they – as lay people – remain steadfast in their efforts to make the "church safer" (Wexler 2016, 138–9). For more on the potential of acts of remembrance to bring about change by bearing witness (i.e., naming abuse and identifying injustice) in the Church, see Heyder (2022).

25 Compared to the structural changes required to eradicate the race-, gender-, and age-based superiority underlying such abuses, micro-level therapeutics may be viewed as limited in their capacity for transformation. Nevertheless, we recognize that the need for, and provision of, counselling and therapy for survivors has been overlooked and underfunded for far too long and such care must be prioritized and fully funded by both Church and state entities.

26 Although some sisters interviewed did make reference to the exact opposite: the Church's very deliberate tactics to protect such assets in order to mitigate financial losses related to settlements with survivors.

27 Beyond the criminal conviction and imprisonment of priests.

28 Another, and arguably an even more literal, crumbling of sorts in relation to clerical abuse allegations may be recognized by some critics in the burning and damaging of several churches in Canada in the immediate aftermath of the confirmation of the unmarked graves at former residential schools in British Columbia and Saskatchewan in the spring of 2021 (Major 2021; Malone 2021).

29 We cannot overlook the Church's ongoing hypocrisy when it comes to children's safety and well-being; for example, in an exclusive CBS interview in May 2024, ahead of the Catholic Church's first World's Children's Day, Pope Francis referred to the importance of listening to children and of "always" taking care of them (CBS News 2024). Yet, his statement seems hypocritical considering the Church's harmful history of clerical abuse and calculated cover-ups. As such, while he advocated for children's right to be heard, his Church has not fully respected their right to be safe.

30 Advocates have been steadfast in their pursuits of truth, justice, reparation, and change. They include, but are not limited to, Concerned Lay Catholics in Canada and Survivors Network of those Abused by Priests (SNAP) in the United States, as well as wider networks such as Voices of Faith and #ChurchToo and #NunsToo activists (Colwell and Johnson 2020; Manning 2002; McPhillips 2019; McPhillips and McEwan 2022; Poggioli 2019; Wexler 2016). These efforts have been met with backlash from the institutional Church and conservative Catholics, even when they agitate for greater inclusion in the Church, not its abolition. Written over two decades ago, activist Joanna Manning's (2002, 160–1) provocative "Blueprint for the Next Pope" addressed patriarchal power and abuse and the legacy of John Paul II. This call to action is now two popes ago. Survivors deserve a much swifter response to the abuses they continue to suffer. Yet, the Church does not seem amenable to changes that challenge the patriarchal dominance established in its hierarchy.

CHAPTER SIX

1 This encyclical was issued by Pope Paul VI in 1968 and was defended by Popes John Paul II and Benedict XVI.
2 In reference to the "Brazilian girl" who had been sexually abused by her stepfather (Congregation for the Doctrine of the Faith 2009).
3 See, for examples, the Knights of Columbus 2020 "March for Life Map" (http://www.kofc.org/un/campaigns/en/march-for-life/index.html), sisters pictured at the "National March for Life" in Ottawa in 2018 (http://ipolitics.ca/2018/05/10/ipolitics-am-march-for-life-rally-set-to-take-anti-abortion-message-to-parliament-hill/), Sisters of Life anti-abortion advocates in Toronto (http://sistersoflife.org), and the Catholic Women's League anti-abortion brochure (http://www.cwl.ca/wp-content/uploads/2023/04/305-ProLife-Brochure-no-bleeds.pdf).
4 *R. v. Morgentaler* [1988], 1 SCR 30.
5 In conveying this example, Sister Joelle recalled the late-1960s context of *Humanae Vitae* in which a Canadian bishop allegedly advocated for the right to choose among married couples. She drew upon that stance to formulate her opinion at the time of her interview in 2010.
6 The name was removed to protect the sisters' identity (given their closely connected geographic locations). She was referring to a Canadian case in which a priest was found guilty of sexually abusing over forty girls under the age of fifteen over a period of four decades.

7 Sister Josephine's point about God not likely being upset refers to the institutional Church rules related to excommunication, and not to the sexual assault of a nine-year-old girl.

8 For more on the Vatican's statement in *L'Ossevatore Romano*, see Congregation for the Doctrine of the Faith (2009).

9 Similar refusals and the non-involvement in anti-abortion efforts by American nuns were considered a form of dissent, and thus grounds for the Vatican's investigation and extended monitoring of sisters in the United States between 2008 and 2015 and beyond (Araujo-Hawkins 2016).

10 For more details on the complex implications of Sister Mary Mansour's role as a sister in public office, and of the consequences for the nuns who signed the ad in 1984, see Thompson (2022b).

11 Birthright, founded by Louise Summerhill, is now an international anti-abortion agency that describes itself as "non-judgemental" and "non-political" while using deception and misinformation to discourage abortion (Smith 2010). It is interesting in this context to consider Carol's perception of Summerhill as compassionate once a young woman made the decision to pursue an abortion despite Summerhill's efforts to convince her otherwise.

12 While some individual CWL members and some CWL groups opposed the CWL participation in the Women's March in 2000, and some may have withdrawn, the League's national president advocated that while the CWL "stands firm on all life issues from conception to natural death," that League members "stand in solidarity with women around the world on the issues of poverty and violence against women" and thus strongly encouraged CWL members to participate in the March (Pellerin 2000, 10). See also Joan M. Hastie's article in the spring 2000 edition of *The Canadian League* magazine on how some CWL members opposed the participation, but, like the national president, she underscored the importance of demonstrating the League's position on poverty and violence (14) – some members of the national executive walked in the march and attended the Mass and sat up in the sanctuary with the bishop that Sr Adele mentioned.

13 The allegations against Development and Peace were investigated by the Canadian Conference of Catholic Bishops (CCCB) and deemed unfounded. See The Interim (2009).

14 The survey responses included here were found on page 4 of the congregation's file of submitted statements.

15 Such an alleged presumption is similar to how some traditionalist nuns in the United States joined the Church's male clerics in critiquing feminist

sisters and the Leadership Conference of Women Religious (LCWR) for not participating in anti-abortion endeavours – an accusation that led, in part, to the Vatican investigations and doctrinal assessments of some American women's religious orders and their leadership council between 2009 to 2015 (Araujo-Hawkins 2016).

16 Discussion of reproductive health in this context primarily referred to *women's* reproductive health, perhaps overshadowing the critical need for abortion access across genders.

CHAPTER SEVEN

1 Chastity, expected of all Catholic people, is defined in the *Catechism of the Catholic Church* as a moral virtue involving the "integration of sexuality within a person" and "includes an apprenticeship in self-mastery" (Catholic Church 2005, paras. 2331–2400) through which one's appropriate sexual conduct reflects one's moral purity. Celibacy refers specifically to the unmarried state expected of those who dedicate their lives to religious service as priests or nuns. The Constitution and Rules of 1966, responding to a political climate of gender equality and expanding ideas about human sexuality, shifted the language of chastity to that of consecrated celibacy – presenting the status of celibacy on equal footing to the sacrament of marriage and emphasizing the motive of celibacy to attract those who are called to the work of the apostolate whose devotion inspires one to freely accept its burdens (Catholic Church 1967).

2 Including c. 573.1, c. 573.2, c. 598.1, and c. 599 (Vatican n.d.).

3 For more on the gendered dimensions of virginity constructed and controlled via Church doctrine and religious representations, see Elliott (2004, 2012). For what has been both constructed and perceived as the liberating dimensions of virginity, see Castelli (1986). For a contemporary example of the hypocritical ways in which nuns' alleged sexual experiences are controlled and manipulated by Church clerics, see Stockman (2023) and Wiering (2023).

4 Given the sensitive nature of the issues discussed in this chapter, including disclosures of intimate or romantic relationships, we have changed the interview participants' pseudonyms herein to protect the women's identity and that of their congregations. To further ensure anonymity, we have also removed any reference to the women's status as sister or former sister.

5 Sister Ava, who is from the same congregation as Sister Carmel, also confirmed the shift in language that was first applied during her own renewal of vows: "We had changed some years ago … from chastity to

consecrated celibacy." For more on contemporary considerations of the vow of chastity/celibacy, see The Life Panelists (2021).

6 Ava's emphasis on "freedom of mobility" parallels "the notion of virginity [and arguably celibacy] as liberation" from the confines of marriage (Castelli 1986, 71).

7 "Why stay?" has become a renowned, recurring, and duly posed question among women religious, not only due to challenges associated with the vows, but also and especially in light of the Church's intransigence toward gender equality (Coco 2013; Daly 1991; Molesky-Poz 2003; Schneiders 2004; Winter et al. 1994). For an expanded analysis on the sisters' responses to this question, see chapter 3, "Understanding How and Why They Stay," in Gervais (2018). For a more recent theological consideration of why and how one might stay within the Church from both feminist and Catholic perspectives, see Rubio (2024).

8 Diarmuid Ó'Murchu is a priest with the Sacred Heart Missionary Order and a social psychologist who is renowned for his insights and writings on the connections between God and nature, science, and theology (including a quantum theory–informed spirituality, and an evolutionary-oriented theology). In his writings on reclaiming spirituality, including its feminist and feminine variations, he emphasizes relationality, to which Evelyn refers here (Ó'Murchú 1997, 2011).

9 The verbatim excerpts noted here are drawn from pages 1–5 of the congregation's statements submitted to the Canadian Religious Conference's survey; as with all previous excerpts from the same document, the source remains anonymous for confidentiality reasons.

10 While the sisters' calls to action were both ignored and disparaged in the early 2000s, it remains to be seen how similar calls for reconsiderations of celibacy and sexuality by Catholic Church members worldwide, including by nuns, are addressed and acted upon during and after the ongoing Synod of 2023 and 2024, especially since discussions on such "controversial" topics have been postponed until 2025 (Giangravé 2024; Wooden 2024).

CHAPTER EIGHT

1 For Naomi, the second issue was clerical sexual abuse and the Church's problematic mishandling of it.

2 As referenced in the introductory chapter of this book, the acronym 2SLGBTQI+ stands for two-spirit, lesbian, gay, bisexual, transgender, queer, intersex, and diverse sexual communities using additional language.

We use this language inconsistently here as the sisters are primarily referring to resistance to *compulsory heterosexuality* (Rich 1980), which presumes that men are innately sexually drawn to women and women are sexually drawn to men and instinctually drawn to care for children. The derogatory language of "homosexuality" or the binary and identity-first description of "gays and lesbians" is common in Catholic culture. As such, we have retained the sisters' original language instead of using the more inclusive acronym to make clear that the sisters' comments in these interviews pertain to sexual orientation and not to trans and nonbinary expressions of gender identity. The sisters are specifically referring to gay and lesbian sexual orientations in the context of homophobic doctrine and the church's stance on gay marriage. Explaining the derogation inherent in the language of homosexuality, linguist George Lakoff explains for the *New York Times* (Peters 2014) that "Gay doesn't use the word sex … Lesbian doesn't use the word sex. Homosexual does … It also contains 'homo,' which is an old derogatory … They want to say this is not normal sex, this is not normal family, it's going against God." GLAAD, the Gay and Lesbian Alliance Against Defamation, added the word to its list of derogatory terms in 2006.

3 Pope Francis's seemingly inclusive approach was first made known in 2013 through his now-oft-quoted comment about gay priests which he made on a flight from Brazil to Italy: "If they accept the Lord and have good will, who am I to judge them? They shouldn't be marginalized. The tendency is not the problem … they're our brothers" (Allen 2013). When he echoed his original statement on 26 June 2016 on a flight between Armenia and Italy, he pluralized it ("Who are we to judge?") and thus called on others to join in a collective apology and non-judgmental approach (McElwee 2016a). In 2023, Pope Francis claimed that "criminalizing people with homosexual tendencies is an injustice" (Pullella 2023) and repeated his position that same-sex couples deserve the legal and economic protections granted by civil unions.

4 The institutional Roman Catholic Church relies on various Biblical passages to justify its exclusionary position against 2SLGBTQI+ people, particularly as it relates to compulsory heterosexuality. One such passage is from Leviticus 18:22, which reads, "You shall not lie with a male as with a woman; it is an abomination" (New Revised Standard Version of the Bible 1989). Another passage states, "in the same way also the men, giving up natural intercourse with women, were consumed with passion for one another. Men committed shameless acts with men and received in their own persons the due penalty for their error" (Romans 1:27).

5 Canon 2357 and Canon 2358 from *Catechism of the Catholic Church* (Catholic Church 2000, 566).

6 For more detailed historical accounts of how such suspicions have detrimentally impacted women religious, see Brown (1986) and Elliott (2004).

7 See reflections by Nancy Corcoran (2017). Corcoran elaborates the notion of "queer" as a verb, explaining how nuns have challenged gender binaries in numerous ways through their self-presentation and work. For a feminist and queer theological grounding of inclusivity, reciprocity, solidarity, and advocacy in this regard, see Hunt (2024).

8 Referring to Canon 2357.

9 Claire was not the only one to notice omissions and hypocrisy when it came to the issues selected by the diocese for parishioner support. In response to the Canadian Bishops CRC Survey in the mid-2000s, one entire community of women religious submitted: "We deplore the fact that the Pastoral Letters written by the Bishops of Ontario and Canada on such issues as Justice and Peace are not widely circulated in the Catholic community. It seems that only for those issues touching on sexuality are the pastors directed to speak and call for a response from the people in the pews."

10 A sister in Murphy's (2022) study revealed how she had intentionally taken extra pamphlets distributed after a Mass one day so that there would be less available for others to read about "the Church's stand on homosexuality" (292).

11 The verbatim excerpts noted here are drawn from pages 3–5 of the congregation's statements submitted to the Canadian Religious Conference's survey. Specific details of the source are omitted to protect the sisters' anonymity.

12 Sister Jeannine Gramick is a Roman Catholic nun and human rights activist in the United States who co-founded New Ways Ministry (see http://www.newwaysministry.org), through which she has been advocating for the rights of 2SLGBTQI+ people both within and outside the Catholic Church from the 1970s onward and for which she has been the target of incessant surveillance and scrutiny by the Vatican ever since (Bonavoglia 2006, 148–60; Kaylin 2000, 183) – that is, until 2021, when Pope Francis thanked and commended her for her outreach, and acknowledged the suffering she endured as a result of the backlash against her ministry (Fraga 2021; Yeagle 2022).

13 Conservative cardinals' problematic statements are not the only sources of stigmatization. Even the progressive Pope Francis, who reiterated his "all are welcome" stance in a media interview that aired on 21 May 2024

(CBS News 2024), found himself apologizing shortly thereafter, on 28 May 2024, for having used homophobic language in a private meeting on 20 May (Thomson Reuters 2024). Just weeks later, on 11 June, reports surfaced that the pope had used the same slur a second time in a closed-door meeting with priests (White 2024b).

EPILOGUE

1 Such feminist writers and advocates include but are certainly not limited to Broz and Flynn (2006); Chittister (2004); Ganim (2013); Hunt (2024); Holtmann (2008); Johnson (2002a); Leonard (2008); Manning (2002); Monk Kidd (1996); Schenk (2017); Schneiders (2021); and Winter (2002).

2 See for example Broz and Flynn (2006); Chittister (2004); McPhillips and McEwan (2022); Osiek (1986); Romey (2022); and Schneiders (2021).

3 While it varies by religious congregation, we recognize that the sisters herein benefit from racial and religious privilege, while others are also sustained by economic privilege.

4 See for example Kinew (2017); Michaelson (2021); Rastello (2023a, 2023b, 2023c); and Voices of Faith (2018).

5 In fairness, we recognize that, to varying degrees, sisters across Canada have already been involved in Indigenous-led reconciliation processes and have thus been intentional in their listening and collaboration efforts (see Rastello 2023a, 2023b, 2023c). We also acknowledge that some men clerics in Canada, including Archbishop of Regina Donald Bolen, have engaged in genuine listening to Indigenous people and residential school survivors, and in critical efforts against colonial practices by the Roman Catholic Church and the Canadian government (Keung 2022; Patterson 2023).

6 For more on the recent re-entrenchment of such patriarchal constraints, see also, for example, Bruni (2015); Chittister (2023); Giangravé (2024); McPhillips and McEwan (2022); Sprows Cummings (2018); Thomson Reuters (2024); Voices of Faith (2018); White (2024a); Wooden (2024); and Zagano (2021b).

7 We acknowledge Sarah Gilliss's insightful observation regarding the abolitionist aspects of the sisters' positions.

8 The Third Age refers to a later stage in life beyond middle age wherein individuals continue to engage relatively fully and productively in society (Radtke et al. 2016).

9 We acknowledge that not all women's religious congregations are in stable financial positions, but among those that are, many are re-allocating their assets to their own or other feminist and social justice projects. The

consideration of financial privilege is also relevant to our illustrations of resistance as it relates to how capacities to resist are conditioned by access to economic resources and social capital on individual and institutional levels (Munn and Bruckert 2010).

10 This thought-provoking recommendation reappeared as the opening statement in the 2020 book entitled *From the Writings of Joan Chittister: On Women*, selected and compiled by Jacqueline Sanchez-Small, Colleen Leathley, and Mary Lou Kownacki, OSB.

11 A fact recognized in the summary report for the October 2023 Synod, which spoke to the acknowledgment among members of the Church that women religious have been treated as "cheap labour" by the institution, and that the exploitation of their unpaid and/or underpaid labour requires attention (XVI Ordinary General Assembly of the Synod of Bishops 2023, 22). Yet, it remains to be seen what change will come from such observations.

12 Church clerics ought to also learn from other men who openly advocate for gender equality in the Roman Catholic Church through their journalistic and academic contributions, including, among others, Frank Bruni (2015), Nicholas Kristof (2010, 2012), Dan Stockman (2017, 2023), Diarmuid Ó'Murchú (1997, 2011), and Ryan Murphy (2014, 2017, 2022). We extend this call to listen and learn to the wider academic community, ourselves included, as part of our shared commitment to a decolonial and feminist approach that invites us to remain open to opportunities and obligations to expose unjust realities (Arvin et al. 2013; Di Mascio 2013), including those known to and/or perpetuated by both men and women religious, and all members of the Roman Catholic Church. Future studies in consultation with implicated individuals can contribute to expanding and evolving understandings of the problematic roles of religious institutions in historical and contemporary colonial practices.

13 The importance of love was underscored in several messages shared by Indigenous elders and survivors on the third National Day for Truth and Reconciliation in Canada / on Turtle Island on 30 September 2023. Among those who emphasized the significance of love in their speeches at the gathering on Parliament Hill that day include Elder Claudette Commanda (Algonquin Anishinaabe from the Kitigan Zibi Anishinabeg First Nation, and chancellor of the University of Ottawa), Wilton Littlechild (former member of Parliament, Truth and Reconciliation Commission commissioner, Grand Chief of Treaty 6 Nation, and residential school survivor), Angie Mercredi Crerar (Métis Elder

and residential school survivor), Evan Adams (Coast Salish physician and actor, former deputy chief medical officer of Indigenous Services Canada, and acting associate dean of Indigenous health at Simon Fraser University's Medical School), and Lavinia Brown (Inuk Elder and residential school survivor) (CBC News 2023). On the fourth National Day for Truth and Reconciliation in Canada in 2024, Elder Claudette Commanda and Actor Tom Jackson, among others, re-emphasized the value of love through prayer and song (National Centre for Truth and Reconciliation 2024).

References

Ahmed, Sara. 2010. "Feminist Killjoys (And Other Willful Subjects)." *The Scholar and Feminist Online* 8, no. 3. http://sfonline.barnard.edu/polyphonic/print_ahmed.htm.

Ajiambo, Doreen. 2022. "Lake Victoria Fishmongers Try to Escape 'Sex for Fish' Trap and HIV Outcome." *Global Sisters Report*, 20 January. https://www.globalsistersreport.org/news/ministry/news/lake-victoria-fishmongers-try-escape-sex-fish-trap-and-hiv-outcome.

Allen, John L. 2013. "Pope on Homosexuals: 'Who Am I to Judge?'" *National Catholic Reporter*, 29 July. https://www.ncronline.org/blogs/ncr-today/pope-homosexuals-who-am-i-judge.

Allen, John L., and Pamela Schaeffer. 2001. "Reports of Abuse: AIDS Exacerbates Sexual Exploitation of Nuns." *National Catholic Reporter*, 12 March. https://natcath.org/NCR_Online/archives2/2001a/031601/031601a.htm.

Ammerman, Nancy T. 2003. "Religious Identities and Religious Institutions." In *Handbook of the Sociology of Religion*, edited by Michelle Dillon, 207–24. Cambridge: Cambridge University Press.

The Anglican Church of Canada. 2022. "Ordination of Women in the Anglican Church of Canada (Deacons, Priests, Bishops and Primate)." https://www.anglican.ca/ask/faq/ordination-of-women/.

AP in Vatican City. 2023. "Pope Francis Calls for End to Anti-Gay Laws and LGBTQ+ Welcome from Church." *The Guardian*, 25 January. https://www.theguardian.com/world/2023/jan/25/pope-francis-calls-for-end-to-anti-gay-laws-and-lgbtq-welcome.

Araujo-Hawkins, Dawn. 2016. "Sisters of Mercy Also Being Asked to Come to Rome for Conversation." *Global Sisters Report*, 6 July. https://www.ncronline.org/sisters-mercy-also-being-asked-come-rome-conversation.

– 2021a. "Leadership Groups Condemn Abuse by Nuns but Leave Solutions to Local Congregations." *National Catholic Reporter*, 25 February. https://www.globalsistersreport.org/news/leadership-groups-condemn-abuse-nuns-leave-solutions-local-congregations.

– 2021b. "Survivors of Sex Abuse by Nuns Suffer Decades of Delayed Healing." *National Catholic Reporter*, 22 February. https://www.globalsistersreport.org/news/survivors-sex-abuse-nuns-suffer-decades-delayed-healing.

Armstrong, Karen. 1981. *Through the Narrow Gate: A Memoir of Life In and Out of the Convent*. London: MacMillan.

Arocho Esteves, Junno. 2022. "Do Not Hide Reality of Abuse, Pope Tells Religious Orders." *National Catholic Reporter*, 14 July. https://www.ncronline.org/news/accountability/news/news/do-not-hide-reality-abuse-pope-tells-religious-orders.

Arvin, Maile, Eve Tuck, and Angie Morrill. 2013. "Decolonizing Feminism: Challenging Connections between Settler Colonialism and Heteropatriarchy." *Feminist Formations* 25, no. 1: 8–34. https://doi.org/10.1353/ff.2013.0006.

Assembly of First Nations. 2018. "Dismantling the Doctrine of Discovery." https://www.afn.ca/wp-content/uploads/2018/02/18-01-22-Dismantling-the-Doctrine-of-Discovery-EN.pdf.

The Associated Press. 2017. "Pope Indefinitely Extends Special Permission on Abortion Forgiveness." CBC News, 10 January. https://www.cbc.ca/news/world/pope-abortion-mercy-1.3860072.

– 2018. "Pope Francis Compares Abortion to Hiring a Hit Man." CBC News, 10 October. https://www.cbc.ca/news/world/pope-compares-abortion-hiring-hit-man-1.4856742.

– 2022a. "Europe's Different Approach to Ukrainian and Syrian Refugees Draws Accusations of Racism." CBC News, 28 February. https://www.cbc.ca/news/world/europe-racism-ukraine-refugees-1.6367932.

– 2022b. "Taliban Cancels Girls' Higher Education Despite Promise." CBC News, 23 March. https://www.cbc.ca/news/world/afghanistan-girls-education-1.6394296.

– 2023. "Blessings for Same-Sex Unions Possible in Catholicism, Pope Francis Wrote to Conservative Cardinals." CBC News, 2 October. https://www.cbc.ca/news/world/pope-same-sex-blessings-1.6984540.

Avishai, Orit. 2008. "Doing Religion' in a Secular World: Women in Conservative Religions and the Question of Agency." *Gender & Society* 22, no. 4: 409–33.

Barlow, Rich. 2022. "Should Women Be Ordained Catholic Deacons?" *Bostonia*, 26 April. https://www.bu.edu/articles/2022/should-women-be-ordained-catholic-deacons/.

Barr Ebest, Sally. 2003. "Evolving Feminisms." In *Reconciling Catholicism and Feminism? Personal Reflections on Tradition and Change*, edited by Sally Barr Ebest and Ron Ebest, 263–79. Notre Dame, IN: University of Notre Dame Press.

BBC News. 2019. "Pope Admits Clerical Abuse of Nuns Including Sexual Slavery." 6 February. https://www.bbc.com/news/world-europe-47134033.

– 2021. "Catholic Church Child Sexual Abuse Scandal." 5 October. https://www.bbc.com/news/world-44209971.

Beattie, Tina. 2014. "Whose Rights, Which Rights? – The United Nations, the Vatican, Gender and Sexual and Reproductive Rights." *Heythrop Journal* 55, no. 6: 1080–90.

Bergen, Rachel. 2022. "Pope's Apology Doesn't Acknowledge Church's Role as 'Co-Author' of Dark Chapter: Murray Sinclair." CBC News, 26 July. https://www.cbc.ca/news/canada/manitoba/murray-sinclair-pope-apology-1.6532525.

Blažek, Petr, Patrik Eichler, Michal Ježek, Eva Nachmilnerová, Jáchym Šerých, and Ivo Šulc. n.d. "Jan Palach." https://www.janpalach.cz/en/default/index/onas (accessed 5 October 2023).

Böhm, Bettina, Hans Zollner, Jörg M. Fegert, and Hubert Liebhardt. 2014. "Child Sexual Abuse in the Context of the Roman Catholic Church: A Review of Literature from 1981–2013." *Journal Of Child Sexual Abuse* 23, no. 6: 635–56.

Bonavoglia, Angela. 2006. *Good Catholic Girls: How Women Are Leading the Fight to Change the Church*. New York: Regan Books.

Bornat, Joanna, and Polly Russell. 2004. "Conference Reports." *Oral History* 32, no. 1: 33.

Bouclin, Marie. 2006. *Seeking Wholeness: Women Dealing with Abuse of Power in the Catholic Church*. Collegeville, MN: Liturgical Press.

Briggs, Kenneth A. 2006. *Double Crossed: Uncovering the Catholic Church's Betrayal of American Nuns*. New York: Doubleday.

Brock, Megan P. 2010. "Resisting the Catholic Church's Notion of the Nun as Self-Sacrificing Woman." *Feminism & Psychology* 20, no. 4: 473–90.

Broner, Esther M. 1999. *Bringing Home the Light: A Jewish Women's Handbook of Rituals*. San Francisco: Council Oak Books.

Brown, Judith. 1986. *The Life of a Lesbian Nun in Renaissance Italy.* New York: Oxford University Press.

Broz, Mary Ruth, and Barbara Flynn. 2006. *Midwives of an Unnamed Future: Spirituality for Women in Times of Unprecedented Change.* Skokie, IL: ACTA Publications.

Bruckert, Chris. 2005. "Resistance." In *Encyclopedia of Prisons & Correctional Facilities*, edited by Mary Bosworth, 844–5. Thousand Oaks, CA: Sage.

Bruni, Frank. 2015. "Catholicism Undervalues Women." *New York Times*, 6 May. https://www.nytimes.com/2015/05/06/opinion/frank-bruni-catholicism-undervalues-women.html.

Bruno-Jofré, Rosa. 2007. "The Process of Renewal of the Missionary Oblate Sisters, 1963– 1989." In *Changing Habits: Women's Religious Orders in Canada*, edited by Elizabeth M. Smyth, 247–73. Ottawa: Novalis.

– 2019. "Encountering Social Change at a Time of Rapid Radicalization of the National Church: The Missionary Oblate Sisters in Brazil." *Historical Studies* 85: 57–72.

Bruno-Jofré, Rosa, and Ana Jofré. 2015. "Reading the Lived Experience of Vatican II – Words and Images: The Canadian Province of the Sisters of Our Lady of Missions in Peru." *Historical Studies* 81: 31–51.

Bruno-Jofré, Rosa, Heidi MacDonald, and Elizabeth M. Smyth. 2017. *Vatican II and Beyond: The Changing Mission and Identity of Canadian Women Religious.* Montreal: McGill-Queen's University Press.

Burke, Kelsy C. 2012. "Women's Agency in Gender-Traditional Religions: A Review of Four Approaches." *Sociology Compass* 6, no. 2: 122–33.

Burns, Kathryn. 1999. *Colonial Habits: Convents and the Spiritual Economy of Cuzco, Peru.* Durham, NC: Duke University Press.

Butler, Patrick. 2022. "Selling Churches to Pay for Sins." CBC News Interactives, 1 June. https://www.cbc.ca/newsinteractives/features/selling-churches-to-pay-for-sins.

Call to Action. 2023. "Mission." http://www.cta-usa.org.

Callaghan, Tonya D. 2018. *Homophobia in the Hallways: Heterosexism and Transphobia in Canadian Catholic Schools.* Toronto: University of Toronto Press.

Canadian Charter of Rights and Freedoms, Part 1 of the *Constitution Act, 1982*, being Schedule B to the *Canada Act 1982* (UK), c. 11. https://www.justice.gc.ca/eng/csj-sjc/rfc-dlc/ccrf-ccdl/resources-ressources.html.

Case, Mary Anne. 2016. "The Role of the Popes in the Invention of Complementarity and the Vatican's Anathemization of Gender." *Religion and Gender* 6, no. 2: 155–72. http://doi.org/10.18352/rg.10124.

Caspary, Anita M. 2003. *Witness to Integrity: The Crisis of the Immaculate Heart Community of California.* Collegeville, MN: Liturgical Press.

Castelli, Elizabeth. 1986. "Virginity and Its Meaning for Women's Sexuality in Early Christianity." *Journal of Feminist Studies in Religion* 2, no. 1: 61–88.

Catholic Church. 1967. "Sacerdotalis Caelibatus: Encyclical of Pope Paul VI on the Celibacy of the Priest." Vatican City: Libreria Editrice Vaticana. https://www.vatican.va/content/paul-vi/en/encyclicals/documents/hf_p-vi_enc_24061967_sacerdotalis.html.

– 2000. *Catechism of the Catholic Church: Revised in Accordance with the Official Latin Text Promulgated by Pope John Paul II.* Vatican City: Libreria Editrice Vaticana.

– 2005. *Compendium of the Catechism of the Catholic Church.* Vatican City: Libreria Editrice Vaticana. https://www.vatican.va/archive/compendium_ccc/documents/archive_2005_compendium-ccc_en.html.

Catholic Church, Archdiocese of St John's. 1990. *The Report of the Archdiocesan Commission of Enquiry into the Sexual Abuse of Children by Members of the Clergy (Winter Commission Report).* St John's: Archdiocese of St Johns.

Catholic Network for Women's Equality. 2020. "About CNWE." http://cnwe.ca/new_cnwe/about-cnwe/.

Catholics for Choice. 2011. "The Truth about Catholics and Abortion." https://www.catholicsforchoice.org/wp-content/uploads/2014/01/TruthaboutCatholicsandAbortion.pdf.

Cavanagh, Catherine. 2010. *Women Priests: Answering the Call.* Brockville, ON: Butternut Publishing.

CBC News. 2022. "Pope Francis in Canada: How You Can Watch and Listen on CBC." 22 July. https://www.cbc.ca/mediacentre/press-release/pope-francis-in-canada-how-to-watch-and-listen-on-cbc.

– 2023. "CBC News Special: National Day for Truth and Reconciliation." 30 September. Video, 2:00:00. https://www.youtube.com/watch?v=ygAdrhJLmbM.

CBC News Edmonton. 2022. "Pope Francis Apologizes for Forced Assimilation of Indigenous Children at Residential Schools." 25 July. https://www.cbc.ca/news/canada/edmonton/edmonton-pope-alberta-apology-1.6530947.

CBC News Manitoba. 2022. "Pope's Residential School Apology Prompts Mixed Emotions from Manitoba Survivors." 26 July. https://www.cbc.ca/news/canada/manitoba/pope-apology-residential-school-mixed-emotions-manitoba-1.6532046.

CBC Radio. 2014. "Magdalene Laundries." Interview by Carol Off with Maureen O'Sullivan. *As It Happens*, 6 June. Audio, 6:41. https://www.cbc.ca/radio/asithappens/friday-moncton-shooting-rcmp-friend-ireland-s-magdalene-laundries-squirrel-cpr-and-more-1.2903540/survivors-of-magdalene-laundries-fight-for-compensation-1.2903549.

– 2017. "Magdalene Laundries, Turo in Canada, CBC Short Story Winner (Part 3)." Interview by Carol Off with JP O'Malley. *As It Happens*. Audio, 27:32. https://www.cbc.ca/player/play/2687191205.

CBS News. 2024."Pope Francis: *The First* with Norah O'Donnell." 21 May. Video, 2:25. https://www.youtube.com/watch?v=D1rRj2ecNew.

Chandra, Uday. 2015. "Rethinking Subaltern Resistance." *Journal of Contemporary Asia* 45, no. 4: 563–73.

Chibnall, John T., Ann Wolf, and Paul N. Duckro. 1998. "A National Survey of the Sexual Trauma Experiences of Catholic Nuns." *Review of Religious Research* 40, no. 2: 142–67.

Chin, Carol. 2003. "Beneficent Imperialists: American Women Missionaries in China at the Turn of the Twentieth Century." *Diplomatic History* 27, no. 3: 327–52.

Chittister, Joan. 1995. *The Fire in These Ashes: A Spirituality for Contemporary Religious*. Kansas City, MO: Sheed & Ward.

– 2004. *Called to Question: A Spiritual Memoir*. Oxford, UK: Sheed & Ward.

– 2012. *Aspects of the Heart: The Many Paths to a Good Life*. New London, CT: Twenty-Third Publications.

– 2013. "'Tainted by Radical Feminism'? More Like 'Living the Gospel.'" *National Catholic Reporter*, 24 April. https://www.ncronline.org/blogs/where-i-stand/tainted-radical-feminism-more-living-gospel.

– 2014. "The Ending Should Have Been the Beginning." *Global Sisters Report*, 17 December. http://globalsistersreport.org/column/where-i-stand/ending-should-have-been-beginning-16791.

– 2020. *From the Writings of Joan Chittister*. Edited by Mary Lou Kownacki. Erie, PA: Benetvision.

– 2022a. "What Are We Seeking? Old Orders or New? Or Not at All?" *NCRonline*, 31 March. https://www.ncronline.org/news/opinion/what-are-we-seeking-old-orders-or-new-or-not-all.

– 2022b. "Will Religious Life Rise Again – And Should It?" *National Catholic Reporter*, 15 September. https://www.ncronline.org/opinion/ncr-voices/religious-life/will-religious-life-rise-again-and-should-it.

– 2023. "Nothing Really Changed after Vatican II. But Synodality May Make a Difference." *Global Sisters Report*, 9 June. https://www.global-sistersreport.org/opinion/ncr-voices/nothing-really-changed-after-vatican-ii-synodality-may-make-difference.

– 2024. "Women Will Call the Church to Truth." *Vision and Viewpoint: A Weekly Newsletter from Joan Chittister*, 22 January. https://mailchi.mp/benetvision.org/doubt-is-the-mother-of-conviction-752077.

Clark, Monica. 2012. "Two Groups, Two Paths for US Women Religious." *National Catholic Reporter*, 26 May. https://www.ncronline.org/news/two-groups-two-paths-us-women-religious.

Coburn, Carol K. 2015. "The Selma Effect: Catholic Nuns and Social Justice 50 Years On." *Global Sisters Report*, 9 March. https://www.globalsistersreport.org/news/selma-effect-catholic-nuns-and-social-justice-50-years-21201.

Coburn, Carol K., and Martha Smith. 1999. *Spirited Lives: How Nuns Shaped Catholic Culture and American Life, 1836–1920*. Chapel Hill, NC: University of North Carolina Press.

Coco, Angela. 2013. *Catholics, Conflicts and Choices: An Exploration of Power Relations in the Catholic Church*. Durham, UK: Acumen.

Cole, Teju. 2012. "The White-Savior Industrial Complex." *The Atlantic*, 21 March. https://www.theatlantic.com/international/archive/2012/03/the-white-savior-industrial-complex/254843/.

Colwell, Kelly, and Sheryl Johnson. 2020. "#MeToo and #ChurchToo: Putting the Movements in Context." *Review & Expositor* 117, no. 2: 183–98.

Condon, Brian. 2000. *Letters and Documents in 19th Century Australian Catholic History*. https://unisa.alma.exlibrisgroup.com/view/delivery/61USOUTHAUS_INST/12178158800001831.

Congregation for the Doctrine of the Faith. 1995. "Responsum ad Propositum Dubium Concerning the Teaching Contained in 'Ordinatio Sacerdotalis.'" http://www.vatican.va/roman_curia/congregations/cfaith/documents/rc_con_cfaith_doc_19951028_dubium-ordinatio-sac_en.html.

– 2009. "Clarification on Procured Abortion." https://www.vatican.va/roman_curia/congregations/cfaith/documents/rc_con_cfaith_doc_20090711_aborto-procurato_en.html.

– 2012. "Doctrinal Assessment of the Leadership Conference of Women Religious." http://www.vatican.va/roman_curia/congregations/cfaith/documents/rc_con_cfaith_doc_20120418_assessment-lcwr_en.html.

Connell, R.W. 2003. "The Role of Men and Boys in Achieving Gender Equality." *United Nations Division for the Advancement of Women.* http://www.un.org/womenwatch/daw/egm/men-boys2003/Connell-bp.pdf.

Cooke, Ryan. 2022. "Teacher Exonerated at Mount Cashel Abused Kids in B.C. Until at Least 2009, Lawsuit Alleges." CBC News Newfoundland & Labrador, 5 August. https://www.cbc.ca/news/canada/newfoundland-labrador/vancouver-college-mount-cashel-joseph-burke-1.6541951.

Corcoran, Nancy. 2017. "Nuns as Queer." *New Ways Ministry*, 20 May. https://www.newwaysministry.org/2017/05/20/nuns-as-queer/.

Corwin, Anna. 2021. *Embracing Age: How Catholic Nuns Became Models of Aging Well.* New Brunswick, NJ: Rutgers University Press.

CPAC. 2022. "Pope Francis Attends Community Event in Iqaluit (With English Interpretation)." Cable Public Affairs Channel (CPAC Canada), 29 July. Video, 1:39:43. https://www.youtube.com/watch?v=yxdwCVuS2Gw.

Csillag, Ron. 2005. "Nun Draws on Zen Buddhism to Enrich Catholicism." *The Huntsville Times*, 30 December. https://www.buddhistchannel.tv/index.php?id=2,2123,0,0,1,0#.VCMUU03wtyo.

Cuneo, Michael W. 1989. *Catholics against the Church: Anti-Abortion Protest in Toronto, 1969–1985.* Toronto: University of Toronto Press.

Curb, Rosemary, and Nancy Manahan. 1985. *Lesbian Nuns: Breaking Silence.* Tallahassee, FL: The Naiad Press Inc.

D'Allaire, Micheline. 1983. *Vingt ans de crise chez les religieuses du Québec 1960–1980.* Montreal: Éditions Bergeron.

Daly, Mary. 1968. *The Church and the Second Sex.* New York: Harper and Row.

– 1973. *Beyond God the Father: Toward a Philosophy of Women's Liberation.* Boston: Beacon Press.

– 1991. "The Spiritual Dimension of Women's Liberation." In *A Reader in Feminist Knowledge*, edited by Sneja Gunew, 335–41. London: Routledge.

Davidson, Madeleine. 2021. "Joy, Frustration and Humor: Reactions to Vatican Law Change on Lectors, Altar Servers." *National Catholic Reporter*, 22 January. https://www.ncronline.org/news/parish/joy-frustration-and-humor-reactions-vatican-law-change-lectors-altar-servers.

Demasure, Karlijn. 2021. "Vulnerability of Women Religious in the Context of Abuse." *Studia Canonica* 55, no. 1–2: 275–88.

Democracy Now! 2010. "Percy Schmeiser vs Monsanto: The Story of a Canadian Farmer's Fight to Defend the Rights of Farmers and the Future of Seeds." Interview by Amy Goodwin. *Democracy Now!*, 17 September. Video, 38:37. https://www.democracynow.org/2010/9/17/percy_schmeiser_vs_monsanto_the_story.

Di Mascio, Anthony. 2013. "Beyond Church and State: Rethinking Who Knew What When about Residential Schooling in Canada." *First Peoples Child & Family Review* 7, no. 2: 85–96.

Donadio, Rachel. 2010. "Comments by Cardinal on Sexuality Create a Stir." *New York Times*, 14 April. https://www.nytimes.com/2010/04/15/world/europe/15vatican.html.

Dugan, Kate, and Jennifer Owens, eds. 2009. *From the Pews in the Back: Young Women and Catholicism*. Collegeville, MN: Liturgical Press.

Dumont, Micheline. 1995. *Les religieuses sont-elles féministes?* Quebec: Bellarmin.

Dunne, Veronica. 2008. "A Force of Nature: Canadian Catholic Women Shifting the Ecclesial Landscape." In *Feminist Theology with a Canadian Accent*, edited by Mary Ann Beavis, Elaine Guillemin, and Barbara Pell, 179–99. Ottawa: Novalis.

Ebaugh, Helen R.F. 1993. *Women in the Vanishing Cloister: Organizational Decline in Catholic Religious Orders in the United States*. New Brunswick, NJ: Rutgers University Press.

Edward, John. 2014. "Study on the Impacts of the Doctrine of Discovery on Indigenous Peoples, Including Mechanisms, Processes and Instruments of Redress." *United Nations Economic and Social Council: Permanent Forum on Indigenous Issues*, E/C.19/2014/3. https://digitallibrary.un.org/record/767270?ln=en.

Elliott, Dyan. 2004. *Proving Woman: Female Spirituality and Inquisitional Culture in the Later Middle Ages*. Princeton, NJ: Princeton University Press.

– 2012. *The Bride of Christ Goes to Hell: Metaphor and Embodiment in the Lives of Pious Women, 200–1500*. Philadelphia: University of Pennsylvania Press.

– 2020. *The Corrupter of Boys: Sodomy, Scandal, and the Medieval Clergy*. Philadelphia: University of Pennsylvania Press.

Elmúdesi Espaillat, Leonor R. 2017. *El milagro de Consuelo: Una historia con valor para la educación Dominicana*. Santo Domingo: Acción Empresarial por la Educación (EDUCA).

– 2024. "Abstract of the Book: *The Miracle of Consuelo: A Story with Value for Dominican Education.*" Santo Domingo: Acción Empresarial por la Educación (EDUCA).

Evangelista, Jaesen. 2022. "To Be Part of Womankind Is to Be Limitless." *Global Sisters Report*, 9 March. https://www.globalsistersreport.org/news/spirituality/blog/be-part-womankind-be-limitless.

Faulkner, Ellen, and Gayle MacDonald, eds. 2009. *Victim No More: Women's Resistance to Law, Culture and Power*. Black Point, NS: Fernwood Publishing.

Feminist Majority Foundation Blog. 2001. "Coalition Calls Vatican to Accountability for Abuse of Nuns." *Feminist Majority Foundations*, 16 July. https://feminist.org/news/coalition-calls-vatican-to-accountability-for-abuse-of-nuns/.

Fernandes, Dorothy. 2022. "Mulakkal Verdict Signals a Need for Structural and Systemic Change." *Global Sisters Report*, 23 February. https://www.globalsistersreport.org/news/religious-life/column/mulakkal-verdict-signals-need-structural-and-systemic-change.

Figueroa, Rocío, and David Tombs. 2022. "Living in Obedience and Suffering in Silence." In *Sexualisierte Gewalt in Kirchlichen Kontexten: Neue interdisziplinäre Perspektiven* [Sexual violence in the context of the Church: New interdisciplinary perspectives], edited by Mathias Wirth, Isabelle Noth, and Silvia Schroer, 45–74. Boston and Berlin: De Gruyter Press.

Filipovic, Jill. 2008. "Offensive Feminism: The Conservative Gender Norms that Perpetuate Rape Culture and How Feminists Can Fight Back." In *Yes Means Yes! Visions of Female Sexual Empowerment and a World without Rape*, edited by Jaclyn Friedman and Jessica Valenti, 13–28. Berkeley, CA: Seal Press.

– 2013. "Rape Is about Power, Not Sex." *Guardian*, 29 August. https://www.theguardian.com/commentisfree/2013/aug/29/rape-about-power-not-sex.

Finkel, Alvin. 2006. *Social Policy and Practice in Canada: A History*. Waterloo, ON: Wilfrid Laurier University Press.

Fisher, Fran. 2012. *In the Name of God, Why? Ex-Catholic Nuns Speak Out about Sexual Repression, Abuse & Ultimate Liberation*. Granite Bay, CA: Griffin Publishing.

Foisy, Catherine. 2012. "Preparing the Quebec Church for Vatican II: Missionary Lessons from Asia, Africa, and Latin America, 1945–1962." *Historical Studies* 78: 7–26.

Foley, Mary Ann. 2015. "Prophets on the Bus? Women Religious's Self-Understanding since the Second Vatican Council." *New Theology Review* 28, no. 1: 12–19.

Forester, Brett. 2022. "Catholic Church Must 'Address Deniers' Following Apology Says Murray Sinclair." APTN National News, 1 April. https://www.aptnnews.ca/national-news/catholic-church-must-address-deniers-following-apology-says-murray-sinclair/.

Fraga, Brian. 2021. "Pope Francis Thanks New Ways Ministry in Recent Correspondence." *National Catholic Reporter*, 8 December. https://www.ncronline.org/news/people/pope-francis-thanks-new-ways-ministry-recent-correspondence.

Freire, Paulo. 1970 [1968]. *Pedagogy of the Oppressed*. Translated by Myra Bergman Ramos. New York: Herder.

Friedman, Jaclyn, and Jessica Valenti. 2008. *Yes Means Yes! Visions of Female Sexual Empowerment and a World without Rape*. Berkeley, CA: Seal Press.

Gaillardetz, Richard. 2023. "Pope Francis' New Vatican Doctrinal Chief Signals Enormous Change for Catholic Church." *National Catholic Reporter*, 19 July. https://www.ncronline.org/opinion/guest-voices/pope-francis-new-vatican-doctrinal-chief-signals-enormous-change-catholic.

Ganim, Carole. 2013. *Being Out of Order: The Prophetic Generation of Nuns and Sisters*. St Petersburg, FL: Vandamere Press.

Gatehouse, Jonathon. 2014. "Catholic Church Sex Abuse Scandals." *The Canadian Encyclopedia*, 29 May. https://www.thecanadianencyclopedia.ca/en/article/catholic-church-sex-abuse-scandals.

Gautier, Mary L. 2018. "How Is the Diaconate Changing? Trends in the Presence and Ministry of Deacons." In *Word, Liturgy, Charity: The Diaconate in the U.S. Catholic Church, 1968–2018*, edited by Center for Applied Research in the Apostolate, 29–43. Lanham, MD: Lexington Books.

Gebara, Ivone. 1999. *Longing for Running Water: Ecofeminism and Liberation*. Minneapolis: Augsburg Fortress.

– 2002. *Out of the Depths: Women's Experience of Evil and Salvation*. Minneapolis: Augsburg Fortress.

Gervais, Christine. 2012. "Canadian Women Religious' Negotiation of Feminism and Catholicism." *Sociology of Religion* 73, no. 4: 384–410.

– 2018. *Beyond the Altar: Women Religious, Patriarchal Power, and the Church*. Waterloo, ON: Wilfrid Laurier University Press.

Gervais, Christine, and Shanisse Kleuskens. 2019. "Beyond Their Mission: Solidarity, Activism and Resistance among Ontario-Based Women Religious Serving in Latin America." *Historical Studies* 85: 73–97.

Gervais, Christine, and Claire Turenne Sjolander. 2015. "Interrogating and Constructing the 'Authentic' Roman Catholic Church: Feminist Perspectives among Canadian Women Religious." *Review of Religious Research* 57, no. 3: 365–96.

Gervais, Christine, and Amanda Watson. 2014. "Discipline, Resistance, Solace and the Body: Catholic Women Religious' Convent Experiences from the Late 1930s to the Late 1960s." *Religions* 5, no. 1: 277–303.

– 2018. "Countering Renewed Patriarchal Commitments in the Institutional Catholic Church: Feminist Perspectives among Women Religious in Canada." In *Global Currents in Gender and Feminisms: Canadian and International Perspectives*, edited by Glenda Bonifacio, 49–63. Bingley, UK: Emerald Press.

Giangravé, Claire. 2023. "Synod Raises Hopes for Long-Sought Recognition of Women in the Catholic Church." *Global Sisters Report*, 21 August. https://www.globalsistersreport.org/vatican/vatican-news/news/synod-raises-hopes-long-sought-recognition-women-catholic-church.

– 2024. "Vatican Puts the Brakes on Synod on Synodality, Pushes 'Controversial' Topics to 2025." *Religious News Service*, 14 March. https://religionnews.com/2024/03/14/vatican-pulls-the-break-on-synod-on-synodality-pushes-hot-topics-to-2025/.

Gibson, David. 2016. "Is Pope Francis Alone on Apologizing to Gays?" *National Catholic Reporter*, 30 June. https://www.ncronline.org/news/vatican/pope-francis-alone-apologizing-gays.

Gill, Rosalind. 2008. "Commodity Feminism." In *International Encyclopedia of Communication*, edited by Wolfgang Donsbach, 1–3. Hoboken, NJ: John Wiley & Sons, Ltd.

Gillis, Heather. 2022. "Court Approves Sale of 43 Catholic Church Properties to Settle Abuse Victims Claims." CBC News Newfoundland & Labrador, 18 July. https://www.cbc.ca/news/canada/newfoundland-labrador/court-approves-catholic-church-sales-1.6523788.

Glatz, Carol. 2022. "Update: Women Speakers Emphasize Need for 'Reciprocity' in Church's Ministry." *Catholic Diocese of Saginaw*, 29 February. https://saginaw.org/news/update-women-speakers-emphasize-need-reciprocity-churchs-ministry.

Glick, Peter, and Susan T. Fiske. 2018. "The Ambivalent Sexism Inventory: Differentiating Hostile and Benevolent Sexism." In *Social*

Cognition: Selected Works of Susan Fiske, edited by Susan Fiske, 116–60. Boca Raton, FL: Routledge.

Global Sisters Report. n.d. "Steps and Stages of the Formation Process for Women Religious." https://www.globalsistersreport.org/steps-and-stages-formation-process-women-religious (accessed 25 May 2023).

Globe Spotlight Team. 2002. "Church Allowed Abuse by Priest for Years." *The Boston Globe*, 6 January. https://www.bostonglobe.com/news/special-reports/2002/01/06/church-allowed-abuse-priest-for-years/cSHfGkTIrAT25qKGvBuDNM/story.html.

Gott, Chloë K. 2021. "Productive Bodies, Docile Women and Violence: Exploring 'Respectable Work' as Physical Abuse within Ireland's Magdalene Laundries." *Religion and Gender* 11, no. 2: 167–91.

– 2022. *Experience, Identity & Epistemic Injustice within Ireland's Magdalene Laundries*. London: Bloomsbury Academic.

Gresko, Jacqueline. 1975. "White 'Rites' and Indian 'Rites': Indian Education and Native Responses in the West." In *Western Canada: Past and Present*, edited by A.W. Rasporich, 163–81. Calgary: University of Calgary Press.

– 2007. "Gender and Mission: The Sisters of Saint Ann in British Columbia." In *Changing Habits: Women's Religious Orders in Canada*, edited by Elizabeth M. Smyth, 274–95. Ottawa: Novalis.

Grimshaw, Patricia, and Peter Sherlock. 2008. "Women and Cultural Exchanges." In *Missions and Empire*, edited by Norman Etherington, 175–93. Oxford, UK: Oxford University Press.

Gutiérrez, Gustavo. 1973 [1971]. *A Theology of Liberation: History, Politics, and Salvation*. Translated and edited by Sister Caridad Inda and John Eagleson. Maryknoll, NY: Orbis Books.

Gutiérrez, Luis T. 2016. "Fostering Gender Balance in Religion." *Mother Pelican: A Journal of Solidarity and Sustainability* 12, no. 6. http://www.pelicanweb.org/solisustv13n06supp6.html.

Ḥāfiẓ and Daniel James Ladinsky. 1999. *The Gift: Poems by the Great Sufi Master*. New York: Arkana.

Hastie, Joan M. 2000. "World March of Women 2000: March 8 to October 17, 2000." *The Canadian League* (Spring): 14–15.

Hatton, Barry. 2022. "Portugal Cardinal Meets Pope as Sex Abuse Allegations Swirl." *National Catholic Reporter*, 5 August. https://www.ncronline.org/news/accountability/portugal-cardinal-meets-pope-sex-abuse-allegations-swirl.

Hertzler-McCain, Aleja. 2023. "Theologians Praise Expanding Synod to Lay Voting Members as 'Very Significant.'" *Global Sisters Report*,

27 April. https://www.globalsistersreport.org/news/theologians-praise-expanding-synod-lay-voting-members-very-significant.

– 2024. "Despite Pope's Clear 'No' on CBS, Promoters of Women Deacons Hold Out Hope." *National Catholic Report*, 23 May. https://www.ncronline.org/news/despite-pope-s-clear-no-cbs-promoters-women-deacons-hold-out-hope.

Heyder, Regina. 2022. "Narrating and Remembrance in the Face of Abuse in the Church." *Religions* 13, no. 4: 348. https://doi.org/10.3390/rel13040348.

Hidalgo, Myra L. 2007. *Sexual Abuse and the Culture of Catholicism: How Priests and Nuns Become Perpetrators*. New York: The Haworth Maltreatment and Trauma Press.

Hoffman, Elizabeth. 1991. *The Liturgy Documents: A Parish Resource*, vol. I. Chicago: Liturgy Training Publications.

Holtmann, Cathy. 2008. "Resistance Is Beautiful: The Growth of the Catholic Network for Women's Equality in New Brunswick." In *Feminist Theology with a Canadian Accent*, edited by Mary Ann Beavis, Elaine Guillemin, and Barbara Pell, 200–19. Ottawa: Novalis.

– 2011a. "The Vexed Question of Catholic Women, Abortion and Public Policy – Workshop Report." *The Seed Keepers* 23, no. 1: 14–15. Toronto: Catholic Network for Women's Equality.

– 2011b. "Workers in the Vineyard: Catholic Women and Social Action." In *Religion, Spirituality and Everyday Practice*, edited by Giuseppe Giordan and William H. Swatos, 141–52. New York: Springer.

Holy See Press Office. 2021. "Summary of Bulletin. New Book VI of the Code of Canon Law, 01.06.2021. Book VI. Penal Sanctions in the Church." 1 June. https://press.vatican.va/content/salastampa/en/bollettino/pubblico/2021/06/01/210601b.html.

Howard Ecklund, Elaine. 2003. "Catholic Women Negotiate Feminism: A Research Note." *Sociology of Religion* 64, no. 4: 515–24.

Hunt, Mary. 2005. "Keynote: Mary Hunt: Different Voices / Different Choices." *Women's Ordination Worldwide*. http://womensordinationcampaign.org/ottawa-2005/2014/2/2/mary-hunt-different-voicesdifferent-choices-feminist-perspectives-on-ministry.

– 2009. "Women-Church: Feminist Concept, Religious Commitment, Women's Movement." *Journal of Feminist Studies in Religion* 25, no. 1: 85–98.

– 2024. "Working Together: Feminist and Queer Theology in Conversation with Mary E. Hunt." *FutureChurch*, 5 June. Video, 1:07:43. https://futurechurch.org/justice-in-the-church/working-together-feminist-and-queer-theology-in-conversation-with-mary-e-hunt-ph-d/.

Huygens, Eline. 2023. "Navigating the Catholic Church in Belgium: Catholic Women on Female Authority, Reforms, and Sexual Difference." *European Journal of Women's Studies* 30, no. 2: 234–47. https://doi.org/10.1177/13505068231164595.

Imperatori-Lee, Natalia M. 2024. *Women and the Church: From Devil's Gateway to Discipleship*. Mahwah, NJ: Paulist Press.

The Interim. 2009. "Catholic Bishops Respond to LifeSite D&P Report." 14 August. https://theinterim.com/issues/catholic-bishops-respond-to-lifesite-dp-report/.

Jackowski, Karol. 2004. *The Silence We Keep: A Nun's View of the Catholic Priest Scandal*. New York: Harmony Books.

Jessee, Erin. 2011. "The Limits of Oral History: Ethics and Methodology amid Highly Politicized Research Settings." *The Oral History Review* 38, no. 2: 287–307.

Johnson, Elizabeth A. 2002a. *She Who Is: The Mystery of God in Feminist Theological Discourse*. New York: Crossroad.

– 2002b. *The Church Women Want: Catholic Women in Dialogue*. New York: Crossroad.

– 2014. "Remarks for Leadership Award Dinner." Leadership Conference of Women Religious, 15 August. https://lcwr.org/sites/default/files/calendar/attachments/elizabeth_johnson_csj_response_-_8-15-14.pdf.

Johnson, Val Marie. 2019. "'I'm Sorry Now We Were So Very Severe': 1930s Colonizing Care Relations between White Anglican Women Staff and Inuvialuit, Inuinnait, and Iñupiat People in an 'Eskimo Residential School.'" *Feminist Studies* 45, no. 2–3: 335–71.

Kalven, Janet. 2003. "Feminism and Catholicism." In *Reconciling Catholicism and Feminism? Personal Reflections on Tradition and Change*, edited by Sally Barr Ebest and Ron Ebest, 32–46. Notre Dame, IN: Notre Dame University Press.

Kavi, Jose. 2022. "Catholic Women Demand Church Accountability, after Bishop Mulakkal's Acquittal." *Global Sisters Report*, 7 February. https://www.globalsistersreport.org/news/news/news/catholic-women-demand-church-accountability-after-bishop-mulakkals-acquittal.

Kaylin, Lucy. 2000. *For the Love of God: The Faith and Future of the American Nun*. New York: Perennial.

Keeley, Theresa. 2016. "Reagan's Real Catholics vs. Tip O'Neill's Maryknoll Nuns: Gender, Intra-Catholic Conflict, and the Contras." *Diplomatic History* 40, no. 3: 530–58.

Kerr, Joanna. 1993. *Ours by Right: Women's Rights as Human Rights.* Ottawa: North-South Institute.

Keung, Nicholas. 2022. "This Canadian Cleric Has Been a 'Bridge' between the Vatican and Indigenous People. And He, Too, Wants to Hear an Apology from Pope Francis." *Toronto Star*, 27 March. https://www.thestar.com/news/canada/this-canadian-cleric-has-been-a-bridge-between-the-vatican-and-indigenous-people-and-he/article_3033b981-0e74-5a1b-8826-fcc30d66edf9.html.

Kinew, Wab. 2017. *The Reason You Walk.* Toronto: Penguin Canada.

Kirchgaessner, Stephanie. 2018. "Pope Francis Tells Gay Man: 'God Made You Like This.'" *The Guardian*, 20 May. https://www.theguardian.com/world/2018/may/20/pope-juan-carlos-cruz.

Koehlinger, Amy L. 2007. *The New Nuns: Racial Justice and Religious Reform in the 1960s.* Cambridge, MA: Harvard University Press.

Kristof, Nicholas D. 2010. "A Church Mary Can Love." *New York Times*, 17 April. http://www.nytimes.com/2010/04/18/opinion/18kristof.html.

– 2012. "We Are All Nuns." *New York Times*, 28 April. https://www.nytimes.com/2012/04/29/opinion/sunday/kristof-we-are-all-nuns.html.

Lee, Becky R. 1996. "The Purification of Women after Childbirth: A Window onto Medieval Perceptions of Women." *Florilegium* 14, no. 1: 43–55.

Leonard, Ellen. 2007. "The Process of Transformation: Women Religious and the Study of Theology, 1955–1980." In *Changing Habits: Women's Religious Orders in Canada*, edited by Elizabeth M. Smyth, 230–46. Ottawa: Novalis.

– 2008. "The Emergence of Canadian Contextual Feminist Ideologies." In *Feminist Theology with a Canadian Accent: Canadian Perspectives on Contextual Feminist Theology*, edited by Mary Ann Beavis, Elaine Guillemin, and Barbara Pell, 23–38. Toronto: Novalis Publishing.

The Life Panelists. 2021. "Love with a Hundred Hearts: How Do Sisters Live the Vow of Chastity?" *Global Sisters Report*, 28 June. https://www.globalsistersreport.org/news/spirituality/news/love-hundred-hearts-how-do-sisters-live-vow-chastity.

Lilja, Mona. 2022. "The Definition of Resistance." *Journal of Political Power* 15, no. 2: 202–20.

Loughlin, Gerard. 2018. "Catholic Homophobia." *Theology (Norwich)* 121, no. 3: 188–96.

Lux-Sterritt, Laurence, and Carmen M. Mangion. 2011. *Gender, Catholicism and Spirituality.* Basingstoke, UK: Palgrave Macmillan.

MacDonald, Heidi. 2019. "Women Religious' New Educational Approaches in the Global South, 1968–80." In *Educationalization and Its Complexities: Religion, Politics, and Technology*, edited by Rosa Bruno-Jofré, 129–50. Toronto: University of Toronto Press.

Mahmood, Saba. 2012. *The Politics of Piety: The Islamic Revival and the Feminist Subject*. Princeton, NJ: Princeton University Press.

– 2006. "Agency, Performativity, and the Feminist Subject." In *Bodily Citations: Religion and Judith Butler*, edited by Ellen T. Armour and Susan M. St Ville, 177–221. New York: Columbia University Press.

– 2009. "Feminism, Democracy, and Empire: Islam and the War on Terror." In *Gendering Religion and Politics: Untangling Modernities*, edited by H. Herzog and A. Braude, 193–216. New York: Palgrave MacMillan.

Major, Darren. 2021. "Residential School Survivors Call for an End to Arson Attacks on Churches." CBC News, 5 July. https://www.cbc.ca/news/politics/residential-school-survivors-end-church-arson-1.6090511.

Malone, Kelly Geraldine. 2021. "Politicians, Indigenous Leaders Say Burning Churches Not the Way to Get Justice." The Canadian Press, 1 July. https://www.cbc.ca/news/canada/edmonton/burning-churches-unmarked-graves-1.6087602.

Mangion, Carmen. 2008. *Contested Identities: Catholic Women Religious in Nineteenth-Century England and Wales*. Manchester, UK: Manchester University Press.

– 2020. *Catholic Nuns and Sisters in a Secular Age*. Manchester, UK: Manchester University Press.

Manning, Joanna. 1999. *Is the Pope Catholic? A Woman Confronts Her Church*. New York: Crossroad.

– 2006. *The Magdalene Moment*. Vancouver: Raincoast Books.

– 2002. *Take Back the Truth: Confronting Papal Power and the Religious Right*. New York: Crossroad.

Marcel, Mary. 2013. "Victim Gender in News Coverage of the Priest Sex Crisis by the Boston Globe." *Women's Studies in Communication* 36: 288–311.

Mason, Corinne. 2017. *Manufacturing Urgency: The Development Industry and Violence Against Women*. Regina: University of Regina Press.

Mayer, Andre. 2014. "Catholic Church's Overture to Gays 'Encouraging' but Unlikely to Change School Teaching." CBC News, 15 October. https://www.cbc.ca/news/catholic-church-s-overture-to-gays-encouraging-but-unlikely-to-change-school-teaching-1.2797956.

McCue, Duncan 2022. "Kuper Island: Episode 2: Nights on the Boys' Side." *Telling Our Twisted Histories*, 24 May. Audio, 39:19. https://www.cbc.ca/listen/cbc-podcasts/1062-kuper-island/episode/15914269-e2-nights-on-the-boys-side.

McDonald, Henry. 2009. "Endemic Rape and Abuse of Irish Children in Catholic Care, Inquiry Finds." *The Guardian*, 20 May. https://www.theguardian.com/world/2009/may/20/irish-catholic-schools-child-abuse-claims.

McElwee, Joshua. 2013. "Pope Francis Reaffirms Critique of LCWR, Plan for Reform." *National Catholic Reporter*, 15 April. https://www.ncronline.org/news/vatican/pope-francis-reaffirms-critique-lcwr-plan-reform.

– 2016a. "Francis: Christians Must Apologize to Gay People for Marginalizing Them." *National Catholic Reporter*, 26 June. https://www.ncronline.org/news/vatican/francis-christians-must-apologize-gay-people-marginalizing-them.

– 2016b. "Loretto Sisters Summoned to Rome, Raising Questions on Closure of Apostolic Visitation." *Global Sisters Report*, 9 June. http://globalsistersreport.org/news/trends/loretto-sisters-summoned-rome-raising-questions-closure-apostolic-visitation-40306.

– 2016c. "Vatican Contacting About 15 Orders of US Sisters for 'Serene' Dialogue." *National Catholic Reporter*, 14 June. https://www.ncronline.org/news/vatican/vatican-religious-congregation-contacting-15-orders-us-sisters-serene-dialogue.

– 2018. "Vatican's Doctrinal Prefect Reaffirms Ban on Women Priests, Calls Teaching 'Definitive.'" *National Catholic Reporter*, 29 May. https://www.ncronline.org/news/vatican/vaticans-doctrinal-prefect-reaffirms-ban-women-priests-calls-teaching-definitive.

– 2019a. "Francis: Decision on Women Deacons Cannot Be Made 'Without Historical Foundation.'" *National Catholic Reporter*, 10 May. https://www.ncronline.org/news/vatican/francis-decision-women-deacons-cannot-be-made-without-historical-foundation.

– 2019b. "Francis: Women Deacons Commission Gave Split Report on Their Role in Early Church." *National Catholic Reporter*, 7 May. https://www.ncronline.org/vatican/francis-women-deacons-commission-gave-split-report-their-role-early-church.

– 2019c. "In New Letter, Benedict Blames Clergy Abuse on Sexual Revolution, Vatican II Theology." *National Catholic Reporter*, 11 April. https://www.ncronline.org/news/accountability/new-letter-benedict-blames-clergy-abuse-sexual-revolution-vatican-ii-theology.

– 2020. "Several Members of New Vatican Commission Appear Opposed to Women Deacons." *National Catholic Reporter*, 9 April. https://www.ncronline.org/news/vatican/several-members-new-vatican-commission-appear-opposed-women-deacons.

McFarland Taylor, Sarah. 2007. *Green Sisters: A Spiritual Ecology.* Cambridge: Harvard University Press.

McGuinness, Margaret M. 2013. *Called to Serve: A History of Nuns in America.* New York: New York University Press.

McPhillips, Kathleen. 2019. "The Catholic Church Is Heading for Another Sexual Abuse Scandal as #NunsToo Speak Up." *The Conversation*, 15 February. https://theconversation.com/the-catholic-church-is-headed-for-another-sex-abuse-scandal-as-nunstoo-speak-up-111539.

McPhillips, Kathleen, and Tracy McEwan. 2022. "The Sexual Economies of Clericalism: Women Religious and Gendered Violence in the Catholic Church." *Religions* 13, no. 10: 916. https://doi.org/10.3390/rel13100916.

McPhillips, Kathleen, Tracy McEwan, Jodi Death, and Kelly Richards. 2022. "Does Gender Matter? An Analysis of the Role and Contribution of Religious Socialisation Practices in the Sexual Abuse of Boys and Girls in the Catholic Church." *Religion and Gender* 12, no. 1: 52–7.

Meyer, Joyce. 2021. "Q & A with Doris Reisinger, Theologian at the Forefront of the #NunsToo Movement." *Global Sisters Report*, 28 April. https://www.globalsistersreport.org/qas/q-doris-reisinger-theologian-forefront-nunstoo-movement.

Michaelson, Valerie. 2021. "A Decolonial Approach to Formation and Discipleship." In *Child Theology: Diverse Methods and Global Perspectives*, edited by Marcia J. Bunge, 172–89. New York: Orbis Books.

– 2023. "Decolonizing Discipline: The Normalization of Violence against Children, Church Parties to the Settlement Agreement, and the Truth and Reconciliation Commission's Call to Action 6." *Canadian Journal of Children's Rights* 10, no. 1: 68–93. https://doi.org/10.22215/cjcr.v10i1.4231.

Million, Dian. 2013. *Therapeutic Nations: Healing in an Age of Indigenous Human Rights.* Tucson, AZ: University of Arizona Press.

Molesky-Poz, Jean. 2003. "The Form Didn't Fit: Charting New Maps, Illuminating New Spaces." In *Reconciling Catholicism and Feminism? Personal Reflections on Tradition and Change*, edited by Sally Barr Ebest and Ron Ebest, 13–31. Notre Dame, IN: University of Notre Dame Press.

Monk Kidd, Sue. 1996. *The Dance of the Dissident Daughter: A Woman's Journey from Christian Tradition to the Sacred Feminine*. New York: HarperCollins.

Morrill, Bruce T., and Susan K. Roll. 2007. "The Duties and Ministries in the Mass." In *A Commentary on the General Instruction on the Roman Missal*, edited by Edward Foley, Nathan D. Mitchell, and Joanne M. Pierce, 199–223. Collegeville, MN: Liturgical Press.

Munn, Melissa, and Chris Bruckert. 2010. "Beyond Conceptual Ambiguity: Exemplifying the 'Resistance Pyramid' through the Reflections of (Ex) Prisoners' Agency." *Qualitative Sociology Review: QSR* 6, no. 2: 137–49.

Murphy, Ryan P. 2014. "Promises Unfulfilled: American Religious Sisters and Gender Inequality in the Post-Vatican II Catholic Church." *Social Compass* 61, no. 4: 594–610.

– 2017. "The Hidden, Unconventional Missionary Spirit of the Sisters of St. Joseph of Philadelphia." *American Catholic Studies* 128, no. 4: 29–54.

– 2022. "A Matter of Conscience: American Women Religious, Feminist Agency, and the Catholic Church." *Review of Religious Research* 64, no. 2: 279–300.

Mustian, Jim. 2022. "FBI Opens Sweeping Probe of Clergy Sex Abuse in New Orleans." *National Catholic Reporter*, 29 June. https://www.ncronline.org/news/accountability/fbi-opens-sweeping-probe-clergy-sex-abuse-new-orleans.

Nakonechny, Simon. 2021. "As Catholic Church Balked at Paying Residential School Settlement, Quebec Nuns Sold Nearly $25M in Real Estate." CBC News Montreal, 9 July. https://www.cbc.ca/news/canada/montreal/residential-school-financial-settlements-quebec-catholic-church-1.6092215.

National Centre for Truth and Reconciliation. 2024. "Remembering the Children: National Day for Truth and Reconciliation 2024." 30 September. https://www.youtube.com/watch?v=wFN2G2jvBIs.

Ní Laoire, Caitríona. 2007. "To Name or Not to Name: Reflections on the Use of Anonymity in an Oral Archive of Migrant Life Narratives." *Social & Cultural Geography* 8, no. 3: 373–90.

NPR Europe. 2019. "'I Just Froze': Former Nun Talks About Experiences of Sexual and Spiritual Abuse." Interview by Michel Martin with Doris Wagner. *All Things Considered*, 9 February. Audio, 8:54. https://www.npr.org/2019/02/09/693062479/former-nun-talks-about-experiences-of-abuse-in-germany.

O'Brien, Anne. 2016. "Catholic Nuns in Transnational Mission, 1528–2015." *Journal of Global History* 11, no. 3: 387–408.

O'Kane, Lydia. 2022. "Pope Francis Apologizes to Canada's Indigenous Peoples." *Vatican News*, 1 April. https://www.vaticannews.va/en/pope/news/2022-04/pope-francis-meets-with-canadian-indigenous-peoples.html.

O'Kane, Michael. 2003. *Beyond Our Vision: Journey of a Married Priest.* Ottawa: Tomiko Publications.

O'Malley, JP. 2016. "How a Global Board Games Giant Exploited Ireland's Magdalene Women: The Penance Industry." *Little Atoms.* https://littleatoms.com/article/how-global-board-games-giant-exploited-irelands-magdalene-women.

Ó'Murchú, Diarmuid. 1997. *Reclaiming Spirituality.* New York: Crossroad Publishing Co.

– 2011. *Christianity's Dangerous Memory.* New York: Crossroad Publishing Co.

Ontario. 1962. *Human Rights Code.* https://www.ontario.ca/laws/statute/90h19.

O'Riordan, Steven. 2016. "The Forgotten Maggies Official Documentary (52 min) Magdalene Laundries." 1 April. Video, 2:00:28. https://www.youtube.com/watch?v=Y4VAdN7HaxQ.

Ormsby, Mary. 2010. "Sex Abuse Victims Say Church Is Still Tenaciously Fighting Claims." *Toronto Star*, 30 May. https://www.thestar.com/news/ontario/2010/05/30/sex_abuse_victims_say_church_is_still_tenaciously_fighting_claims.html.

Orthodox Church in America. 2023. "Ordination of Women." https://www.oca.org/questions/priesthoodmonasticism/ordination-of-women.

Ortiz, Dianna. 2002. *The Blindfold's Eyes: My Journey from Torture to Truth.* Maryknoll, NY: Orbis Books.

Osiek, Carolyn. 1986. *Beyond Anger: On Being a Feminist in the Church.* New York: Paulist Press.

Patterson, Dayne. 2023. "Mixed Feelings from Sask. Indigenous People after Catholic Church Repudiates Doctrine of Discovery." CBC News, 30 March. https://www.cbc.ca/news/canada/saskatoon/mixed-feelings-indigenous-people-repudiation-doctrine-of-discovery-1.6796852.

Pauls, Karen. 2022. "The Pope's Apology Was a Start. Now the Real Work Begins, Some Catholics and Indigenous Leaders Say." CBC News Manitoba, 26 July. https://www.cbc.ca/news/canada/manitoba/the-pope-s-apology-was-a-start-now-the-real-work-begins-some-catholics-and-indigenous-leaders-say-1.6531879.

Payne, Aleta. 2021. "Aleta Payne: The Wise Men Packed Up Their Privilege and Slipped Out the Back." *Faith and Leadership*, 5 January. https://faithandleadership.com/aleta-payne-the-wise-men-packed-their-privilege-and-slipped-out-the-back.

Pellerin, Sheilah. 2000. "Oral Report of National President Sheilah Pellerin – Convention 2000." *The Canadian League* (Fall): 10–11.

Peña, Milagros. 1994. "Liberation Theology in Peru: An Analysis of the Role of Intellectuals in Social Movements." *Journal for the Scientific Study of Religion* 33, no. 1: 34–45.

Pentecostal Assemblies of Canada. 2018. "PAOC Statement of Affirmation Regarding the Equality of Women and Men in Leadership." https://www.paoc.org/docs/default-source/church-toolbox/position-papers/statements/paoc-statement-of-affirmation-regarding-the-equality-of-women-and-men-in-leadership.pdf.

Peters, Jeremy. 2014. "The Decline and Fall of the 'H' Word." *New York Times*, 21 March. https://www.nytimes.com/2014/03/23/fashion/gays-lesbians-the-term-homosexual.html.

Poggioli, Sylvia. 2019. "After Years of Abuse by Priests, #NunsToo Are Speaking Out." National Public Radio (NPR), 18 March. https://www.npr.org/2019/03/18/703067602/after-years-of-abuse-by-priests-nunstoo-are-speaking-out.

Prejean, Helen. 1994. *Dead Man Walking: An Eyewitness Account of the Death Penalty in the United States*. New York: Vintage Books.

Pullella, Philip. 2023. "Pope Francis Says Laws Criminalising LGBT People Are a 'Sin' and an Injustice." Reuters, 6 February. https://www.reuters.com/world/pope-francis-says-laws-criminalising-lgbt-people-are-sin-an-injustice-2023-02-05/.

Queen, Lisa. 2019. "York Region Mental Health Centre Speaks Out Months after Explosive Report on Abusive Priests." *Toronto Star*, 1 April. https://www.thestar.com/news/gta/2019/04/01/york-region-mental-health-centre-speaks-out-months-after-explosive-report-on-abusive-priests.html.

Radtke, H. Lorraine, Jenna Young, and Janneke van Mens-Verhulst. 2016. "Aging, Identity, and Women: Constructing the Third Age." *Women & Therapy* 39, no. 1–2: 86–105.

Rashid, Raphael. 2022. "'Devastated': Gender Equality Hopes on Hold as 'Anti-Feminist' Voted South Korea's President." *The Guardian*, 11 March. https://www.theguardian.com/world/2022/mar/11/south-korea-gender-equality-anti-feminist-president-yoon-suk-yeol.

Rastello, Sandrine. 2023a. "A Year after Pope Francis' Canada Trip, Sisters Walk Long Road to Reconciliation amid Boarding Schools' Bitter Legacy." *National Catholic Reporter*, 24 July. https://www.ncronline.org/news/year-after-francis-canada-trip-sisters-walk-long-road-reconciliation-amid-boarding-schools.

– 2023b. "For Catholic Sisters in Canada, Reconciliation Is a Mosaic of Action." *National Catholic Reporter*, 27 July. https://www.ncronline.org/news/catholic-sisters-canada-reconciliation-mosaic-action.

– 2023c. "Taking Part in Reconciliation: Inside the Process of Life-Changing Workshops." *National Catholic Reporter*, 27 July. https://www.ncronline.org/news/taking-part-reconciliation-inside-process-life-changing-workshops.

Reed, Cheryl L. 2004. *Unveiled: The Hidden Lives of Nuns*. New York: Berkley Books.

Rimer, Sara. 2002. "Scandals in the Church: The Shanley Case. A Nun Feels Betrayed in a Male-Led Scandal." *New York Times*, 27 April. https://www.nytimes.com/2002/04/27/us/scandals-church-shanley-case-nun-feels-betrayed-male-led-scandal.html.

Roberts, Terry. 2024. "This Irish Loop Church Is for Sale, but Defiant Local Catholics Have Changed the Locks." CBC News, 12 September. https://www.cbc.ca/news/canada/newfoundland-labrador/church-sale-locks-1.7320147.

Rogers, Carol Garibaldi. 1998. "Overlooked Narrators: What Women Religious Can Contribute to Feminist Oral History." *Frontiers* 19, no. 3: 157–70.

Roll, Susan K. 2003. "The Old Rite of the Churching of Women after Childbirth." In *Wholly Woman Holy Blood: A Feminist Critique of Purity and Impurity*, edited by Kristin De Troyer, Judith A. Herbert, Judith Ann Johnson, and Anne-Marie Korte, 117–41. Harrisburg, PA: Trinity Press International.

– 2015a. "Mystery without Mystique: The Question of Sacred Language, Post Roman Missal 2011." In *Mediating Mysteries, Understanding Liturgies*, edited by Joris Geldhof, 67–82. Leuven, Belgium: Peeters.

– 2015b. "(Un)Completed Touch: The Presence and Touch of Women in the Roman Catholic Liturgy Today." In *Noli Me Tangere in Interdisciplinary Perspective: Textual, Iconographic and Contemporary Interpretations*, edited by Reimund Bieringer, Barbara Baert, and Karlijn Demasure, 457–74. Bibliotheca Ephemeridum Theologicarum Lovaniensium. Leuven: Peeters.

Roman Catholic Women Priests. 2023. "About Us." https://www.romancatholicwomenpriests.org/about-us/.

Romey, Linda. 2022. "It's Time to Find Out Where Religious Life Can Go without Patriarchy." *Global Sisters Report*, 18 January. https://www.globalsistersreport.org/news/religious-life/column/its-time-find-out-where-religious-life-can-go-without-patriarchy.

– 2023. "Sisters' Communities Can Spur a New Economic Perspective." *Global Sisters Report*, 25 March. https://www.globalsistersreport.org/columns/sisters-communities-can-spur-new-economic-perspective.

Rubio, Julie Hanlon. 2024. *Can You Be a Catholic and a Feminist?* New York: Oxford University Press.

Ruether, Rosemary Radford. 1983. *Sexism and God-Talk: Toward a Feminist Theology*. Boston: Beacon Press.

– 1992. *Gaia & God: An Ecofeminist Theology of Earth Healing*. San Francisco: HarperSanFrancisco.

– 2003. "American Catholic Feminism: A History." In *Reconciling Catholicism and Feminism? Personal Reflections on Tradition and Change*, edited by Sally Barr Ebest and Ron Ebest, 3–12. Notre Dame, IN: University of Notre Dame Press.

– 2005. "Keynote: Rosemary Radford Ruether: The Church as Liberation Community from Patriarchy." Women's Ordination Worldwide. http://womensordinationcampaign.org/ottawa-2005/2014/2/2/rosemary-radford-ruether.

– 2008. "Women, Reproductive Rights and the Catholic Church." *Feminist Theology* 16, no. 2: 184–93.

– 2011. "Sex and the Body in the Catholic Tradition." In "Rosemary Radford Ruether: A Commemorative Issue," *Conscience: The NewsJournal of Catholic Opinion*, 25–31. https://docplayer.net/20796504-Rosemary-radford-ruether.html.

– 2014. "Sexism and Misogyny in the Christian Tradition: Liberating Alternatives." *Buddhist-Christian Studies* 34, no. 1: 83–94.

Rukavina, Steve. 2019. "Man Abused by Priest Launches Class Action Suit against Montreal Catholic Archdioceses." *The Inquiry*, 3 April. https://www.theinquiry.ca/wordpress/accused/charged/accused-a-to-l/boucher-father-brian-boucher/man-abused-by-priest-launches-class-action-suit-against-montreal-catholic-archdiocese-related-article/.

Rutherdale, Myra. 2003. *Women and the White Man's God: Gender and Race in the Canadian Mission Field*. Vancouver: UBC Press.

Saldanha, Virginia. 2022. "Mulakkal Verdict Leaves Nuns More Vulnerable to Clergy Sex Abuse." *Global Sisters Report*, 19 January.

https://www.globalsistersreport.org/news/religious-life/blog/mulakkal-verdict-leaves-nuns-more-vulnerable-clergy-sex-abuse.

Salgado, Soli. 2022. "Nuns and Nones Project Teaches Sisters How to Create Land Legacies for Justice." *Global Sisters Report*, 19 January. https://www.globalsistersreport.org/news/environment/news/nuns-and-nones-project-teaches-sisters-how-create-land-legacies-justice.

Salvian, Hailey. 2018. "Percy Schmeiser Looks Back 20 Years at Fight against Monsanto." CBC, 3 August. https://www.cbc.ca/news/canada/saskatchewan/percy-schmeiser-monsanto-legal-battle-1.4771673.

San Martín, Inés. 2018. "Pope Reaffirms Women Can't Be Priests, Says Church Has 'Woken Up' on Sex Abuse." *Crux*, 20 June. https://cruxnow.com/vatican/2018/06/pope-reaffirms-women-cant-be-priests-says-church-has-woken-up-on-sex-abuse.

Saurette, Paul, and Kelly Gordon. 2016. *The Changing Voice of the Anti-Abortion Movement: The Rise of "Pro-Woman" Rhetoric in Canada and the United States*. Toronto: University of Toronto Press.

Schenk, Christine. 2014. "The Apostolic Visitation Report Was Laudatory, but Sisters Remain Caught in Ambiguity." *National Catholic Reporter*, 18 December. http://ncronline.org/blogs/simply-spirit/apostolic-visitation-report-was-laudatory-sisters-remain-caught-ambiguity.

– 2017. *Crispina and Her Sisters: Women and Authority in Early Christianity*. Minneapolis: Fortress Press.

– 2021. "Women Believers Changed the Roman Empire – Now We Must Change the Roman Church." *National Catholic Reporter*, 22 July. https://www.ncronline.org/news/opinion/simply-spirit/women-believers-changed-roman-empire-now-we-must-change-roman-church.

– 2022. "Gay Catholics Refuse to Give Up on a Church that Too Often Gave Up on Them." *National Catholic Reporter*, 20 January. https://www.ncronline.org/news/opinion/gay-catholics-refuse-give-church-too-often-gave-them.

Schneiders, Sandra M. 2001. *Selling All: Commitment, Consecrated Celibacy, and Community in Catholic Religious Life*. New York: Paulist Press.

– 2004. *Beyond Patching: Faith and Feminism in the Catholic Church*. Mahwah, NJ: Paulist Press.

– 2009. "Why They Stay(ed)." *National Catholic Reporter*, 17 August. https://www.ncronline.org/news/why-they-stayed.

– 2011. *Prophets in Their Own Country: Women Religious Bearing Witness to the Gospel in a Troubled Church*. Maryknoll, NY: Orbis.

– 2013. *Buying the Field: Catholic Religious Life in Mission to the World*. Mahwah, NJ: Paulist Press.

– 2014. "Engage the Future: Reflections on the Apostolic Visitation Report." *Global Sisters Report*, 18 December. http://globalsistersreport.org/column/trends/engage-future-reflections-apostolic-visitation-report-17046.

– 2021. "Women's Religious Life Is Undergoing a Transformation that Will Help It Survive." *Global Sisters Report*, 19 May. https://www.globalsistersreport.org/news/spirituality/news/sr-sandra-schneiders-womens-religious-life-undergoing-transformation-will.

Schüssler Fiorenza, Elisabeth. 1993. *Discipleship of Equals: Feminist Theology as a Critical Theology of Liberation*. New York: Crossroads.

– 2001. *Wisdom Ways: Introducing Feminist Biblical Interpretation*. Maryknoll, NY: Orbis Books.

– 2005. "Keynote: Elisabeth Schüssler Fiorenza: We are a Church – A Kingdom of Priests." Women's Ordination Worldwide. http://womensordinationcampaign.org/ottawa-2005/2014/2/2/elizabeth-schussler-fiorenza-we-are-a-church-a-kingdom-of-priests.

– 2016. *Congress of Wo/Men: Religion, Gender and Kyriarchal Power*. Cambridge: Feminist Studies in Religion Books.

Scott, Jamie S. 2005. "Cultivating Christians in Colonial Canadian Missions." In *Canadian Missionaries, Indigenous Peoples: Representing Religion at Home and Abroad*, edited by Alvyn Austin and Jamie S. Scott, 21–45. Toronto: University of Toronto Press.

Sethi, Sanyam. 2022. "In Wake of Roe v Wade, Canadians Becoming Firmer in Their Conviction for a Women's Right to Choose." *Ipsos*, 29 July. https://www.ipsos.com/en-ca/news-polls/canadians-becoming-firmer-in-their-conviction-womens-right-to-choose.

Shine, Robert. 2024. "'The Church Can't Operate without Gay Priests'; And More Reactions to Pope's Use of Slur." *New Ways Ministry*, 4 July. https://www.newwaysministry.org/2024/07/04/the-church-cant-operate-without-gay-priests-and-more-reactions-to-popes-use-of-slur/.

Simpson, Audra. 2014. *Mohawk Interruptus: Political Life across the Borders of Settler States*. Durham, NC: Duke University Press.

Sinclair, Niigaan. 2022. "The House: TRC Calls to Action – What's Next?" CBC Radio, 30 July. Audio, 48:32. https://www.cbc.ca/radio/thehouse/cbc-the-house-july-30-1.6536307.

Sisters of Providence of St Vincent de Paul. 2005. *Providence Pages* 3, no. 1: 1–24. https://www.yumpu.com/en/document/view/53316048/providence-pages.

Smith, Joanna. 2010. "Deception Used in Counselling Women against Abortion." *Toronto Star*, 7 August. https://www.thestar.com/news/canada/2010/08/07/deception_used_in_counselling_women_against_abortion.html.

Smyth, Elizabeth M., ed. 2007. *Changing Habits: Women's Religious Orders in Canada*. Ottawa: Novalis.

Sprows Cummings, Kathleen. 2018. "For Catholics, Gradual Reform Is No Longer an Option." *New York Times*, 17 August. https://www.nytimes.com/2018/08/17/opinion/catholic-church-reform.html.

Stefanovich, Olivia. 2022. "Pope Francis Apologizes to Indigenous Delegates for 'Deplorable' Abuses at Residential Schools." CBC News, 1 April. https://www.cbc.ca/news/politics/pope-francis-responds-indigenous-delegations-final-meeting-1.6404344.

Stockman, Dan. 2017. "Apostolic Visitation Brought Dialogue with Rome, New Unity of Women Religious with Laity." *Global Sisters Report*, 14 February. https://www.globalsistersreport.org/news/trends/apostolic-visitation-brought-dialogue-rome-new-unity-women-religious-laity-44941.

– 2023. "Allegations of Adultery and Abuse of Power Embroil Texas Bishop, Carmelite Monastery in Complex Scandal." *Global Sisters Report*, 9 June. https://www.globalsistersreport.org/news/allegations-adultery-and-abuse-power-embroil-texas-bishop-carmelite-monastery-complex-scandal.

Stone, Merlin. 1976. *When God Was a Woman*. New York: Harcourt Brace & Company.

Sullivan, Rebecca. 2005. *Visual Habits: Nuns, Feminism, and American Postwar Popular Culture*. Toronto: University of Toronto Press.

– 2007. "Blasphemes of Modernity: Scandals of the Nineteenth-Century Quebec Convents." In *Changing Habits: Women's Religious Orders in Canada*, edited by Elizabeth M. Smyth, 103–28. Ottawa: Novalis.

Supreme Court of Canada. 2018. "Case in Brief: Highwood Congregation of Jehovah's Witnesses (Judicial Committee) v. Wall." 2018 SCC 26. https://www.scc-csc.ca/case-dossier/cb/37273-eng.aspx.

Taylor, Stephanie. 2022. "Canada Agreed to 'Forever Discharge' Catholic Entities from Raising $25M for Residential School Survivors." *The Canadian Press*, 21 August. https://www.cbc.ca/news/politics/canada-deal-catholic-church-fundraising-1.6557533.

Te Rōpū Tautoko. 2022a. "Information Gathering Project (IGP) Fact Sheet." https://tautoko.catholic.org.nz/wp-content/uploads/2022/06/3-20220201-February-2022-Tautoko-IGP-Fact-Sheet-1.pdf.

– 2022b. "Information Gathering Project (IGP) Information Sheet #2." https://tautoko.catholic.org.nz/wp-content/uploads/2022/06/20220601-Tautoko-IGP-Information-Sheet.pdf.

Thomas, Saji. 2022. "Accuser, Prosecution File Appeals against Bishop Franco Mulakkal's Acquittal in Rape Case." *Global Sisters Report*, 31 March. https://www.globalsistersreport.org/news/news/accuser-prosecution-file-appeals-against-bishop-franco-mulakkals-acquittal-rape-case.

Thompson, Margaret Susan. 2016a. "Circles of Sisterhood: Formal and Informal Collaboration among American Nuns in Response to Conflict with Vatican Kyriarchy." *Journal of Feminist Studies in Religion* 32, no. 2: 63–82.

– 2016b. "Sisters in the Public Square: Persuasion, Politics and Prayer." *Global Sisters Report*, 30 June. http://www.globalsistersreport.org/column/justice-matters/trends/sisters-public-square-persuasion-politics-and-prayer-40711.

– 2018. "An Outsider Studies the Insider World of Women Religious." *Global Sisters Report*, 30 April. https://www.globalsistersreport.org/blog/gsr-today/trends/outsider-studies-insider-world-women-religious-53482.

– 2021. "The 'Cult of True Womanhood' and American Catholic Sisters: An Example of Creative Subversion." *Encounters in Theory and History of Education* 21: 268–85.

– 2022a. "The History of Women Religious & Resistance Part I." FutureChurch: Women Erased online presentation sessions, 5 April. Video, 1:00:42. https://futurechurch.org/women-in-church-leadership/women-religious-and-resistance/.

– 2022b. "The History of Women Religious & Resistance Part II." FutureChurch: Women Erased online presentation sessions, 26 April. Video, 59:08. https://futurechurch.org/women-in-church-leadership/women-religious-and-resistance/.

Thomson Reuters. 2013. "Pope Francis Says He Won't Judge Gay People." CBC News, 29 July. https://www.cbc.ca/news/world/pope-francis-says-he-won-t-judge-gay-people-1.1358335.

– 2024. "Pope Francis Apologizes over Use of Homophobic Slur, Vatican Says." CBC News, 24 May. https://www.cbc.ca/news/world/pope-francis-gay-slur-apology-1.7216846.

Titley, B. 1986. *A Narrow Vision: Duncan Campbell Scott and the Administration of Indian Affairs in Canada.* Vancouver: University of British Columbia Press.

– 2006. "Heil Mary: Magdalen Asylum and Moral Regulation in Ireland." *History of Education Review* 35, no. 2: 1–15.

– 2017. *Into Silence and Servitude: How American Girls Became Nuns, 1945–1965*. Montreal and Kingston: McGill-Queen's University Press.

Traina, Cristina. 2018. "'Intrinsically Disordered': How We Got There, Why It Matters, and What We Should Do About It." *New Ways Ministry*, 9 May. https://www.newwaysministry.org/2018/05/09/intrinsically-disordered-how-we-got-there-why-it-matters-and-what-we-should-do-about-it/.

Truth and Reconciliation Commission of Canada. 2015a. *Canada's Residential Schools: The History, Part 1, Origins to 1939. The Final Report of the Truth and Reconciliation Commission of Canada*, vol. 1. Montreal and Kingston: McGill-Queen's University Press.

– 2015b. *Canada's Residential Schools: The History, Part 2, 1939 to 2000. The Final Report of the Truth and Reconciliation Commission of Canada*, vol. 1. Montreal and Kingston: McGill-Queen's University Press.

– 2015c. *Canada's Residential Schools: The Métis Experience*, vol. 3. Montreal and Kingston: McGill-Queen's University Press.

Tucker, Amy. 2022. "A Shared Understanding: Northerners Take In Pope's Apology while Looking to Next Steps." CBC News, 26 July. https://www.cbc.ca/news/canada/north/pope-francis-north-reaction-apology-1.6531625.

UCA News. 2022. "Sr. Ann Rose Nu Tawng, Myanmar's Famed Kneeling Nun, Has Become a Global Icon of Peace." *Global Sisters Report*, 23 February. https://www.globalsistersreport.org/news/news/news/sr-ann-rose-nu-tawng-myanmars-famed-kneeling-nun-has-become-global-icon-peace.

United Church of Canada. 2023. "Historical Timeline." https://united-church.ca/community-and-faith/welcome-united-church-canada/history-united-church-canada/historical-timeline.

United Nations. 2022a. "Sexual Violence 'Most Hidden Crime' Being Committed against Ukrainians, Civil Society Representative Tells Security Council." *Meetings Coverage Security Council*, 6 June. https://press.un.org/en/2022/sc14926.doc.htm.

– 2022b. "UNHCR Chief Condemns 'Discrimination, Violence and Racism' against Some Fleeing Ukraine." *UN News*, 21 March. https://news.un.org/en/story/2022/03/1114282.

United Nations General Assembly. 1948. *Universal Declaration of Human Rights*. https://www.un.org/sites/un2.un.org/files/2021/03/udhr.pdf.
– 1979. *Convention on the Elimination of All Forms of Discrimination against Women*. https://www.ohchr.org/en/instruments-mechanisms/instruments/convention-elimination-all-forms-discrimination-against-women.
– 1993. *Declaration on the Elimination of Violence against Women*. https://www.ohchr.org/en/instruments-mechanisms/instruments/declaration-elimination-violence-against-women.
Vatican. n.d. "Code of Canon Law. Book II. The People of God. Part III. Institutes of Consecrated Life and Societies of Apostolic Life. Section I: Institutes of Consecrated Life. Title I: Norms Common to All Institutes of Consecrated Life." The Holy See. https://www.vatican.va/archive/cod-iuris-canonici/eng/documents/cic_lib2-cann573-606_en.html.
– 2010. "Substantive Norms." The Congregation for the Doctrine of the Faith. The Holy See. https://www.vatican.va/resources/resources_norme_en.html.
– 2016. "Code of Canon Law. Book IV. Function of the Church." The Holy See. http://www.vatican.va/archive/cod-iuris-canonici/eng/documents/cic_lib4-cann998-1165_en.html#TITLE_VI.
Vatican News. 2021. "Pope Francis: Ministries of Lector and Acolyte to Be Open to Women." 11 January. https://www.vaticannews.va/en/pope/news/2021-01/pope-francis-opens-ministries-lector-acolyte-women.html.
Vatican Radio. 2016. "UISG President Issues Statement on Meeting with Pope Francis." 13 May. http://www.archivioradiovaticana.va/storico/2016/05/13/uisg_president_issues_statement_%20on_meeting_with_pope_francis/en-1229597.
Voices of Faith. 2018. "Overcoming Silence: Women's Voices in the Abuse Crisis." November 27, 2018. http://xn--vulnerabilittsdiskurs-h2b.de/wp-content/uploads/Breaking_the_Silence-VoicesofFaith Magazine2019.pdf.
Voisard, Pauline, dir. 2010. *Je vous salue Mariette*. Video Femmes. 33 min.
Wagner, Doris. 2018. "#NunsToo: Sexual Abuse of Religious Women. Facts and Questions." *Stimmen Der Zeit* 6 (June): 374–84. https://www.herder.de/stz/hefte/archiv/143-2018/6-2018/nunstoo-sexueller-missbrauch-an-ordensfrauen-fakten-und-fragen/.
Warick, Jason. 2021. "'Where Is Their Soul?': Inside the Failed Push to Make Catholic Church Pay for Its Residential School Abuses."

CBC News, 9 August. https://www.cbc.ca/news/canada/saskatoon/church-residential-school-compensation-1.6082935.

Watts, Rachel. 2024. "Abuse Allegations at Quebec Orphanage: Health Authority, Religious Order Agree to $65M Settlement." CBC News, 24 May. https://www.cbc.ca/news/canada/montreal/65m-settlement-alleged-abuse-mont-d-youville-orphanage-1.7213090.

Weaver, Mary Jo. 1985. *New Catholic Women: A Contemporary Challenge to Traditional Religious Authority*. San Francisco: Harper & Row Publishers.

Wexler, Celia Viggo. 2016. *Catholic Women Confront Their Church: Stories of Hurt and Hope*. Lanham, MD: Rowman & Littlefield.

White, Christopher. 2023a. "Synodality Is 'Radically Inclusive,' Says Vatican Committee Member Sr. Filo Hirota." *Global Sisters Report*, 12 April. https://www.globalsistersreport.org/news/synodality-radically-inclusive-says-vatican-committee-member-sr-filo-hirota.

– 2023b. "The Synod Will Meet in a Different Vatican Hall. This Could Be Groundbreaking." *National Catholic Reporter*, 20 July. https://www.ncronline.org/vatican/view-vatican/synod-will-meet-different-vatican-hall-could-be-groundbreaking.

– 2024a. "Pope Francis Voices Firm Opposition to Women Deacons in CBS Interview." *Global Sisters Report. Vatican News*, 21 May. https://www.globalsistersreport.org/vatican/vatican-news/pope-francis-voices-firm-opposition-women-deacons-cbs-interview.

– 2024b. "Pope Francis: The Unintentional Star of Rome's 2024 LGBTQ Pride Parade." *National Catholic Reporter*, 16 June. https://www.ncronline.org/vatican/vatican-news/pope-francis-unintentional-star-romes-2024-lgbtq-pride-parade.

Whitfield, Janani. 2019. "Archdiocese Issues Open Letter, Apology to Victims of Sexual Abuse on Ash Wednesday." *The Inquiry*, 8 March. https://www.theinquiry.ca/wordpress/rc-scandal/canada-2/canada/its-not-our-shame-to-carry-victim-of-sexual-abuse-says-archdiocese-of-regina-on-right-path-related-articles/.

Wiering, Maria. 2023. "Texas Carmelites Say They No Longer Recognize Bishop Olson's Authority." *Global Sisters Report*, 19 August. https://www.globalsistersreport.org/news/texas-carmelites-say-they-no-longer-recognize-bishop-olsons-authority.

Williams, Shannen Dee. 2022. *Subversive Habits: Black Catholic Nuns and the Long African American Freedom Struggle*. Durham, NC: Duke University Press.

Wilson-Raybould, Jody. 2022. *True Reconciliation: How to Be a Force for Change*. Toronto: McClelland & Stewart.

Winfield, Nicole. 2023. "Indigenous Leaders Hope Vatican's Repudiation of Oppressive Colonial Concepts Leads to Real Change." CBC News, 30 March. https://www.cbc.ca/news/canada/vatican-reject-discovery-doctrine-indigenous-demands-1.6795728.

Winkel, Thomas, and Joachim Heinz. 2022. "German Leaders See Crisis as Catholics Resign from the Church." *National Catholic Reporter*, 30 June. https://www.ncronline.org/news/accountability/german-leaders-see-crisis-catholics-resign-church.

Winter, Miriam Therese. 2002. "Feminist Women's Spirituality: Breaking New Ground in the Church." In *The Church Women Want: Catholic Women in Dialogue*, edited by Elizabeth Johnson, 23–31. New York: Crossroad.

Winter, Miriam Therese, Adair Lummis, and Allison Stokes. 1994. *Defecting in Place: Women Taking Responsibility for Their Own Spiritual Lives*. New York: Crossroad.

Wittberg, Patricia. 1994. *The Rise and Decline of Catholic Religious Orders: A Social Movement Perspective*. Albany: State University of New York Press.

Women's Ordination Conference. 2021a. "Updates to Canon Law Fail to Correct the 'Crime' of Women's Ordination." 1 June. https://www.womensordination.org/2021/06/updates-to-canon-law-fail-to-correct-the-crime-of-womens-ordination/.

– 2021b. "WOC Responds to Canon Law Development Permitting All Laity in Roles of Acolyte and Lector." 11 January. https://www.womensordination.org/2021/01/woc-responds-to-canon-law-230-development-to-include-all-laity/.

– 2022a. "The Ministry of Irritation." 7 April. Video, 8:31. https://www.youtube.com/watch?v=des1NZ4mCso

– 2022b. "WOC Welcomes Appointment of Women to the Dicastery for Bishops." 13 July. https://www.womensordination.org/2022/07/woc-welcomes-appointments-of-women-to-the-dicastery-of-bishops/.

Wooden, Cindy. 2024. "Pope Sets Up Groups to Study Most Controversial Issues Raised at Synod." *National Catholic Reporter*, 14 March. https://www.ncronline.org/vatican/vatican-news/pope-sets-groups-study-most-controversial-issues-raised-synod.

Woolf, Virginia. 1929. *A Room of One's Own*. London: Hogarth Press.

XVI Ordinary General Assembly of the Synod of Bishops. 2023. *XVI Ordinary General Assembly of the Synod of Bishops, First Session*

(4–29 October 2023), Synthesis Report, A Synodal Church in Mission. Vatican City: XVI Ordinary General Assembly of the Synod of Bishops. https://www.synod.va/en/news/a-synodal-church-in-mission.html.

Yeagle, Stephanie. 2022. "Soul Seeing for Lent with Loretto Sr. Jeannine Gramick." *National Catholic Reporter*, 7 March. https://www.ncronline.org/news/people/soul-seeing-lent-loretto-sr-jeannine-gramick.

Zagano, Phyllis. 2021a. "New Canon on Women's Ordination Nothing New, Can Be Changed." *National Catholic Reporter*, 7 June. https://www.ncronline.org/news/opinion/just-catholic/new-canon-womens-ordination-nothing-new-can-be-changed.

– 2021b. "New Women Deacons Commission to Meet with Unclear Agenda." *National Catholic Reporter*, 31 August. https://www.ncronline.org/news/just-catholic/new-women-deacons-commission-meet-unclear-agenda.

Zimonjic, Peter. 2022. "American Women Can Obtain Abortions in Canada if Roe v. Wade Falls, Minister Says." CBC News, 3 May. https://www.cbc.ca/news/politics/canada-provide-abortion-access-american-women-1.6440238.

Index